T0309372

CLASSICAL MEMORIES/MODERN IDENTITIES
Paul Allen Miller and Richard H. Armstrong, Series Editors

Virginia Woolf, Jane Ellen Harrison, AND THE Spirit of Modernist Classicism

Jean Mills

THE OHIO STATE UNIVERSITY PRESS
COLUMBUS

Copyright © 2014 by The Ohio State University.
All rights reserved.

Library of Congress Control Number
2014931257

Cover design by Mary Ann Smith
Type set in Adobe Sabon

♾ The paper used in this publication meets the minimum requirements of the American
National Standard for Information Sciences—Permanence of Paper for Printed Library
Materials. ANSI Z39.48–1992.

9 8 7 6 5 4 3 2 1

For Martha Lou Haag,
Potnia Theron and Tenth Muse

CONTENTS

LIST OF ILLUSTRATIONS

KEY TO TITLES

Virginia Woolf

Jane Ellen Harrison

AAR   *Ancient Art and Ritual*

A&O   *Alpha and Omega*

E   *Epilegomena to the Study of Greek Religion*

EOW   "Epilogue on the War: Peace with Patriotism"

P   *Prolegomena to the Study of Greek Religion*

R   *Reminiscences of a Student's Life*

SSF   "Scientiae Sacra Fames"

T   *Themis: A Study of the Social Origins of Greek Religion*

Archives

AR Papers   Alexei Remizov, Papers. Amherst Center for Russian Culture. Amherst College

HMH   Hope Mirrlees, Papers. Hornbake Library, University of Maryland

HMN   Hope Mirrlees, Papers. Newnham College Archives, Newnham College, Cambridge

JC Papers   Janet Case, Papers. Girton College Archives, Girton College, Cambridge

JH Papers   Jane Ellen Harrison, Papers. Newnham College Archives, Newnham College, Cambridge

MH Papers   Monks House Papers. Manuscript Collections. University of Sussex Library

VWBerg   Virginia Woolf and Leonard Woolf, Papers. Henry W. and Albert A. Berg Collection. New York Public Library

ACKNOWLEDGMENTS

I WISH TO THANK my own intellectual mothers, mentors, and friends, especially Jane Marcus, Blanche Wiesen Cook, Clare Coss, and Alison Bernstein. In many ways, this book is not only inspired by them, but is about them. Their impatience with injustice in all its guises and their enduring contributions in mentoring and empowering women are extensions of the conversation continued here. I am particularly grateful for the archival support and expertise of Anne Thomson and Pat Ackerman, at The Jane Ellen Harrison Papers (and more recently, The Hope Mirrlees Papers), Newnham College, Cambridge University; Robert Ackerman, Clare College, Cambridge; Jay Barksdale of the Wertheim Room in the Research Division of The New York Public Library; Isaac Gerwitz, of The Henry W. and Albert A. Berg Collection of The New York Public Library; Stanley Rabinowitz and Isabel Duarte-Gray at The Amherst Center for Russian Culture; Kate Perry of The Janet Case Papers, Girton College, Cambridge; Karen Watson of Monks House Papers, Sussex University; Trevor Bond, Special Collections, Holland Library, Washington State University; Karen Kukil of Rare Book Room, William Allen Nielsen Library, Smith College; Kings College Archives, Kings College,

Cambridge; The Hornbake Library, University of Maryland; and the curators of Antikensammlung at the Altes Museum and Pergamon Museum in Berlin.

I wish to thank the International Virginia Woolf Society and the Virginia Woolf Society of Great Britain for providing such intellectually vibrant forums for presenting and testing my ideas and essays over the course of writing this book. In particular, I'd like to thank Leslie Hankins, Suzanne Bellamy, Judith Allen, Georgia Johnston, Bonnie Kime Scott, Helen Southworth, Vara Neverow, Merry Pawlowski, Suzette Henke, Anne Fernald, Mark Hussey, Helen Wussow, Gillian Beer, Frances Spaulding, and Christine Froula for their own work in Woolf Studies, and for their intellectual insight and generosity. I wish to acknowledge the memory and important work of scholars, Julia Briggs and Eve Sedgwick, each of whom were early backers of my work on Woolf and Harrison. Thanks to friends and scholars Sandi E. Cooper; the indomitable Ruth Gruber; Deborah Lutz; Rebecca Wisor; Ashley Foster; Deryn Rees-Jones; June Dunn; Linda Camarasano; Elias Theodorakopoulos; Cori Gabbard; Claire Buck; Michael Marcus; Christopher Stray; and Dr. Sarah Sheftel. At Sissinghurst, I'd like to thank Frances Brooks and Cathy Hickey for the return ride home.

For their generous support of my research, I wish to thank John Jay College's Office for Sponsored Programs; the Professional Staff Congress; The Office for the Advancement of Research; and my incredible colleagues in the John Jay College English Department. I wish to acknowledge early support from The Graduate Center of the City University of New York; the Mario Cappeloni Fellowship; Nina Fortin Memorial Award; Florence Howe Award; and Robert Adams Day Prize award committees.

At The Ohio State University Press, I am indebted to my readers Richard H. Armstrong and Paul Allen Miller; to the expertise and professionalism of my editor, Eugene O'Connor; and to members of the production and marketing staff, whose efforts kept the book on track and on point, from farm to table, as we like to say Upstate. Thanks to Spirit Wilson, Jr. for the Index and to my brother, Scott Mills, for his help in securing the photographs.

I wish also to thank my family and my 'found families' of friends for their support during the years spent writing this book: my wife, Martha, my daughter, Abby, my stepsons, Max, Peter, and Harrison Basch, my mother, Alice Jean Mills; my brothers, Robert, Scott, and Todd; friends Rachel Hyman, Richard David, Sharon Klein, Harriet Lyons, Karen

Katz, Gary Richards, Ivy and Lance Lappin; my tennis family, especially Chris, Linda, Sandi, and Lorna; and the baby group, Debi Wierum, Shari Werner, and Helen Lorell. Thanks for listening and reading, and also for feeding me and often giving me a place to sleep while I took this trip. Lastly, I wish to acknowledge the memory of the following people who I'd like to think would have enjoyed reading this: my father, Stanley Robert Mills; my mother-in-law, Audrey L. Haag; and my sister-in-law, Kathryn Haag Clauss. *Nox est perpetua una dormienda.*

Virginia Woolf, Jane Ellen Harrison, and the Spirit of Modernist Classicism

A Transpersonal Modernism

THIS INTERDISCIPLINARY study re-examines the origins and sources of Virginia Woolf's intellectual, literary, and political views by decisively positioning her work in dialogue with the theories and practices of Cambridge classicist, Jane Ellen Harrison. Drawing on the discourses of feminist historicism, feminist theory, cultural studies, and literary analysis, I argue that a distinctive model of relations between women intellectuals emerges by cross-reading Jane Harrison and Virginia Woolf that does not rehearse the linearity of influence, but outlines an intertextuality, an active and transformative use of one body of writing by another writer that makes of Virginia Woolf's modernism a specifically feminist amplification. This cross-reading reveals a dimension of modernism that has been overlooked or minimized, but which has far-reaching significance in its totality across the writing lives and professional careers of both women, as I argue that the questions preoccupying Harrison resonated with Woolf as she adapted these ideas to her own intellectual, political, and literary pursuits. What is the relationship of the family and women to the state? What are the sources of violence and war? What role can gender play in effecting social change? What are the roots of patriarchy and the possibilities of alternative social systems? How do universal structures, like language and time, function and govern culture? And what role can art play in changing our lives?

To an extent, this study participates in an act of recovery, and is an effort to revive and reclaim Harrison's work, and to point to the degree to which her cultural, political, and scholastic example informed one of the major modernist voices of the twentieth century. As such, it becomes a challenge to a critical climate, which suggests that the most important acts of feminist recovery have already been accomplished, a contention that has created no small degree of critical anxiety in feminist scholarship, especially among young women scholars who often struggle to find their place and their voices in an increasingly compulsory intellectually polyamorous world. In concert with Lizzie Hutton and others, I reject "the implication that we ought to—or can be—'through'" (Hutton 128). Jane Harrison's work becomes renewed and re-vitalized precisely because Virginia Woolf can be read through the prism of Harrison's work. Woolf is an astute and thoughtful reader of Jane Harrison, but also a creative writer who sought to use her own writing to see the present and to see it differently because of her reading of Harrison's work. This is not a matter of Joycean intertextuality with myth or of cross-reading Eliot and the classics. The classical presence in English and Irish modernism is difficult to ignore, but unlike an inquiry into the classicism of Eliot or Pound, Lawrence or Yeats, for example, this study is distinctive, because it is not a looking back, which is classicism, but a transforming forward of a particular version and interpretation of classicism into a feminist modernism.

Despite trends in transnationalism and digital "one world, we're all connected" technologies in Modernist Studies, much of current scholarship in literary modernism continues to focus on Joyce, Pound, Eliot, and Yeats, "the men of 1914," and their male contemporaries as comprising the dominant narratives of early twentieth-century literary and political history. Recent examples in Woolf Studies have also attempted to send Virginia Woolf back to Bloomsbury, linking her politics, ethics, and philosophy to a male homosexual community she may have geographically resided near, but whose intellectual and political ambitions she often did not share.[1] Furthermore, despite important interventions,

1. Most recently in *Modernist Commitments: Ethics, Politics, and Transnational Modernism* (Columbia 2012) Jessica Berman links Woolf's ethics and politics to G. E. Moore, who was, indeed, favored by Lytton Strachey, Maynard Keynes, E. M. Forster, Leonard Woolf, and other Cambridge Apostles, but not necessarily by Virginia Woolf, who shared more of an ethical and political affinity with Jane Harrison, and with the ethicist and phi-

our Kristevan "raids from the margins," and efforts to re-map modernism with texts such as Bonnie Kime Scott's *The Gender of Modernism:
A Critical Anthology* (1990), and more recently, *Gender in Modernism:
New Geographies, Complex Intersections* (2007), publishing lists and syllabi demonstrate that "the hero's journey," continues to be the story that
is respected and learned. What is different about this project is precisely
what made Jane Harrison relevant to what Virginia Woolf was seeking as
a writer: a voice that registered an alternative perspective on gender relations and power.

When I began this study, I thought I would be mainly exploring Virginia Woolf's work, but what I discovered was that in order to understand Woolf's modernism, I'd have to recover Harrison, instead. This has
led me to the belief that much of the work of my own generation of feminist critics is not so much to recover the work of women writers, as it
may be to recover the work of their mentors—the women philosophers,
aestheticians, anthropologists, archaeologists, intellectuals—not necessarily the women behind the women, so to speak, but, in this case, women
locked in intellectual and political orbit with one another. The Harrison–
Woolf relationship begins initially by reading, evolves into an intellectual
mentorship, but shifts ultimately away from any notion of descent to one
of shared ambitions, overlapping politics, and friendship. I have, therefore, found it useful to characterize this study as participating in a ritual
Woolf encouraged all women to take part in, to "think back through our
mothers" with the aim of creating and reclaiming women's writing and
women's lives, but I've also found it productive to discuss this relationship in terms of what Nancy K. Miller has called "transpersonal,"[2] a connection sideways. In "Getting Transpersonal: The Cost of an Academic
Life" (2009) and more recently in "A Feminist Friendship Archive"
(2011), Miller asks "when we shift the emphasis from the vertical axis,
the bonds that shape our identities through our family and intergener-

---

losopher who co-founded Newnham College and advocated for women's higher education,
Henry Sidgwick.

2. The term "transpersonal" in relation to psychology is used to characterize states
of consciousness or esoteric mental experiences beyond the limits of personal identity, but
I am borrowing it from Miller's more specific use of the term in relation to women's writing. The term, Miller writes ("A Feminist Friendship Archive" 75), has also been used in
this way by feminist critics Estella Lauter, "perhaps originally," in *Women as Mythmakers:
Poetry and Visual Art by Twentieth-Century Women* (1984); Alicia Ostriker, in "Anne
Sexton and the Seduction of Audience," *Seduction and Theory* (1989), to discuss Sexton's
idea that "personal truth is also transpersonal"; and Deborah Nelson, in *Pursuing Privacy
in Cold War America* (2002), which explores the "transpersonal" as political in relation to
Sexton's work.

ational ties, to the horizontal axis of chosen relations, what kind of a story emerges?" ("A Feminist Friendship Archive" 69). Miller has used the term to explore memoir, biography, and life-writing between women poets, such as Anne Sexton and Maxine Kumin, to create what she has called "a feminist friendship archive," but the "transpersonal," as she defines it, as encompassing "other categories of significant others, those to whom one is related by affinity (profession, passion, politics) but not (or not necessarily) by blood or marriage" (74) helps to articulate the shift away from the vertical axis of mentorship to the aspects of the Harrison–Woolf relationship that were also lateral, or interjacent in nature, becoming ultimately an interactive project of shared ambitions and objectives.

Many feminist critics have invoked Woolf's famous passages in Chapter 5 of *A Room of One's Own* when "Chloe liked Olivia perhaps for the first time in literature" (81) in order to explore the nature of women's friendships as mutually beneficial and constructive, rather than stereotypically reductive, destructive, or based on jealousy and competition for a male gaze. Sharon Marcus, for example, instructively points out that these moments in *A Room* illustrate "a symptom of exactly the problem [Woolf] hoped it would correct: our lack of knowledge about women's relationships" (258). In her own exploration of Woolf's discussion, Miller finds an intimacy between women based on intellectual passions and work. She writes:

> The reason that "Chloe liked Olivia," [. . .] has provoked so much discussion is not solely, I think, what Woolf did or did not imply by positing a friendship between two women at the heart of a new literature by women (the temperature of the emotion registered by the verb *to like*) but also what liking between women turns out to mean when combined with work. ("A Feminist Friendship Archive" 69)

As Woolf goes on to explore the implications of their relationship, we learn that in addition to liking each other, Chloe and Olivia "share a laboratory, which of itself will make their friendship more varied and lasting because it will be less personal" and if that is the case "then something of great importance has happened" (AROO 82–83). Miller writes that "[k]ey here for Woolf is not simply the power of affection that binds women but also the extraordinary, if as yet untested, power of friendship combined with work" ("A Feminist Friendship Archive" 70). This study deploys both Woolf's theories on the importance of mentorship as "thinking back through our mothers," in order to recover and reclaim Harrison's writing and to illustrate the vertical axis of mentoring, and Miller's "transpersonal" frame to explore the shift in their relationship as a more lateral and entwined intellectual intimacy, a shared "laboratory" of ideas.

My argument lies in Harrison's intellectual and political significance as Woolf's mentor and friend over a twenty-four year period, as it investigates the kind of story, and the kind of modernism, that emerges as a result of their many points of contact. As Woolf spent her early years trying to find her own voice as a writer, years she once referred to as her "Greek slave years," (MB 106) she was inspired and encouraged by Harrison's research and re-visioning of Greek ritual and mythology that she hoped quite possibly could free, if not her body, then her imagination and her exceptional intellect. As a mature woman, she paid homage to Harrison in *A Room of One's Own* (1929) and by publishing Harrison's translation from the Russian, *The Life of the Archpriest Avvakum, by Himself* (1924), and finally her memoir, *Reminiscences of a Student's Life* (1925). Woolf helped to secure Harrison's reputation as an international scholar, "thinking back" through her intellectual mother, but also demonstrating, that by the end of Harrison's life, theirs was a friendship of mutual respect, ideologies and goals.

Jane Harrison was mid-Victorian by birth and Virginia Woolf late-Victorian, but they each belonged intellectually to a younger and to succeeding generations. Woolf did not complete a major novel until she and her sister set up "a home of their own" after their father's death in 1904, and she continued to struggle with conflict and depression associated with the oppressive constraints placed on her in a strict Victorian household. She feared marriage and was often exhausted by the emotional and physical efforts necessary for a woman to carve out a place and time for her art. Harrison, similarly burdened by restrictive Victorian mores, and an often hostile professional environment, was unable to complete her most significant work until she was in her fifties. Both women, separated by a span of thirty-two years in age, found themselves in conversation with one another, intellectually and politically, as they asked detailed and profound questions about their own experience in relation to the social systems they inhabited. Harrison's work offered Woolf the intellectual, emotional and psychic space to challenge the foundations and systems upon which she was raised. Her research gave Woolf the necessary tools to reject patterns and structures made by others and to seek out alternatives, different ways of knowing, of being, and different literary and political approaches.

Studying Harrison's work gives us a revised classicism and by extension a revised modernism, in a relationship with Woolf, which I characterize as "transpersonal." As one of the most astute readers of Harrison's research and example, Woolf saw in her work on ancient Greece and later on Russian language and literature, issues of immediate feminist significance for the culture of war, heroism, and death she recognized in her patriarchal and imperialistic present. Two issues stand out here: the acknowledgment of a pre-classical Greek culture centered on women, and pacifism, some would say, the most powerfully important component of Virginia Woolf's intercalated philosophy of feminism, socialism, and pacifism. Reading Harrison, Woolf transforms academic scholarship in the fields of archaeology and classical literature into a foundation for a new kind of writing and thinking by means of creating her novels and essays for their elucidation. She uses Harrison both as a role model in making herself into a public intellectual, but her reading across Harrison, transpersonally, reveals the potential in a study of an ancient world to illuminate and navigate issues in the present. The specific nature of Harrison and Woolf's relationship was between classical scholarship and contemporary literature, between studying a pre-patriarchal world and contemporary political aspirations whose underlying feminisms evolve into anti-war positions. Neither Harrison nor Woolf was a declared feminist, but each engaged publicly and profoundly in the manner of the period with questions of power, oppression, and gender. In Harrison's work, Woolf was not seeking ready-made models in the past for the future in such reductive or simple terms. Like Harrison, she was seeking alternatives, drawing from ancient world resources, she read as feminist, to explore language and revise questions, often in response to the failed language of the state. As this study argues, they each were seeking, transpersonally, to propose ways of being and ways of thinking that specifically differed from the dominant ideologies of their time—ideologies that too frequently are accepted or promoted as inevitable, timeless and justified by the glorification of past heroic civilizations, and read as mirrors of the present, or, even more dangerously, as excuses for the present. In *Virginia Woolf, Jane Ellen Harrison, and the Spirit of Modernist Classicism*, I argue that by reading Harrison's work, Woolf is seeking to discern new plots, new models, which she then could translate, revise, or recreate into a basis for a modern vision, by way of a modern literary project, and she uses Harrison's reinterpretations of Greek myth and ritual, and her work on psychology, linguistics, and Russian language and literature, as sources for this project.

Harrison and Woolf: Reticulate Lives, an Overture

While Jane Harrison is often known to historians of anthropology and those searching for the origins of Structuralism,[3] many outside of academic or specialist circles are unfamiliar with her biography and the nature of her scholarly contributions. The following two main sections provide a brief biographical overview to introduce the more significant events in her life to readers less familiar with her oeuvre and to give a basic frame of reference for the Harrison–Woolf encounter. Harrison is more frequently remembered as a founder of myth-ritual criticism and the intellectual leader of the Cambridge Ritualists, or The Cambridge Group of Classical Anthropologists, as they were called at the time, a community of scholars pushing the disciplinary boundaries of the Classics as they created new fields in anthropology and archaeology. She was a well-known scholar with an international reputation and respected among her colleagues, despite frequent attacks on her work, politics, and personal life from the academic establishment. Harrison is most notably remembered for her three foundational texts on the matrifocal beginnings of the Olympian Gods: *Prolegomena to the Study of Greek Religion* (1903); *Themis: A Study of the Social Origins of Greek Religion* (1912), and *Epilegomena to the Study of Greek Religion* (1921), each of which Virginia Woolf read. The introduction of the theory of a pre-classical culture based on women that is communal and collective in nature is among her greatest contributions as a Ritualist, along with her articulation of Dionysus as a Year-Spirit or *eniautos daimon* rather than as a drunken, pot-bellied Bacchus. She also portrayed and outlined the goddess Themis as representative of *polis,* as the integument or fabric of society, itself, especially when characterized by a sense of community (see Chapter 2). Each of these new ideas was considered radical and controversial as her work shifted the focus in the Classics away from philology and the myths of a pantheon of named and individuated gods to the communal, women-guided ritual practices of ancient Greek culture.

Woolf knew Jane Harrison personally from 1904 until Harrison's death in 1928. Her *Ancient Art and Ritual* (1913) was given to Woolf as a Christmas gift, inscribed by the author in 1923 (J. Marcus, *Languages of Patriarchy* 195). She owned a number of Harrison's books, including *Aspects, Aorists, and the Classical Tripos* (1919) on the structure of Rus-

---

3. See Shelley Arlen's commentary in *The Cambridge Ritualists,* referencing Claude Lévi-Strauss's debt to Harrison.

sian linguistics, and was familiar with Harrison's lectures on religion, art, women's rights and war, later collected as essays in *Alpha and Omega* (1915). In her letters and diaries, Woolf's allusions to Jane Harrison demonstrate a deeply held respect for her scholarship, intellect, and political views, as we find their relationship moving from one of indirect contact to a participation in Miller's transpersonal "zone." Miller describes this space as "the many complex processes of identification and disidentification," which form "in the connective tissue that binds together language, custom, practice, cultural memory, and the archive" ("Getting Transpersonal" 168). This study locates Woolf and Harrison along the transpersonal interstices of gender, the classics, politics, ethics, religion, and the intellectual lives of women.

A young, intellectually curious Virginia Stephen first met Miss Harrison "and all the other learned ladies at Newnham" (L 1: 145) in 1904, and one can imagine her private exhilaration at encountering the renowned scholar, who had traveled to Greece, published and lectured on Greek art and archaeology, and smoked a pipe on the steps of the Parthenon. As F. M. Wilson writes in *A Newnham Anthology*, "Jane Harrison with her originality and her penetration into the world of Ancient Greece brought glamour into scholarship" (67). Their relationship continued off and on for the next twenty-four years, with their contact increasing once Woolf added the role of publisher to her own accomplishments in the founding of the Hogarth Press. She writes of "Jane" in a letter to her friend, the artist Jacques Raverat, the husband of Gwen Raverat, née Darwin, whom Jane Harrison knew well, describing her as "a gallant old lady, very white, hoary, and sublime in a lace mantilla" who "took my fancy greatly." In the letter, she not only realizes that she shares the same "superb high thinking agnostic ways" (L 3: 58) with Jane Harrison, but she also likes the way she looks. Both Woolf and Harrison are shocked and dismayed by the trend among the younger generation, especially at Oxbridge, who are flocking to patriarchal religion and converting to Catholicism in droves. The exchange recorded by Woolf reveals their camaraderie, a transpersonal "liking," between two women:

> "Alas," she [Jane Harrison] said, "you and your sister and perhaps Lytton Strachey are the only ones of the younger generation I can respect. You alone carry on the traditions of our day." This referred to the miserable defection of Fredegond [Shove] (mass; confession; absolution, and the rest of it.) "There are thousands of Darwins" I said, to cheer her up. "Thousands of Darwins!" she shrieked, clasping her mittened hands, and

raising her eyes to Heaven. "The Darwins are the blackest traitors of them all! With that name!" she cried, "that inheritance! That magnificent record in the past!" "Surely," I cried, "our Gwen is secure?" "Our Gwen" she replied, "goes to Church, (if not mass, still Church) every Sunday of her life. Her marriage [. . .] may have weakened her brain. Jacques is, unfortunately, French. A wave of Catholicism has invaded the young Frenchmen. Their children are baptized; their–" Here I stopped her. "Good God," I said, "I will never speak to them again!" (L 3: 58).

Woolf, feigning outrage, proclaims that she was on the verge of ending her longtime friendship with Raverat over the issue, when she thankfully received his letter assuring her that his wife "Gwen is a militant atheist: The world renews itself," she wrote, and she "at once sent word to dear old Jane," who met the news with relief and "a little inconsistently, 'Thank God.'"

A month before Harrison's death, at the age of seventy-eight, in April 1928, Woolf remembers having "tea with Jane, raised in bed, with her old white head lifted up, on pillows, very aged & rather exalted" (D 3: 176). On her last visit, she describes her as "like a very old person, whom life has tossed up, & left; exalted, satisfied, exhausted" as Virginia returned home "to work & work, as hard as I can" (D 3: 180). She would produce her "talks" to women, later published as A Room of One's Own, by October of that year. When Harrison died, Woolf comments on the funeral arrangements, which followed a typical script from the Protestant liturgy of Jane's Northern, nonconformist relations, and represented a system of thought and belief that neither Woolf nor Harrison shared. Afterwards, Woolf wrote in her diary "[. . .]as usual the obstacle of not believing dulled & bothered me. Who is 'God' & what the Grace of Christ? & what did they mean to Jane?" (D 3: 181).

Years later, in Downhill All the Way: An Autobiography of the Years 1919 to 1939, Leonard Woolf remembers Harrison as

One of the most civilized persons I have ever known. She was also the most charming, humorous, witty, individual human being. When I knew her she was old and frail physically, but she had a mind which remained eternally young. (26)

This depiction of Harrison as "eternally young" was universally shared by her friends, her students, and many of her colleagues, and supports an understanding of Harrison as transcending time, and of her ability to meet Virginia Woolf across time in a shared, inter-generational space that is also transpersonal in nature. The transpersonal, as Miller notes, "is always about entanglement," and "entanglement is generational" ("Getting Transpersonal" 171, 175), as she explores the current trend to reject the term "autobiography" in favor of memoir, creative non-fiction, or the lyrical essay, in discussing the theory and practice of women's autobiographical and life writings. Because "autobiography" (and "biography," for that matter) have recently been regarded as "old-fashioned," or narrow designations, which presume linearity, and a fully integrated, autonomous sense of self, Miller discusses these relationships as transpersonal in order to embrace autobiography and extend it, as the transpersonal encompasses the entanglements of both the chronological frame of a life and the intermittent, partial, sometimes completely silent intersections of the self with other selves, across the boundaries of time, but on the basis of work and ideas that become shared. Sometimes this interaction occurs imaginatively or sometimes through what Carolyn Heilbrun calls "an unmet friend" (138), relationships we share based on reading. Here, I argue that Woolf apprehends Harrison as an intellectual chosen relation which comprises both the generational notion of "these are the people I come from" (Miller, "Getting Transpersonal" 175), the looking-backward, as well as, the transforming forward via the knots, cross-roads, and intersections of a life, the interrupted, sometimes circuitous, fits and starts of the transpersonal. The Harrison–Woolf relationship ultimately becomes one characterized by a transpersonal reticulation, an intellectual, cultural, political, and historical interweaving and sharing which is distinctive in its ability to support, inform, and transform Woolf's modernist project, and, in turn, adjusts the ways we think about and read Virginia Woolf.

Revival, Ritual, and Reputation: Recovering "J—H—"

While it can be argued that Virginia Woolf actively participated in Jane Harrison's "disappearance" from the public record by including only her initials J—H— in *A Room of One's Own*,[4] it was and continues to be a

---

4. If one tries to google J—H—, as Woolf mysteriously identifies Harrison in the early pages of *A Room*, "J&H Tackle" pops up—"Your fishing tackle super store!"—leaving contemporary, and especially undergraduate, readers a bit perplexed by the reference as well as the efforts required, in an age of information immediacy, to discover exactly to whom this J—H— refers.

landmark gesture pointing out the invisibility and anonymity of women writers, artists, and thinkers of which her essay as a whole was an unveiling. As one of the few professional women scholars with an international reputation by the time she died in 1928, Jane Harrison would have been easily identified by her audiences at Newnham and Girton Colleges, where Woolf claimed to have told the "starved but valiant young women" to "drink wine & have a room of their own" (D 3: 200), but by providing only her initials Woolf was also making a political point about the absence of women from the history of culture. Her essay was an invocation not only of Harrison's example of an educated woman of genius, but also of her work, where in her own essay on women's access to education, "Scientiae Sacra Fames," Harrison wrote: "One of the most ominous signs of the times is that woman is beginning to demand a study" (128) (see Chapter 3). In *Prolegomena*, in a chapter called "The Placation of Ghosts," Harrison discusses the ancient and universal desire to appeal to ghosts for absolution and purification, usually from guilt. She gives an historical case in which a ghost is "wrenched out of the sanctuary" after a ritual is performed and finds its parallel in the mythological example of Orestes, when she writes "It needed a Euripides to see that this ghost was a purely subjective horror, a disordered conscience," as Orestes is plagued, pursued, and undone by his conscience, and becomes aware of his "fell deeds" (P 71). For our purposes, this study is an attempt to correct the "disordered conscience" of the public record which continues to obscure or dismiss her and revivify Harrison's "ghost," especially in relation to her work, her significance to Virginia Woolf and in turn to the literature and internationalism of modernism.

A glimpse into her early life gives us a degree of insight into many of the literary and political passions and preoccupations we find in her lectures, articles, and major work, and about which Virginia Woolf was well aware. Harrison was born 9 September 1850 to an upper-middle-class Northern Yorkshire family of Nonconformists. Her father was a timber merchant with business connections in Russia, and as Annabel Robinson notes, "though it was Greece that inspired her life's work, her life began and ended with ties with Russia" (*The Life and Work of Jane Ellen Harrison* 15), a subject she returns to later in life, when she translates the Russian classic *The Life of the Archpriest Avvakum* (1924) and Russian folktales in *The Book of the Bear* (1926) with her companion, the poet and novelist Hope Mirrlees, in Paris. Harrison's mother died from puerperal fever within days of giving birth to Jane, her third daughter. The children were cared for by an aunt, until her father remarried their governess, Gemimi Merredith, whom Harrison would later describe in her memoir as "the fervent semi-revivalist type" (R 19). In a passage that reveals the seeds of her atheistic principles illustrated in Woolf's letter to Raverat, above, and her early love of languages, she writes of her stepmother:

> She gave us Scripture lessons every Sunday. Her main doctrines were that we must be "born again" and that "God would have our whole hearts or nothing." I think I early felt that this was not quite fair. Why, if we were to care for Him only, had He made this delightful world full of enchanting foreign languages? (19)

As Virginia Woolf asks: "Why, why did my father teach me to read?" ("A Society" 125), Harrison, who learned to read at an extremely young age, cannot remember a time when she did not know how (R 10). One of "the daughters of educated men," Woolf taught herself from the books in her father's library until she could take Greek classes and later study with private tutors, which she paid for out of her own pocket. Like many women of her class in mid- to late-Victorian England, Harrison was basically educated by a series of governesses, who, though frequently surpassed by Harrison's abilities, quickly discovered their pupil's talents and linguistic gifts. At the age of seventeen, after years of navigating the conflicts that arose between her desire to cobble together an education and her social and domestic responsibilities and strict religious training from her stepmother, Harrison was accepted into Cheltenham Ladies College, where she claims she was "summarily dispatched in dire disgrace" (R 27). Her older sister Lucy gave evidence to bolster this claim, because in notes given to Hope Mirrlees after Jane's death, included today in the Jane Harrison Papers at Newnham College, we learn that the real reason Jane was allowed to attend the school was because she had fallen "madly in love" with a local curate. She writes that "their chief opportunity for flirting was choir practices where Jane played the organ. It began to be noticeable that Mr Houseman seemed to have a great deal to say to the organist, and was for ever popping behind the red curtains" (Mirrlees biography notebook, JH Papers). Harrison was sent away to school in 1867 in order to quell rumors and gossip, and she never returned to Yorkshire for any extended period of time. After doing well at Cheltenham, she returned to her family, which had since moved to Wales, to teach her younger step siblings as was expected of young women who had received an education. It was not until 1871, at the age of twenty-

FIGURE 1. Jane Harrison as a young Classics student at Newnham College, Cambridge University, ca. 1880. Photo Credit: The Jane Harrison Papers, Newnham College Archive, The Principal and Fellows, Newnham College, Cambridge.

one, that she received an annuity of £300 from her mother's inheritance, like Virginia Woolf's £500 a year from her aunt, and used the money to travel abroad. During this time she continued to study in natural philosophy and chemistry for the University of London Examination for women and earned a "special certificate of higher proficiency" in 1871 (Robinson, *Life and Work* 33). A childhood friend, Mary Paley, who was one of the original five students to attend the newly established Newnham College, claimed that Harrison was "the cleverest woman in England" (qtd. in Robinson 33), and encouraged her to take the Cambridge University Examination for Women. Harrison said she would take it "for fun," but ended up winning the scholarship.

1. Lectures, *LIKNONS,* and Lantern Slides: Navigating Gender Bias in the Classical Academy

Arriving at Cambridge in 1874, among the first generation of English women to earn a college education, Harrison distinguished herself in her studies. At Newnham, she found a fellowship of women, who were intellectually curious and with whom she made many life-long attachments. She met Ellen Crofts, who introduced her to the Darwin family, through her marriage to Frank Darwin, and Margaret Merrifield who would go on to marry A. W. Verrall, Harrison's teacher and the translator of Aeschylus' *Oresteia,* from which Harrison taught and which Virginia Woolf used to learn Greek (see Chapter 1).

Upon graduation from Newnham, she was passed over for a teaching post for being "insufficiently 'sound'" (Ackerman, *Myth and Ritual School* 74), despite scoring high on the Classical Tripos, the Cambridge Honours degree examinations. Despite initial gestures in the 1860s and 1870s in support of women's higher education at Cambridge, the university devolved into an obstinate prejudice against women that would last until 1948, when women were finally given membership to the University. Their exams were informally marked until 1881, when they were allowed to officially sit for exams. They took their tests in the same manner as male students, but were not allowed a degree or degree title until 1923, when they were given the right (versus the privilege) of attending lectures and earning a degree title. They could not officially hold University posts until 1926. Devastated by the college's lack of support, Harrison traveled abroad and studied at museum collections on Greek art, visited archaeological sites and worked with some of the preeminent German classical archaeologists, honing her skills in the analysis and interpretation of vase fragments and artifacts.

Harrison, rejecting the tradition she was trained in that believed "it was far more important to parse a word than to understand it" (R 57–58), learned and lectured by personal examination of the artifact itself. She studied vase fragments in Cambridge and the Parthenon Marbles and Greek art at the British Museum, but, after Newnham, worked steadfastly again on vase fragments in the museum collections of Berlin, Munich, Florence, Rome, Naples, Palermo, and Athens and later Copenhagen, St. Petersburg (her only trip to Russia), Vienna, and Constantinople. In an interview published 24 August 1889 in *Women's Penny Paper*, she was asked, "You did not find being a woman in your way?" to which she replied:

> Not at all. A woman was a novelty in this field, and my being one was in my favour with regard to professional popularity. Indeed the kindness of foreign archaeologists knew no bounds. Although I had no access to lectures it was made up for by the personal kindness of the professors. In Greece I always meet with a cordial reception, and the papers chronicle my movements. I travel in the remoter parts riding on mules. (JH Papers)

Although, here, she puts a positive gloss on the restrictions she was forced to endure on the basis of her sex, privately she expressed exhaustion at her life-long struggle to promote women's access to education, a battle she waged publicly by her example as well as in print as her scholarly reputation became more established.

Invited to study at The British Museum by Sir Charles T. Newton (the Keeper of the Greek and Roman Antiquities at the time), who took a professional risk in asking her, she continued her analysis of vase fragments, becoming an expert at their interpretation, a skill that would serve her later work well, when she used the narratives depicted on these artifacts to demonstrate the rituals behind Greek myths. During this time, she also began giving lectures at the museum on Greek art that quickly became wildly popular, complete with "oxy-hydrogen lantern illustrations," or hand-painted slides, of primitive Greek art. She made it a rule never to lecture on an object she had not seen herself. In an interview she gave on 24 August 1889 for *Women's Penny Paper: The Only Paper in the World Conducted, Written, Printed, and Published by Women*, the interviewer notes that it was "a difficult standard, but one to which she rigidly adhere[d]" (JH Papers). In the piece, a front page, illustrated feature article, Harrison described her lectures as "working classes," where students would have the opportunity to analyze "problem photographs." She outlines a typical class, when she related in an interview that "when the objects cannot be seen, I give each student a photograph, and they give me their ideas at the next lesson. I thus have a working class. The plan answers excellently" (JH Papers). The photographs were on loan to the students, but if they decided they wanted to keep them permanently, they had to pay 2 s. 6d. (JH Papers). In addition to producing original research, Harrison was an innovative educator. Her lectures are early examples of today's interactive or "smart" classrooms, which support visual pedagogies in classroom settings. Her methods also herald present day theoretical strategies such as "slow looking" at objects in order to instruct and guide students not only in the visual arts, but in all disciplines, including literature, the classics, and history. These "working classes" also serve as early examples of collaborative models for undergraduate research in concert with and guided by a professor's own scholarly research.

In her memoir, Harrison recalls learning the importance of bringing the actual artifact into the classroom or as evidence into her research after a scolding from her friend, Francis Darwin, who was a Cambridge botanist, and son of Charles Darwin (R 57). But Harrison had been augmenting her lectures with archaeological specimens and illustrations long before this memorable episode. In a lecture linking a *liknon* or "winnowing fan," a basket for sifting grain to Dionysus as a fertility god, she had no material example of such a basket, when Darwin had asked her what it was exactly that she was talking about. He exclaimed *"you are writing about a thing you have never seen"* [. . .] Oh, you classical people!" (R 57-58). Darwin ultimately went on a search and found an example of just such a "mystic fan" that was still in use in provincial France, which he sent to her in Cambridge. In the article that resulted from the lecture, published in *the Journal of Hellenic Studies* 23 (1903), she charts the shape, function, and representation of the *liknon* or winnowing fan, on fragments of an Etruscan kylix depicting Hermes in a *liknon,* on two coins of Hadrian, on terracotta plaques in the British Museum, and Hellenistic bas reliefs in the Louvre and Munich, to which she added a photograph of the actual basket Darwin sent her from France.

But she had ultimately devised her public lecture methods on her own, and popularized them as her audiences quickly became so overcrowded she had to limit the classes to thirty per session. Her classes, which lasted until 1887, extended to schools and halls in the provinces, where she taught mainly mothers with young children, members of the working class, and high-school-age boys. At South Kensington's museum, she had audiences of 100–250 people, and at Toynbee Hall and the Midland Institute in Birmingham, nearly 1,000 attendees. Her largest audience was in Dundee, Scotland, where 1,600 men and women assembled to hear her lecture on grave-reliefs. She slowly built a reputation as one of the most entertaining and knowledgeable public lecturers of her day, and points out in an article in the *Pall Mall Gazette* in 1891, that "in those early days, ten years ago, there was nothing of the wide interest of the present day. I have lectured to two or three people only, at the Museum, and see what audiences there are now!" (JH Papers). Advertisements publicized her talks along with her newly published book *Introductory Studies in Greek Art* (1885), and noted that the book was "lucidly conveyed" by "this gifted Lady." She was heralded as a role model and the press instructed, "Englishwomen ought to be proud that one of their sisterhood has accomplished so considerable a work, and done it so thoroughly" (JH Papers). She was a brilliant and dedicated educator, whose syllabi and pamphlets publicizing her lectures quoted Demosthenes, pleading with her audience: "In God's name, I beg of you to think."

Her interactive style of teaching also resonates with the transpersonal and with Woolf's rejection of the masculine lecture voice and her own conversational style opening in *A Room of One's Own* "But, you may say—" inviting participation and dialogue. Like Harrison, Virginia Woolf also taught for nearly two years (without pay), volunteering at Morley College, a night school, to teach history classes and composition. Both Harrison and Woolf were keenly aware of the disparities in their own educations compared to men, but also often conflicted about the objectives and core values of a formal education. As Woolf questioned in *Three Guineas,* "What, then, is this 'university education'?" (31), which required the sacrifices of the educated man's sister, but which was denied her and then, once given, demeaned, denounced, underfunded, and underserved. She questioned and was skeptical about an educational system, "the finest education in the world" that "does not teach people to hate force, but to use it?" (38). Both Woolf and Harrison loathed and were horrified by what Woolf described as "the education of the private house, with its cruelty, its poverty, its hypocrisy, its immorality, its inanity" (TG 49), but they each were also aware of the deeply entrenched flaws of a formal education to the point where Woolf raises the possibility that it may be worse to be included in such a system. After being denied access to the chapel and library at Cambridge and being famously chased off the grass by a beadle, Woolf writes in *A Room of One's Own,* "I thought how unpleasant it is to be locked out; and I thought how it is worse perhaps to be locked in" (24). Both Harrison and Woolf encouraged insubordination in relation to authority, whether in the text or in the university as institution, as they each promoted alternatives and revisions that resisted the status quo of a formal education they each desired but also sought to change.

2. MENTORSHIP AND MONEY: A CHANGE IN DIRECTION

At the turn of the century, as an independent woman scholar in the international academy, Harrison was active in a number of professional societies, but she also lacked the kind of institutional mentoring and support Woolf would later articulate as being essential to producing meaningful work and to advancing a legacy or women's tradition after the work is done. She was Vice-President of the Society for the Promotion of Hellenic Studies from 1889 to 1896 and was elected Corresponding Member of the Berlin Archaeological Institute in 1896. She received honorary degrees from the University of Aberdeen (1895) and University of Durham (1897) as the first female recipient of such honors, but the fact that she was a woman continued to marginalize her intellectual efforts and scholarly ambitions. Despite having a long list of letters of recommendation and testimonials from many of the foremost and internationally renowned scholars in the fields of Classics, Anthropology, and Archaeology,[5] she was passed over twice for the Yates Professorship of Archaeology at University College, London. Each time she was one of two final candidates, but, as Shelley Arlen records, "In the 1888 search, two search committee members signed a minority report stating

5. The list of her supporters is long and distinguished. Reference letters strongly and enthusiastically recommending her for the position were provided by Ernest Babelon, Director of the Bibliothèque Nationale, Paris; Otto Benndorf, Professor of Archaeology, University of Vienna; Henry Craik, Secretary to the Scotch Education Department; Ernst Curtius, Professor of Archaeology, University of Berlin; Richard Garnett, Keeper of the Printed Books, British Museum; Henry Jackson, Fellow and Praelector in Ancient Philosophy, Trinity College, Cambridge; Wilhelm Klein, Professor of Archaeology, University of Prague; Walter Leaf, Trinity College, Cambridge; E. Maunde Thompson, Principal Librarian, British Museum; Luigi Milani, Director of the Archaeological Museum, Florence; Arthur Sidgwick, Fellow and Tutor of Corpus Christi College, Oxford; Henry Sidgwick, Praelector in Moral Philosophy, Trinity College, Cambridge; A. W. Verrall, Fellow of Trinity College, Cambridge; and Paul Wolters of the Kaiserlich Deutsches Archaologisches Institut in Athens. JH Papers.

it "undesirable that any teaching in University College be conducted by a woman" ("'For Love of an Idea'" 168). The 1896 all-male committee pointed out Harrison's inferior education and that she "had not enjoyed the same opportunities for a thorough scholarly grounding in the details of the various branches" as had her male competitor (168). At the final hour, when Harrison seemed just about to be appointed, "committee member W. M. Flinders Petrie put in a good word for the other candidate, his ex-student Ernest Gardner, and "that carried the day," for Harrison had no such mentor on the committee (Calder, qtd. in Arlen 168). The incident points to the crucial importance of mentoring and the ways in which the academy furthered the interests and reputations of its male constituents, realities which led both Harrison and Woolf to theorize the recovery and reclamation of women's writing, research, and lives, in their essays as well as, the need, once recovered, to fund and properly support their reputations in the forms of Chairs, Scholarships, Fellowships, and Foundations, in women's names (see Chapter 3).

Harrison was unable to focus her economic resources and intellectual energies on her major work until she finally received a research fellowship from Newnham College in 1898 at the age of 48, which gave her the time and space to write *Prolegomena*. As she had said in an interview once, despite the popularity and public demand for her talks, "by nature I am more learner than lecturer," and the need to lower the level of the discourse so relentlessly for popular audiences also became a strain, pointing out that "the lecturer has to make the subject as light and as varied as possible [. . . and] must be prepared to generalize a good deal, which is apt to result in much personal demoralization" (*Pall Mall Gazette* [1891]) (JH Papers). The research fellowship changed her life, and she lived and taught at Newnham permanently until she left with "measureless regret" after World War I to live in Paris, more permanently, in 1922. She was discouraged by the failure again of women to be granted degrees, by the attacks on her work, and by the marginalization of her colleagues, who were not elected to academic positions she believed they deserved. In an undated letter, but likely in 1922, she wrote to her longtime colleague and friend Gilbert Murray:

It looks as if this wld be my last year in Cambridge. I retire forcibly the year after & I think it is better not to wait till one is hoofed out. Old Cambridge is gone. I felt that so at the praelections [public lectures given for a Chair to fill the position of the Regius Professor of Greek] . . . write sometimes please. (JH Papers)

Her students felt her departure with deep sadness, and even the students, one of whom would later refer to herself as Harrison's "failure par excellence" (see Chapter 1), were devastated by her move to Paris. Victoria Buxton wrote to her former teacher on 25 May 1922, "To think you are going away from N.C. is very desolating. You *are* it—to me. And I do wish it was to be London, not far-off Paris. Still perhaps you will be able to do more there, there are greater possibilities, & I wonder what language it will be next?" (JH Papers). Harrison moved in with Hope Mirrlees and turned her sights to Russian literature and the Russian language (see Chapter 5), which she learned quickly and well enough to teach it for a short time at Newnham before she retired.

3. EARLY WORK AND "THE BLUE JANE"

Harrison's early work, stylistically speaking, has been linked to a Paterian aestheticism. Given the restrictions placed upon Harrison in her evangelical Christian household during her childhood where beauty was forbidden, it is not surprising that she would identify with the aesthetic movement's Paterian determination to live life "as beautifully and passionately as possible" (Ackerman *Myth and Ritual* 79). Harrison describes meeting Pater in her memoir, writing that he was like a "soft, kind cat" who "purred so persuasively that I lost the sense of what he was saying" (R 46). At Newnham, she had adored the Pre-Raphaelites, decorated her "cave" in Morris wallpaper and Burne-Jones photographs, and was remembered by other Newnham graduates as "the dominating figure in a group of friends; like a Rembrandt picture, with a highlight on her vital imposing figure, tall, willowy, the tight-fitting olive-green serge of the days of the aesthetic craze, her hair in a Greek coil" (qtd. in Prins, "Greek Maenads" 62). In her essay "Greek Maenads, Victorian Spinsters," Yopie Prins writes that Harrison "recognizes in his [Pater's] writing a desire for sensation that also inspires her own writing" (61). Harrison's early work, stylistically, calls to mind Virginia Woolf's own early experimental writings that can be linked to Pater, as well. Her idea of capturing "moments of being" in her prose, intense instances that climax into deeply felt flashes of insight, for example, in her shorter works, such as "Slater's Pins Have No Points," which comprises an intensely felt female mentorship into a matter of seconds, or the more well-known "The Mark on the Wall," which expands and amplifies the meaning of a moment, echoes a Paterian sensibility. As a young woman, Woolf bought Pater's work, and she was briefly tutored in Greek by Pater's sister.

Harrison's focus as a young scholar was largely devoted to Greek art and the stories of the Olympian gods. The early work includes *Myths of the Odyssey in Art and Literature* (1882), *Introductory Studies in Greek Art* (1885), *Mythology and Monuments of Ancient Athens* (1890), and *Greek Vase Paintings* (1894). Of this scholarly production, *Mythology and Monuments of Ancient Athens* marked a dramatic shift in terms of the content of her research, away from myth and art history to the deployment of anthropological approaches in discovering the social origins of ancient Greek religion. This text marked Harrison's arrival as a mature, interdisciplinary scholar, whose early forays into aestheticism gave her a literary gift for writing the visual or eidetic images she analyzed in her work. With its publication, Harrison began to seriously formulate ideas and theories she would later fully realize in her "big books," *Prolegomena, Themis,* and *Epilegomena.*

Mythology and Monuments was known colloquially as "The Blue Jane" for its blue cover and quickly became a standard travel guide for British travelers to Greece at the turn of the century. Harrison had an opportunity to explore the ruins of Athens with some of the leading archaeologists of her day. Robert Ackerman notes, "Dr. Dorpfeld, the director of the excavations being conducted by the German Archaeological Institute, personally led her over the ruins of the ancient city, showing her how closely and strongly cultic reality stood behind mythic narrative (whether narrated in a story or depicted on a vase)" (*Myth and Ritual* 83). This was Harrison's first trip to Greece in 1888 with her friend the art historian and later curator of the Tate D. S. MacColl. She and MacColl traveled to other major classical sites, and Ackerman argues that it was "the Greek experience, combined with a readiness to rethink her basic approach to the past that led her to the theory of the precedence of ritual over myth" (83).

The trip to Greece was transformative for Harrison. Her book, although scholarly, was also accessible to everyday travelers exploring the ruins and relics of Athens. In her vibrant introductory essay to *Mythology and Monuments,* she was suddenly able to write from a much broader canvas and from personal experience, with many more resources available to her from the fields of archaeology, evolution, and ethnography. Ackerman notes:

> Her emphasis on topography and vases implies that myths are not importantly (or at least primarily) to be thought of as verbal constructions (which ultimately might be analyzed philologically) but as secondary developments of a cultic reality that was located in the physical existence

of Greece (not in the Greek imagination) and which therefore had to be
studied with that scene in mind. (82)

The book represented an important turning point for Harrison in actual-
izing her ideas, and can be seen as the beginning of what was perceived
by academic circles as an assault on the discipline of the classics. A trim,
thick, blue-covered text, *Mythology and Monuments* boasts the latest
archaeological commentary with analysis and interpretations by Harrison
based on Dr. Dorpfeld's and others' most recent discoveries in Athens. She
reveals her debt to his work and assistance, as well as marking the turn in
her own work towards the importance of using archaeological evidence in
her own projects. She writes:

> During the spring of 1888 I had the privilege of attending his [Dorp-
> feld's] lectures at Athens on the Dionysiac theatre [. . .] and the succes-
> sive temples at Eleusis. Up to that time the study of topography had been
> to me a weary and most distasteful necessity; then, and not till then, I
> began to realize its close and intimate relation to my own special study,
> and I saw with constantly increasing clearness that the juxtaposition of
> shrines and cults must be a constant factor in the interpretation of both
> ritual and myth. With a rare generosity Dr. Dorpfeld has allowed me to
> make use of many of his as yet unpublished views [. . .]. (*Mythology
> and Monuments* xiv)

In addition to the latest out of Athens, the book is a treasure complete
with fold-out maps, diagrams of Dionysus' theatre, and photographs of
the ruins of the Acropolis, the City of Hadrian, the Street of the Tripods to
the shrine of Demeter, and the west slope of the Acropolis, including the
Areopagus and Academy suburb. Illustrations of vase fragments and photographs of artifacts showing the narratives of local rituals and cults of
Athens fill the pages of the guidebook. Although the translation of Pausanias by Harrison's friend, and wife of her teacher Arthur Verrall, Margaret
de G. Verrall, is the subtitle and claims to be the *raison d'être* of the text,
it is Harrison's commentary which takes the reader along the route Pausanias adopted through the ancient city and which makes up the majority of
the text in the book.

This trip, which resulted in *Mythology and Monuments,* was pre-
cipitated by a profound crisis outlined in her correspondence with D. S.
MacColl, who had criticized her lecturing style. Harrison, in her typical
willingness to see another's point, began a correspondence with MacColl

and soon a friendship, as a result. Initially, however, his rebuke stung as he characterized her lectures as "performances of an overheated, sensationalistic, and superficial kind and related them to her desire to live her life" with a Paterian intensity (Ackerman *Myth and Ritual* 79), and his remarks were meant to insult and provoke her as an emotional woman and a dated aesthete. Despite his equally over-heated, one might argue, shrill comments in his letter, his remarks nevertheless, led her to re-think her methods and approach and to re-focus her considerable talents and intellectual energies towards more rigorous scholarly objectives, and ultimately to pull away from MacColl and exceed many of his own scholarly achievements.

4. THE CAMBRIDGE RITUALISTS AND HARRISON'S "BIG" BOOKS

In addition to being travel partners and friends, Harrison and MacColl collaborated on *Greek Vase Paintings* (1894), but when she returned to Newnham in 1898, she widened her intellectual circle as she began corresponding and working with the like-minded individuals who soon made up the group that would become known as The Cambridge Ritualists. With Jane Harrison as their intellectual leader, the Ritualists were scholars, who were distinguished men in their respective fields: Gilbert Murray was Regis Professor of Greek at Oxford; Francis M. Cornford, a young lecturer, later became the Laurence Professor of Ancient Philosophy at Trinity College, Cambridge; and Arthur Bernard Cook was Reader and then Laurence Professor of Classical Archaeology at Trinity College, Cambridge. When beginning work on The Cambridge Ritualists in 1969, the critic Robert Ackerman quickly realized that the group was "best approached by focusing on the career of Jane Harrison, with Murray, Cornford, and Cook considered in their relationship to her" (*Myth and Ritual* 67), although he curiously leaves her name out of the title for his book. He points to a number of factors for making her the focal point in the content of his research, beginning with Harrison's "need for making passionate intellectual friendships" (68), as well as the reality that "she had a broader conception of their common subject matter than any of the others." She intellectually stimulated them and influenced and encouraged each one in their own individual projects. Murray, whose correspondence with Harrison comprises the majority of her surviving letters, was best known for his *The Rise of the Greek Epic* (1907) and *Four Stages of*

Greek Religion (1912) (later expanded into *Five Stages of Greek Religion* [1925]) and for his work on and translations of Euripides' *Bacchae*. He also contributed "Excursus on the Ritual Forms Preserved in Greek Tragedy" to Harrison's *Themis* (1912). The young Francis M. Cornford, with whom Jane Harrison had an intimate friendship, despite their thirty-year age difference, continues to be read for his work on the Greek philosophers. His books, which fall under the Ritualist aegis, include *Thucydides Mythistoricus* (1907), *From Religion to Philosophy* (1912), and *The Origin of Attic Comedy* (1914). A. B. Cook was not as prolific and although a gifted researcher, was the least talented of the group in terms of writing, which often went painstakingly slowly (Ackerman *Myth and Ritual* 164). He published a five-volume set called *Zeus* (1914–40) and *The Rise and Progress of Classical Archaeology* (1931). As a group they shared the same anthropological comparative approach to classics, but Harrison enriched and expanded their research "by introducing them to material to which they were largely strangers" (Ackerman *Myth and Ritual* 68). Ackerman writes:

> Specifically, she was able to offer a wide and deep knowledge of Greek art and archaeology, and later of contemporary work on religion, psychology, sociology, and philosophy that was invaluable to Cook, primarily a classical folklorist; to Murray, primarily a literary and textual scholar; and to Cornford, primarily a student of ancient philosophy. (68–69)

These three men, of disparate backgrounds, areas of interest, and ages (Murray was ten years Cornford's senior, and formerly a Greek professor at Glasgow without a Cambridge affiliation) were an unlikely band of close colleagues who "first came together in their affection for Jane Harrison [. . . and] each man in the group, especially in the early years, was closer to her than to any of the others" (69). In general, their work examined archaeological evidence and ancient artifacts in order to discover the origins of religion and literature. Harrison, however, in an unorthodox and bold move that resulted in *Prolegomena,* proposed studying Greek religion not by looking at the Olympian gods, which had been the convention in classical study, but at the cultic deities that had come before, and in which, she discovered, women played a significant role.

By the time she returned to Newnham in 1898, Harrison was increasingly attached to using a comparative method to explore similarities and differences between cultures, an approach characteristic of the nineteenth-century anthropology movement, used by ethnographers, archaeologists, folklorists, and anthropologists, like Andrew M. Lang and E. B. Tylor, whose *Primitive Culture* (1871) put forth the idea of "survivals," characteristics, objects, or attitudes that "survived" from one developmental stage to another. The comparative method was applied also by some philologists, such as, Max Muller (whom Harrison had read) who analyzed linguistic "survivals" in primitive cultures. For the purposes of her own research, as Shelley Arlen points out, Harrison adapted a version of structural-functionalism from anthropologist A. R. Radcliffe-Brown that "analyzed these forms to ascertain social and literary structures which in turn, they hypothesized, functioned to meet underlying preconscious, instinctual needs in mankind" ("'For Love of an Idea'" 168). Indeed, the drive behind Harrison's mature work was to plumb the depths of emotion, to look for the deeper patterns, "the hidden shapes" that exist behind our rationalizations in general, by looking at the rituals behind Greek myths. Inspired by French sociologist Emile Durkheim's ideas on religion as a collective representation of the group, she posited in her essay "Unanism and Conversion" that religion "is not the aspiration of the individual soul after a god, or after the unknown, or after the infinite; rather it is the expression, utterance, projection of the emotion, the desire of a group [. . .]. Religion, in its rise, is indistinguishable from social custom, embodying social emotion" ("Unanism and Conversion" 50–51). Her emphasis and theories on group dynamics in relation to Greek myth and ritual find their way into Woolf's fiction, especially, and Woolf's own exploration in her work of family rituals and group dynamics in relation to social mores and group pathology, an area we'll more closely explore in Chapter Two.

Themis, Harrison's second major work, built on her ideas set forth in *Prolegomena* and continued to explore the relationship between Greek ritual and myth. Her ideas on women-based cults, Dionysus as Year-Spirit, and Themis presented in these two texts definitively challenged the content and the boundaries of the discipline (see Chapter 2), and altered the way we speak about and understand the classics. The third in the trilogy of Harrison's "big books," *Epilegomena* (1921), synthesized many of the key ideas presented in her two previous works, but amplified and extended its discussion beyond Greek religion to a discourse on religion itself. *Epilegomena* also included added insights she now had in hand from her readings in Freud, Jung, and Russian philosophy. In her article "The Pillar and the Maiden" (1907), Harrison was already using Freud, whom she had read in German, to talk about the connection between primitive Greek rituals and our deeply-held impulses and emotions. She writes:

Finally it has been suggested to me that *eikonism* and *aneikonism* in their ultimate analysis represent the workings of those two factors of our being with which modern science is now and rightly, but so tardily, much concerned, the conscious and the subconscious. The subconscious makes for fusion, union, emotion, ecstasy; the conscious for segregation, discrimination, analysis, clarity of vision. On the action and interaction of these two our whole spiritual vitality would seem to depend. It is a far-reaching thought. I believe it to be true. ("The Pillar and the Maiden" 13)

Here, are early signs of the interrelations between psyche, myth, and the development of society and culture we find more fully conceptualized in *Epilegomena* in 1921. In its first two chapters, she delineates the distinctions she had made between primitive ritual and primitive theology in earlier texts, but the third chapter, "The Religion of Today" takes her into a new discussion on mysticism, the need for asceticism in the younger generations, philosophy, and psychology. She begins with an Orphic saying in the subtitle of her first chapter, which translates as "I have fled the evil, I have found the better" and ends by promoting the crucial importance of "the setting out of the soul towards a higher value" (E 38) based on interaction and collaboration instead of heroics and a poetics of violence, jealousies, and war.

Harrison writes *Epilegomena* from the vantage point of a post-war Europe, nine years after the publication of *Themis*, at the age of seventy-one. Just as "Old Cambridge was gone," she understood that Europe would be irrevocably changed by the war in 1914, but "alien to her was the wartime glow of her colleagues and students [. . . and] she refused to blind herself to the fact that the war was savagery and a setback to civilization" (Wilson, preface to *Themis* viii–ix). Her essay "Epilogue on the War: Peace with Patriotism," collected in 1915 in *Alpha and Omega*, grew out of her unbending pacifist stance, a position she shared with Virginia Woolf and a work that gestures toward Woolf's later pacifist polemic, *Three Guineas* (see Chapter 4). During the war years, from 1914–1916, she traveled to Paris, at great risk, when she was referred to a specialist there for medical reasons. She also discovered the École des Langues Orientales, which taught classes in Russian, and she and her companion, Hope Mirrlees, soon began to take classes. However, by 1921 with the publication of *Epilegomena,* she was writing not only with the horrors of war fresh in her mind, but also with the physical distance afforded by what would become a permanent break with Cambridge. *Epilegomena* gestures towards religion as the preservation of the group, much in the same way that primitive ritual invokes a singular individual, the young god, the Year-Spirit of *Prolegomena* and *Themis*, whose role and function was connected with the group, with regeneration and with life's preservation, not its destruction.

After writing *Epilegomena*, Harrison feared that the book was a failure and that it would not or could not be heard by a generation that had suffered as much as had the survivors of World War I. On 30 July 1921, however, Gilbert Murray, whom she respected and admired, wrote to her:

> The Epilegomena are a wonderful achievement. They ought to be read
> before, not after, your big books—they provide exactly the key that was
> wanted, and the unification. It is a very great thing to have got the state-
> ment of your whole position into 40 coherent pages. (JH Papers)

In the 1962 edition, *Epilegomena* is usefully published as Murray suggested, *before Themis* in a two-in-one volume set. The book makes important connections between Greek religion and myth, but its main contribution was in raising brave questions about the nature of religion, and in its ability to reveal Harrison as a scholar continuing to stay open to new ideas brought about by the nascent fields of psychology and sociology.

5. REPUTATION: "OH DAMN"

In a memorable scene in Virginia Woolf's *Jacob's Room,* Jacob and other male students copy out poetry and wait for their books in the Reading Room of The British Museum, while the forlorn feminist, Miss Julia Hedge, feels uncomfortable and unwelcome as she daydreams and struggles to think through her flawed and silly argument about women's work potentially leading to their extinction. Her books do not arrive as she gazes up at the museum's glorious and lofty dome and begins reading "the names of great men" (JR 111), when she interrupts herself and curses "Oh damn [. . .] why didn't they leave room for an Eliot or a Brontë?" The passage is marked by Hedge's outsidership, her untenable position and her bitterness as the male readers are given "every consideration" as they set to their intellectual tasks, and the scene is one of many in Woolf's work which insists on the importance of tangible, material support in encouraging, creating, recovering, and sustaining women's writing and women's lives. The fictional Miss Hedge finds herself surrounded and targeted by the "enormous mind" that is housed in the Reading Room and supported and displayed on the dome. Woolf writes "[c]losely stood together in a ring round the dome were Plato, Aristotle, Sophocles, and Shakespeare; the literatures of Rome, Greece, China, India, Persia" (112), but there is no room for the writings by a woman. Even though she has newly been allowed access to "the mind," Hedge might as well be "the woman in the mews behind Great Ormond Street who has come home drunk and cries all night long, "Let me in! Let me in!" (114). Her awkward, annoying presence, however, while outlining a symptom of women's lack of access to education, also acts as the beginning of a solution, and a plea for women students and researchers, despite false starts, disappointments, indifference, and sometimes outright hostility, to write the lives, collect the work, and further the reputations of the women scholars and writers who will make up a tradition of their own, and this study notes the ongoing need to participate in that practice and that theory as outlined by Woolf throughout her writing life, as it questions Harrison's own obscurity and diminishment in the discourse today.

While Jane Marcus was the first to allude to Harrison as a source of Virginia Woolf's work (as early as 1977 in Marcus's essays on *The Years* and *The Pargiters,* first published in the *Bulletin of the New York Public Library* and reprinted in *Virginia Woolf and the Languages of Patriarchy* in 1987), Robert Ackerman was the first to resurrect Jane Harrison's work based on its own merits (in his doctoral dissertation, "The Cambridge Group and the Origins of Myth Criticism," in 1969). When I interviewed Professor Ackerman in June 2006 at Cambridge University, he remembered his director trying to persuade him to choose another topic, because "they [the Cambridge Ritualists] were wrong." After reading *Prolegomena,* however, Ackerman fell in love with Jane Harrison's writing style, the passion, intellect, and generosity she brought to her subject, and her original mind. Like any good researcher who is told "no," he resolved to at least entertain the possibility of "yes," to keep the conversation going, to make note of the imperfections, but also explore what the Cambridge Ritualists "got right." In the book *The Myth and Ritual School: J. G. Frazer and the Cambridge Ritualists* (2002) that grew out of his thesis, Ackerman notes that "reading anything by or about Harrison, one is struck forcefully by her intellectual power and her passionate nature" and he counts her as "one of those rare and fortunate persons who recognize no barriers between specialist knowledge and everyday life, and who bring to both an extraordinary energy and integrity" (70). He writes that she seems to have possessed "a burning insistence on following the truth wherever it leads. One believes it to be true of her as of few others" (73). *Virginia Woolf, Jane Ellen Harrison, and the Spirit of Modernist Classicism* discusses the Ritualists' contributions and the reception of their ideas, but what the Cambridge group "got right or wrong," whether Jane Harrison saw Dionysus as coming from the east or from the west, for example, is of secondary importance to my argument, which is more interested in Harrison's work and how her theories and her politics are read, shared, and revised in a transpersonal, cross-reading by Virginia Woolf in her own work.

Although this study does not attempt to write Harrison's life, a brief look at the biographies published thus far provide context to Harrison as subject and the need for an updated perspective on her life and work. Robert Ackerman, although not one of her biographers per se, remains in my view one of the best writers on the details of Jane Harrison's life to date. Shockingly and disconcertingly, Harrison is frequently disparaged by her biographers in an effort to diminish one's subject that I have yet to come to grips with. As of this writing, the tone and views of her biographers are in serious need of updating and too often do a disservice to a woman who helped to create the disciplines of archaeology and anthropology and whose work continues to be recognized by scholars studying classical Greek thought and culture today. Annabel Robinson's *The Life and Work of Jane Ellen Harrison* (2002) has good information but does not offer a serious analysis of Harrison's work, thought, and influence. Sandra J. Peacock's psychoanalytic *Jane Ellen Harrison: The Mask and the Self* (1988) has a number of inaccuracies; the highly regarded Newnham Classicist Mary Beard, who by all rights is Jane Harrison's successor, wrote a *faux* biography, *The Invention of Jane Harrison* (2000), that is unbalanced and unfair and a factor in the continued erasure and diminishment of Harrison's work and reputation; Hugh Lloyd Jones's brief profile of Harrison in *Cambridge Women: Twelve Portraits* (1996) is conservative and limited in scope; and in his book *The Dons* (1999), Noel Annan soberly records the accomplishments of nearly every male educator at Cambridge over the last two hundred years, but feels compelled to comment on Harrison's sex life when he writes in a kind of adspeak that "She liked good-looking, brainless girls as well as her favourite student, Jessie Steward [*sic*], her first first" (237–38). When I pointed out this passage to an archivist at Newnham she replied, "he'd be hard-pressed to find a 'brainless girl' at Newnham. Jessie Stewart, notwithstanding, Hope Mirrlees spoke at least four languages." In general, however, Harrison's example during her own times and after her death has provoked hostility and a less than objective response, either damning her or elevating her to sainthood, which this project explores and seeks to address.

After Harrison's death, both Hope Mirrlees and Jessie Stewart attempted to write her official biography. The Jane Harrison Papers at Newnham College are filled with notes and pages of manuscript of Hope Mirrlees's false starts and Mirrlees's and Stewart's increasingly divergent views on how best to move forward with the book. Perhaps because she was too close to her subject and unable to talk candidly about their intimate relationship, Hope Mirrlees's efforts never materialized and the project was ultimately abandoned. Jessie Stewart went on to publish some of Harrison's surviving letters in *Jane Harrison: A Portrait from Letters* (1959), but these do not represent the entire collection or a faithful transcription of much of the original correspondence in the archive. An accurate rendering of Harrison's papers with annotations is due, and such a project is said to be in its early stages, but underway, by the classicist Annabel Robinson. In any case, there are no full-length studies which adequately convey the importance of Harrison's work to modernist writers, early twentieth-century thought, or to Virginia Woolf, in particular, which this study is an attempt to begin to rectify.

With few exceptions, the academic community, generally speaking, has marginalized or ignored the work of The Cambridge Ritualists. Their ideas, however, were not dismissed because they were superseded by new evidence. The evidence had always been challenged and even admitted to with some very important caveats by the Ritualists themselves as being theoretically based. Their contributions faded as the fields they helped to create—anthropology, archaeology, sociology, and psychology— became more specialized and self-contained. As pioneers, in many ways, they did the more difficult work of venturing forth into new areas of inquiry, blazing trails, some more fruitful than others. However, *because* their work was new and radical at the time, they were also open to a great deal of criticism from their own and from succeeding generations. Furthermore, their work focused almost exclusively on the question of origins, a topic that with the advent of deconstructionist and social and cultural theory became of subordinate importance.

The Ritualists have not fared well in non-literary disciplines especially. Not surprisingly with their emphasis on traditional textual and philological study, the Classicists had been their most heated adversaries, with two exceptions. George Thomson and T. B. L. Webster acknowledged Ritualist contributions, but Thomson especially, for whom Jane Harrison's work "remained alive and meaningful," noted his debt to her as he "pursued precisely the path blazed by Harrison in *Themis*" in his classical studies *Aeschylus in Athens* (1941) and *Studies in Ancient Greek Society* (1949) (Ackerman, *Myth and Ritual* 189). Anthropologists and folklorists, as the fields developed, moved away from theory towards treating myths and rituals as primary source material (which Harrison also did), and the Ritualists' work continues to be of value to those studying the history of these disciplines. Philosophy as a discipline today has little interest in the Cambridge group. However, the philosophy of culture, language, and ideas, "in man as a symbol-creating and-using being, and in phenomenology" (195), continues to find the their work useful.

Literary criticism is the one field that has continued to value to a certain degree the Ritualists' contributions for the very reason that their work, the exploration of the ritual structures that lie behind myths and how language governs culture, offers insight into literature. Since the 1950s, critics have explored the contributions of the Cambridge Ritualists as a whole or in terms of its individual members in relation to literature of the twentieth century, but they have more frequently dismissed, denied, or completely overlooked Jane Harrison's influence on major modernist texts, with rare exceptions. In addition to Jane Marcus and Robert Ackerman, who have essays on Harrison in larger collections or works, Martha C. Carpentier's *Ritual, Myth, and the Modernist Text* (1999) has important chapters on Harrison's contributions to T. S. Eliot, James Joyce, and Woolf, and my own study is indebted to their earlier research in keeping Harrison's work and reputation alive. It is a continuing controversy, as well as a curiosity, however, that modernist critics persist in citing Harrison's contemporary Sir James G. Frazer's *The Golden Bough,* but neglect Harrison's more significant contributions. Carpentier suggests that the publication in 1973 of John B. Vickery's *The Literary Impact of The Golden Bough* overemphasized the influence of James Frazer and his lengthy, data-rich, argument-poor study in *The Golden Bough*. Although he was a colleague of the Cambridge Ritualists, Frazer was its weakest contributor, and known among his peers as an "arm-chair anthropologist" or of the "Covent Garden school of anthropology," because he had "never once been on a field trip" (Vickery 40). Carpentier argues that Vickery's study privileging Frazer continues to this day to overshadow Harrison's work and distort the historical record. For three decades, but as early as Marcus's essays on Harrison and Virginia Woolf's *The Years* in 1977, feminist scholars, including Carpentier, Martha Vicinus, Bonnie Kime Scott, and Melba Cuddy-Keane, and classicists, such as Annabel Robinson, have steadfastly remarked upon the value of Harrison's work.

However, the notion of Frazer as a dominant influence on modernist texts prevails, and few outside of academic circles have ever heard of Harrison's name.

Robert Ackerman has tried to dispel Frazer's shadow by keeping to the historical record. He also discounts any link between the originality of her ideas and those of William Robertson Smith, who was an early proponent of the use of sociology in analyzing religion. He writes:

> *Mythology and Monuments* appeared in 1890, the same year as the first edition of *The Golden Bough.* The simple fact of contemporaneity seems conclusive evidence that any formulation [. . .] which has ritualist criticism emerging from under the shade of *The Golden Bough* is mistaken [. . .]. Nor was William Robertson Smith any more of a factor in influencing her thought, for we should surely have had some mention of her having attended the lectures that were printed as *The Religion of the Semites,* and no evidence to that effect exists. Add to this the fact that she was in Greece during part of the time that Smith was lecturing, and we may safely deny Smith any formative role in her ideas. (*Myth and Ritual* 83)

While Harrison was certainly open to Frazer's use of the comparative method and anthropological approach, his research focused on the folk cults of Continental Europe, not on the Greeks, and his editions of *The Golden Bough* were filled mostly with information and very few ideas or theories. *Mythology and Monuments,* in contrast, was a thorough examination and theoretical study of Greek ritual and myth, supported by archaeological evidence Harrison gained access to from both her trips to Greece and her personal research of vase collections in museum archives in Britain and Russia and in major cities across Europe.

Harrison's work on her own or as a member of the Cambridge Ritualists was interdisciplinary, involving archaeology, anthropology, sociology, psychology, linguistics, as well as her background in traditional classical study. Her scholarly contributions transcend the label of "Ritualist" or even "Cultural Anthropologist," as she was called, and no sooner is she assigned one label than the name does not quite fit and blends and blurs into yet another category that in turn becomes inadequate and unable to hold her. Her politics, her feminism, atheism, and her radical pacifist positions, ideas elaborated in her collection of essays *Alpha and Omega,* are also both contained in and transcend the boundaries of her Greek work. It is truly in the body of her entire work, the Greek texts, but also her essays, her articles, and her memoir, and in the example of her life as a public intellectual that we find the underpinnings of a reputation worth preserving, and it is one of the aims of this study to participate in Harrison's recovery and to argue the centrality of her place in relation to Woolf's own feminism, pacifism, and writing life.

Of Goddesses and Ghosts, A Reprise

I began my own research for this study, curiously enough, with the opening line of a little known poem called *Paris* by Jane Harrison's former student and later companion, Hope Mirrlees,[6] a poem which Virginia Woolf chose and handset in the winter of 1919–1920 for the Hogarth Press. The poem, which Woolf called "very obscure, indecent, and brilliant" (L 2: 384–85), was filled with intriguing references which reminded me of T. S. Eliot's 1922 *The Waste Land,* but which had been published two years before his speakers' more well-known modernist chronicle of a postwar London landscape. *Paris'* female speaker tours a postwar urban landscape in a single day, 1 May 1919, during the signing of The Treaty of Versailles. The opening line "I want a holophrase" intrigued me, along with references, which proved to be as Woolf said, "very obscure." "The Year-Spirit," the strange reproduction of the constellation of Ursa Major, The Great Bear, as a cryptic, dedicatory epigraph at the end of the poem, each turned out to be my introduction to the work of "J—H—," the mysterious, ghostly scholar of pre-Phidias archaic Greek art and pre-Olympian Greek goddesses, haunting the grounds of Virginia Woolf's fictional Fernham College in *A Room of One's Own.* The references, like scarifications upon a relic, are the more obvious marks upon the poem of Jane Harrison's scholarship and passion for learning, by Hope Mirrlees. In an enduring gesture of her respect for Harrison's intellect, "the giant upon

---

6. In addition to *Paris,* Hope Mirrlees is the author of the novels *Madeleine: One of Love's Jansenists,* published by Hogarth Press in 1919, which is suggestive of Harrison and Mirrlees's intimate relationship; *The Counterplot* (1924); *Lud-in-the-Mist* (1926); *A Fly in Amber: Sir Robert Bruce Cotton* (1963); *Poems, Cape Town* (1963); *Moods and Tensions: Poems* (1976); and the articles "Quelques aspects de l'art d'Alexis M. Remizov," *Journal de Psychologie Normale et Pathologique.* 15 January–15 March 1926: 148-159; "Listening to the Past," *Nation and Atheneum,* 11 September 1926; "The Religion of Women," *Nation and Atheneum,* 28 May 1927; "Gothic Dreams," *Nation & Atheneum,* 3 March 1928; and "Bedside Books," *Life and Letters,* December 1928. The science fiction writer Joanna Russ wrote "Zanzibar Cat" (1971) in homage to Hope Mirrlees.

whose shoulders we all stand,"[7] Hope wrote Jane's work like a shadow into nearly every line of *Paris,* and as a kind of last word on their personal relationship and love for each other, encoded in an epigraph that comes, not at the beginning, but at the end of the poem, in symbols rather than words, of the constellation of The Great Bear, one of Mirrlees's many pet names for Harrison.

A "holophrase" in the opening line of *Paris* is a term Mirrlees borrows directly from *Themis* (1912), in which Harrison unveils the "hidden shapes" behind Greek rituals and examines the psychological aspects of language (see Chapter 2). As a mature woman scholar in her sixties, Harrison, I learned, was an early advocate of Sigmund Freud's work in England, which "is only the best example of her amazing willingness to remain open to new thoughts or, what is nearly as good, to recognize her prejudices as such and compensate for them" (Ackerman *Myth and Ritual* 72). She also had a literary gift and passion for words, knew eleven living languages and five dead languages (Vicinus 152), and regardless of her subject consistently reached for linguistic examples in order to illustrate her points. She explains "holophrase" in a passage which echoes with Bernard's "little language unknown to men" in Virginia Woolf's *The Waves,* her "abstract mystical eyeless book" (D 3: 203) that in a letter to the composer Ethel Smyth she said she wrote "to a rhythm and not to a plot" (L 4: 204) as follows:

> Language, after the purely emotional interjection, began with whole sentences, *holophrases,* utterances of a relation in which subject and object have not yet got their heads above water but are submerged in a situation. A holophrase utters a holopsychosis. Out of these *holophrases* at a later stage emerge our familiar 'Parts of Speech,' rightly so called, for speech was before its partition. (T 473–74)

She goes on to give an example of a Fuegian holophrase, *mamihlapinatapai,* which means "*looking-at-each-other,-hoping-that-either-will-offer-to-do-something-which-both-parties-desire-but-are-unwilling-to-do*" (474). According to Harrison, a holophrase was a primitive, pre-literate, fixed meaning-making representation in language for a larger, complex set of ideas, a theory that pre-dates Kristeva's "semiotic" or preoedipal level of language. Far from being impersonal, she states, "the holophrase shows us man entangled as it were in his own activities, he and his environment

---

7. Hope Mirrlees's dedication to Jane Harrison, translated from the Greek, in her first novel, *Madeleine: One of Love's Jansenists* (1919).

utterly involved" (474). A holophrase, and the larger holopsychosis, then, for me, represents a kind of longing for intimacy that is inclusive of but also amplifies both Woolf's theory and practice of "thinking back through our mothers" and Miller's "transpersonal" frame. Harrison's work also resonates with Kristeva's "project from the purely female desire to rejoin the mother" (Marcus, *Languages of Patriarchy* 7), but extends this model with a more universal choral consciousness, an intimacy with what Harrison refers to as the Unbounded Whole, a verbal exposure (similar to those expressed by the six choral voices in *The Waves*), striving to defeat death and reanimate life through language. This communal, collective chant is read by Harrison and Woolf as feminist as it is women-guided and does not yet comprehend the order and linearity of the patriarchal language of the state. The holophrase for Harrison is a meaning-making tool that the speaker in Mirrlees's poem yearns for ("I want a holophrase"), as she begins her mythic passage via the French Underground Railway through the streets of Paris on 1 May 1919.

After discovering *Paris* through the work of feminist critics Jane Marcus and Julia Briggs, I studied the original in the Berg Collection of the New York Public Library.[8] It is an unassuming little book, and I was immediately struck by how tiny it was, with a trim size of 4 ½" wide x 6 ¼" long; how fixed, single, and whole it was in its holiday wrapper of green and red diamonds, with a plain, white, raised label reading on two lines PARIS HOPE MIRRLEES on its cover, and how it gave no hint of the bigness of the history and politics inside—how like a holophrase itself, a physical rendering of this longed-for intimacy, both pre-language, through language, above and below language, "utterances of a relation in which subject and object have not yet got their heads above water but are submerged in a situation" (T 473–74). For *Paris*, as its lines connect the reader to its international politics, history, music, and the arts, connected me, in my own transpersonal process of entanglement, reading across generations, across bodies of writing by women, to the themes of peace-making and peace-building, to the work of Jane Ellen Harrison and Virginia Woolf, to Greek goddesses and Cambridge ghosts. *Virginia Woolf, Jane Ellen Harrison, and the Spirit of Modernist Classicism*

---

8. Hogarth Press printed 175 copies in all, in 160 of which Virginia Woolf made last-minute corrections by hand (Briggs *Reading* 84). In addition to the copies in the Berg Collection at the New York Public Library, there are copies in the special collections of Princeton University, the University of Delaware, and Columbia University. Holdings in the United Kingdom were not available at this writing. Three pages of proofs can be found in the E. J. Pratt Library, Victoria University, Toronto, Canada, and *Paris* was most recently reprinted in *Gender in Modernism*, edited by Bonnie Kime Scott (2007).

restores the connections between these two major feminist, public intellectuals, as it shows the significance of the questions they grappled with in their own time and the relevance of their ideas to today and to future seekers of new plots, new ways of thinking and being that do not rehearse the disparities and hostilities of the past, but insist on more equitable and just alternatives.

Chapter One, "Of the Nymph and the Noun: Jane Harrison, Janet Case, and Virginia Woolf's Greek Education—from Mentorship to Transpersonal Desire," argues that Harrison's connection to Woolf begins through Woolf's Greek education under the tutelage and mentorship of Janet Case, but shifts to a lateral relationship of shared desires and ideas marked by Harrison's own subversion and her challenge to the classics. The discussion examines the methods employed by Janet Case to teach Woolf Greek, and suggests that these "ardent theories" were in fact inspired and developed by Jane Harrison's unorthodox technique for teaching Greek at Newnham College. Reading this early Harrison–Woolf encounter transpersonally allows us to categorize Woolf's desire for Greek myth and ritual as driven by Harrison's pedagogy as well as by her research and political views. The chapter decidedly places Woolf, not within Bloomsbury, but alongside and within a circle of independent women thinkers, a feminist collective articulated by Harrison's "learned community of women" she dreamed of creating in her memoir, *Reminiscences of a Student's Life.*

Chapter Two, "The Making and Re-Making of a God(dess): Re-writing Modernism's War Story—Feminist Ritual Structures as Transpersonal Plots," deploys literary analysis and feminist theory to discuss Harrison's revision of Zeus and her re-interpretation of Greek goddesses in myth and ritual in her major works and their appearances in Virginia Woolf's fiction. I focus on novels that have received little or no critical attention in relation to Harrison's work, choosing *Night and Day, Jacob's Room, Mrs. Dalloway,* and *The Waves* as a representative selection. The chapter also focuses on Woolf's two Greek notebooks, "The Agamemnon Notebook" (1922) and "The Libation Bearers Notebook" (1907), and places Woolf in relation to her contemporaries and within the context, not of modernism's "mythic method," but of Harrison's, whose theories and re-interpretations allow Woolf to create a literary (and political) modernism that is transpersonal, feminist, and distinctive from her male contemporaries.

Chapters Three and Four, "Reading Transpersonally I and II," respectively, explore the parallels between Woolf's two major essays, *A Room of*

One's Own and *Three Guineas,* and Harrison's essays on women's rights, access to education and the professions, and the sources of violence and war. Chapter Three, "Next Comes the Wife's Room . . . ," reads Woolf's *A Room of One's Own* alongside Harrison's "Scientiae Sacra Fames." Chapter Four, "Women Building Peace," reads Woolf's major essay on peace, *Three Guineas,* alongside Harrison's response to World War I, "Epilogue on the War: Peace with Patriotism," analyzing where their feminism and pacifism dovetail and diverge. This chapter argues that Woolf's and Harrison's pacifism should be read as significant texts in the women's international movement for peace and also in helping to create a vocabulary and intellectual discourse on peace that allowed the future discipline of Peace and Conflict Resolution Studies to become established and grow.

Chapter Five, "To Russia with Love: Literature, Language, and a Shared Ideology of the Political Left," discusses Harrison's and Woolf's engagement with Russian language and literature and argues for a revaluation of Woolf's leftist politics as it also examines their transpersonal points of contact with the political and literary fallout from the 1917 Russian Revolution. I also explore Harrison's experiences at the Pontigny Décades, in 1923 and 1924, the Russian writers and philosophers she met there, and her international reputation as a scholar and public intellectual as it intersects with Woolf's own literary and political networks. A version of this chapter has appeared in *Leonard and Virginia Woolf, the Hogarth Press, and the Networks of Modernism, edited by Helen Southworth* (Edinburgh: Edinburgh University Press 2010).

The Afterword, "Modernism's Transpersonal *and:* Re-connecting Women's Lives/Women's Work and the Politics of Recovering a Reputation," explores the interpretive significance of reading Harrison's work alongside Virginia Woolf's writing life in light of their many points of contact. Understanding their relationship transpersonally as a feminist friendship, we see that Woolf's use of Harrison's re-interpretation of the Olympians enriched and informed not only her literary aesthetic, but also a politics she discovered, developed, and shared by way of Harrison's example as a public intellectual. This afterword also explores the politics of Harrison's erasure as it re-visits the need for an updated, accurate biography of Harrison's life and for the work that is yet to be done in looking at Harrison's extensive cultural and literary output in relation to other modernist authors, ethicists, linguists, anthropologists, psychologists, and philosophers.

CHAPTER 1

Of the Nymph and the Noun

Jane Harrison, Janet Case, and
Virginia Woolf's Greek Education—
From Mentorship to Transpersonal Desire

VIRGINIA WOOLF'S connection to Jane Harrison begins through her tutor, Janet Case (1864–1937) and her emulation of Harrison's pedagogy in teaching Woolf Greek, but ultimately expands into a relationship of shared ideas as Woolf's awareness of Harrison's example and her wanderings in the lore of Harrison's published work increases. As she matures, her aesthetic and politics resonate with Harrison's controversial theories and discoveries, with each new text she writes, and it is to a Harrisonian perspective on the classics that Virginia Woolf commits at an early age.

When Woolf writes in *A Room of One's Own* that "we think back through our mothers if we are women" (75), she is theorizing a tradition that has yet to exist, or one that is too partial, short, or so new, that it is difficult to lay claim to it or find secure footing. She makes note of the exceptions, "Jane Harrison's books on Greek archaeology," among other women writer-pioneers who have given us examples of "books by the living" (AROO 79) that we can turn to for role models of women's writing and women's experience. Woolf looked up to Jane Harrison, and their personal and intellectual contact is begun when Janet Case introduces her, as a young woman in her early twenties, to the distinguished scholar "Miss Harrison" at Newnham College in 1904. Harrison's *Prolegomena to the Study of Greek Religion* was newly published and her revolutionary ideas on women's roles in Dionysiac and orgiastic cults, appealed to Virginia Woolf, as they initiated a challenge to a classical discourse dominated by the Olympians and a strict adherence to grammar and translation. As Harrison would go on to write in *Themis* in 1912, "to the orthodox among my contemporaries, and to the younger reactionaries, *Themis* has appeared dangerous. Their fear is justified" because "A hand was laid upon their ark" (T 538). The Harrison–Woolf relationship begins on the vertical axis of mentoring (and mothering) with important intellectual protection provided by Janet Case, but evolves into one characterized by the transpersonal, an intellectual affinity and "friendship," that she would ultimately share with Jane Harrison, and a desire for Greek that Woolf reads laterally, interactively as feminist and subversive. This relationship, as such, locates Woolf, politically and productively, not in Bloomsbury, nor in her father's library, but within a feminist collective of independent women thinkers, Jane Harrison's "learned community of women" (R 89), which she had dreamed of founding in her memoir, *Reminiscences of a Student's Life,* which Woolf had read and published in 1925.

Reading the Harrison–Woolf relationship as shifting from a mentoring axis to the lateral, transpersonal plane adds Harrison with emphasis to Woolf's feminist and classical *bona fides* but also allows us to characterize Woolf's desire for Greek and her later use of the classics in her own work as driven by and embodied in Harrison's scholarship and example. Woolf discovers a refuge of feminist and feminine erotics in Harrison's work, which she transforms initially into a poetics of sensuality and sexual vitality, alternative "moments of being," she exacts with pleasure from the text (under the watchful eye of her tutor, Janet Case), and later into arguments for political theories and positions on women's education, women's work, and pacifism, as she moves intellectually and artistically away from Case and matures as a writer. This common ground is attained through Woolf's access to Harrison's pedagogy, as well as her research, for Case's methods for teaching Woolf Greek and the content of her curriculum were strategies and techniques developed and inspired by Jane Harrison. This chapter explores the nature of Virginia Woolf's Greek education and argues that Janet Case's mentorship allows Virginia Woolf to recognize Harrison's subversion and challenge to the classics as a shared, transpersonal desire and common goal.

"My Varied Experience of Greek Teachers":
Greek Tutor as Mother/Mentor

With the death of her mother in 1895 and then her older half-sister, Stella, in 1897, Virginia Woolf spent much of her life seeking maternal affection and protection (sometimes in the form of male mothers, such as her husband, Leonard Woolf),[1] and Janet Case assumed the role initially of elder mentor, tutor, and mother figure to a young Virginia Stephen. Her early portrait of "Miss Case" gives us an example of Virginia's intellectual curiosity, playfulness, and excitement at meeting her for the first time and provides us with a glimpse into what her new instructor expected of her and was up against in tutoring so "passionate an apprentice:"

> When I first saw her one afternoon in the drawing room, she seemed to me exactly what I had expected—tall, classical looking, masterfull [sic]. But I was bored at being taught, & for some time, only did just what was asked from me, & hardly looked up from my book—that is at my teacher. But she was worth looking at. She had fine bright eyes—a curved nose, the teeth too prominent indeed—but her whole aspect was vigorous & wholesome. She taught well too. My varied experience of Greek teachers makes me a good judge of their merits I think. (PA 182)

By the time her older brother Thoby, whom she referred to in her letters as "a Greek God, but rather too massive for the drawing room" (L 1: 72) had gone off to begin his public school education, Virginia, at the age of fifteen, began her "varied experience of Greek teachers," writing to him on 24 October 1897 that "I am beginning Greek at King's" (L 1: 10–11). Her first tutor, George Warr, had created the Ladies Department of Kings College, and also knew Jane Harrison, as nearly a decade earlier, he had organized fundraisers by putting on what became known in the 1880s as "five o'clock antiquity" short scenes from *The Iliad* and *The Odyssey* linked together by a common theme, and in which Jane Harrison frequently appeared.[2] After George Warr, Walter Pater's sister,

---

1. For a discussion of Leonard Woolf as "good enough" mother, see J. Marcus, "Thinking Back through Our Mothers," in *Art and Anger* 88.

2. The scenes were performed in English on one night and in Greek on the second night (Robinson Life and Work 82). Harrison was given parts in the Greek cast and would frequently appear in his productions. Although Warr's "The Tales of Troy," as his productions were called, were an amateur affair, they attracted talent, a number of celebrities, and many leading lights in the classical academic world. Mrs. Bram Stoker played Calypso on the English night; Lionel Tennyson, Alfred Lord Tennyson's son, played Ulysses on the

FIGURE 2. Virginia Stephen and her nephew Julian Bell at
Moat House, Blean, near Canterbury, ca. 1910. Her tutorial
relationship with Janet Case had ended the year before in 1909.
She is on holiday, here, recovering from an illness. Photo Credit:
© Tate, London 2011.

Clara[3], tutored her, in 1899, the same year Thoby entered Trinity College,
Cambridge with Lytton Strachey, Leonard Woolf, and Clive Bell. Accord-

---

Greek night; and Virginia Woolf's cousin, the volatile J. K. Stephen, the "well-connected
young don about town, later to be in the front rank of celebrity suspects for Jack the Rip-
per" (Beard 39), played Hector. Harrison played Penelope on the Greek night and went on
to play Alcestis at Oxford in 1887.

3. Clara Pater would go on to become the first Classics Tutor and Vice-President of
Somerville College, Oxford. She is often suggested as the model for Woolf's piano teacher,
Miss Craye, in her short story "Slater's Pins Have No Points," first published in January
1928 in *Forum*, but Woolf may very well have had Jane Harrison in mind as well, as her
writing of the story and its publication date took place near the time of Woolf's visits to
Harrison, who died in April of that year, three months after the story was published.

ing to Woolf, Pater was "perfectly delightful," but her most serious and focused study of Greek language and literature began in 1902 with Case, by which time she did indeed have a solid basis of comparison in measuring her new tutor's attributes, and their tutorial relationship continued off and on until 1909.

Woolf's diary entries, early portraits, and letters demonstrate that she respected Janet Case for challenging her intellectually and for putting up with her self-proclaimed ignorance and amateur skills that she felt, similar to Jane Harrison, were more attuned to a love of Greek literature than to the practice of conjugating lists of verbs. Woolf notes that Case "was more professional than Miss Pater though perhaps not so cultivated—she was more genial than Miss Clay & as good a scholar" (PA 182). She casts Janet Case in a maternal role, remarking that her new tutor makes her feel "contradictious," (PA 182), a nursery nonsense word from her childhood, and she claims that she is not looking forward to learning from so formidable a presence as Case, whom she finds to be "too cheerful & muscular." She figured out "her line of teaching" and then "set her back against it" (PA 182). Virginia purposefully feigned "pure idleness" because "it relieved the tedium of Greek grammar," and she relates her frustration with Miss Case when "she used to pull me up ruthlessly in the middle of some beautiful passage with "Mark the *ar*" (PA 182).

Despite these somewhat typical, gentle aspersions and complaints against Janet Case as being a bit of a grammarian and Victorian moralizer, Woolf adored her. As a mentor/mother, Case's "vigorous & wholesome" presence helped to give Woolf the intellectual and emotional protection to rebel, challenge, and question nearly everything. In October 1903, she wrote to Violet Dickinson,[4] another of Woolf's claimed mothers, with whom she carried on an intimate correspondence, that "Case is as regular as a Clock. She's a nice woman really—and sometimes puts her arm around Sparroy!! [one of Virginia's many aliases in corresponding with Violet] [. . .] She is so exquisitely clean and healthy and normal. I feel she bathes one all over—not with talk only" (L 1: 100). Case provided a motherly affection and nurturance, a sense of stability, and a Victorian reserve, which allowed her young student to be, at least, verbally, linguistically, free. On 27 November, she continued to Violet, whose picture she kept on her mantelpiece, "I began to write to you, and then

4. Violet Dickinson cared for Virginia after her first suicide attempt. Virginia wrote a female utopia for her based on the power of maternal love to renew and redeem the young woman artist (Berg Collection).

Case knocked vigorously. She blushes like a maiden (I say nothing against her morals) when I say I am writing to you. She says 'Miss Dickinson (you'll be Violet soon) has such a sensible look in her eyes' but I won't listen to such stuff" (109). Janet Case herself is considered by Virginia to be "sensible," and here we learn she is also prompt and regarded as morally sound, as her presence represents a strength of character she can feel sure of. The level of their closeness increases, as Woolf also confided in Miss Case during her father's illness and eventual death in 1904, which she characterized as "all pure loss," while cautioning her tutor about her own lack of religious belief, when she wrote, "You see I'm not in a pious frame of mind!" (L 1: 124). And it was to Miss Case that she related the sexual abuse she endured at the hands of her half-brother, George Duckworth.[5] In discussing marriage and Case's sister Emphie's encounter with a male doctor, their conversation turned to "the revelation of all Georges malefactions." On 11 [?] July 1911, she writes to her sister Vanessa:

> To my surprise, she has always had an intense dislike of him; and used to say "Whew—you nasty creature," when he came in and began fondling me over my Greek. When I got to the bedroom scenes, she dropped her lace, and gasped like a benevolent gudgeon. (L 1: 472)

Woolf felt a sense of maternal protection from Janet Case, who cared about her and corresponded with her long after the tutelage ended. She took her student's intellectual interests seriously, and her presence gave Woolf a modicum of security in the wake of the deaths of her mother and half-sister, as well as an outlet for her intellect. It's a relationship that allows Woolf to explore "the bedroom scenes" of the Greek text in relative safety while feeling validated, if not avenged, in her disgust at her stepbrother's unwanted sexual attention.

Woolf also feels confident enough in her relationship with Case to tease her and try to shock her more demure sensibilities. Later on, in this same letter, she implies that she has had sex with one of her suitors, the young classicist Walter Lamb.[6] Virginia relates that "Janet C. said sud-

---

5. For a discussion of Woolf's relationship with her step-brothers, George and Gerald Duckworth, see DeSalvo.

6. Walter Lamb left Trinity to become Lecturer in Classics at Newnham College in 1906. As a young woman, Virginia was pursued by at least three different men who had deep ties to the classics. In addition to Lamb, Walter Headlam, sixteen years her senior, was Lecturer in Classics at Kings College. He is known for his exhaustive translation and notes to The Mimes and Fragments of Herodas originally published posthumously in 1922. The Mimes are comic scenarios of the more seedy characters of life and included portrayals

denly in the train 'What are you thinking of, Virginia?' Imprudently I answered 'Supposing next time we meet a baby leaps within me?' She said that was not the way to talk" (L 1: 473). Woolf enjoys and often revels in the attention she is paid by Janet Case as mentor, as mother-figure, and as confidant, and her early contact with the classics is linked to a desire for maternal love that, with Case's protection, evolves into a more fully realized transpersonal exploration of the sensual erotics she'll find in Harrison's feminist revisions of Greek ritual and myth.

This shift away from Janet Case's mentorship demonstrates a kind of cognitive dissonance necessary for growth, which often takes place between teacher and student, if not between mother and daughter, and which was noted by Woolf herself as she assessed their relationship in her diary entries and again, years later, in her anonymous obituary of Case signed simply from "an old pupil"[7] on 22 July 1937. Woolf writes that her former tutor had a "humorous appreciation both of the nymph and of the noun," but she also makes note of her demeanor as being "contemplative, reticent, withdrawn." She mourns the loss of Miss Case, who was both "so sound a scholar and so fine and dignified a presence," but, who, perhaps, "enjoyed too many things" and was burdened by the necessity of having to teach privately, which made it difficult for her to focus her intellectual energies towards a single ambition. The obituary is respectful, but measured, and seems to mourn not only Case, but all women struggling to lead an independent intellectual existence with few role models or opportunities in an environment at the turn of the century still circumscribed by Victorian sensibilities and rigid social and economic constraints. Here, Woolf is assessing a teacher–student relationship that she valued, but from which she had also grown apart. As Henry Alley notes, Case "held both the predictable role of the calm, somewhat staid, classical tutor with the watchful eye, and the warm but parental confidant" (291). But after April 1907, the tutelage came to an end, "with Case feeling somewhat intimidated by 'the new odd Bloomsbury life.'" What Alley calls the beginning of "friction and anger" between teacher and pupil "comes quite gradually in 1916 and 1917" due not only to the

---

of the bawd, the keeper of the whorehouse, and the purveyor of leather dildos. Headlam also pursued Woolf's older half-sister, Stella, and was a friend of her parents. And Sydney Waterlow, who won a first class in the Classics Tripos, was not yet divorced from his wife when he proposed to her.

7. Woolf's obituary of Case was first rediscovered by Jane Marcus and reprinted in 1977 in Marcus, "*The Years* as Greek Drama" 292–93. Quotations from Woolf's obituary of Case were drawn from this source, from Alley, and from the original in the Janet Case Papers at Girton College, Cambridge.

elder mentor's age, but also to "a kind of ossifying of what Woolf feared to be a rigid classical view of literature" (293). This shift away from what Case represented occurs in 1907, I would argue, with the crafting of Woolf's "Libation Bearers Notebook," a notebook she made to help her translate from the Greek (see also Chapter 2), as she becomes more intimately engaged intellectually and politically not to her elder mentor, but transpersonally to the "eternally young" Jane Harrison and her new perspective of the classics.

Harrison's "Direct Method" and Woolf's "Plunge into Tough Greek"

An important part of what made Janet Case Virginia Woolf's most meaningful tutorial relationship is that her teaching strategies followed an unorthodox method for teaching Greek developed by Jane Harrison at Newnham College. Annabel Robinson writes that Harrison, "disdaining the heavy memorization of paradigms that was the hallmark of all traditional methods, [. . .] plunged her students straight into real Greek literature" (*Life and Work* 188). In 1905, a year after Janet Case had introduced Virginia to her at Newnham, Harrison described her "direct method," which she had been fine-tuning with her own students, who had some rudimentary knowledge of Greek, at the college since her appointment to a research position in 1898. She writes in a letter to her Cambridge colleague, Gilbert Murray:

> I am trying an experiment with yr Hippolytus on a girl who has learnt Greek for one fortnight . . . I read a short chunk of it aloud to her—Greek & yr translation—then I just show her roughly how it fits in grammatically & she learns the Greek off by heart. After she knows it thoroughly we discuss the details but never before. She picked up the first chorus metres without any effort apparently—she is musical—she does not at present know a single technical name, it is all by ear. To such base use do you come. (JEH to GM, n.d., JH Papers)

In this example, Harrison was testing her method on a young woman with little or limited exposure to the Greek language. Generally speaking, however, she started her new students at Newnham (women who had some background in the classics before acceptance at college) not with Murray's Euripides, but with Aeschylus' *The Choephori* (*The Libation*

Bearers), one of the most difficult plays in the Greek language. She ultimately presented her teaching technique to the Curriculum Committee
of the Classical Association with "a predictably mixed reception." Robinson points out that the method was remarkably successful with gifted
students, but frequently "a dismal failure (if measured by examination
success)" with the less linguistically talented. One of the less gifted students, Victoria de Bunsen, in a kind of foreshadowing of the sometimes
unfair, blistering critiques in student evaluations, writes ruefully of Harrison and her controversial method:

> Was she a good teacher? I am hardly the one to give an answer for she
> used to single me out as her failure par excellence [. . .] she tried the
> experiment of starting me straight away on the Choephori, expecting that
> the language would come with a rush from the sheer driving force of the
> subject matter. It did not. (Victoria de Bunsen, "Jane Ellen Harrison,"
> *Newnham College Letter*, 1929, 69) (JH Papers)

It is instructive to imagine what results a Greek lesson with Jane Harrison would have exacted if she had had the opportunity of sharing this
"plunge" in person with the more highly motivated Virginia Stephen, a
young mind hungry for a formal education and passionate about the literary aspects of Greek literature and their "lovely descriptions of maidenhood." Robinson counts both de Bunsen and, undeservedly I believe,
Harrison's companion and former student Hope Mirrlees as examples
of Harrison's "failure [s] par excellence" when it came to this "direct
method." Hardly a failure, Mirrlees went on to become a novelist, poet,
and biographer. She was also linguistically gifted, read Greek and Latin
and spoke four languages, one of them Swahili, and de Bunsen, although
she struggled with the direct method, respected Harrison and noted her
retirement from Cambridge with regret.

Although Harrison's teaching method could be "rather daunting to an
undergraduate" (Robinson *Life and Work* 190), by nearly all accounts,
she was regarded as possessing exceptional abilities as a gifted instructor and her direct method was among many contributions she made as
an effective educator. Harrison, whose lectures on Greek art, complete
with illuminated lantern slides of Greek vase paintings showing the dra-
mas Woolf was reading in her texts, brought Greek culture to life for her
students. Annabel Robinson, a classicist herself, embraced a version of
Harrison's teaching method with remarkable success, and she writes of
Harrison as a lively and wildly popular educator who "taught not to any

curriculum [. . .] but taught on the edge of her own research" (188) in Greek art, language, and archaeology. Her colleague, Francis Cornford, wrote of Harrison: "All her teaching glowed with the excitement of discovery: the gleam of an untravelled world had never faded from the second aorist of the most eccentric verb" (qtd. in Robinson 72–73). Contradicting the credence given to Harrison's failure in teaching Victoria de Bunsen, Robinson seconds that "teaching and learning were for Harrison a joint discovery [. . .]" and "her teaching was as one scholar sharing something new and vital with another. She had no interest in simply imparting knowledge, and refused to teach the orthodox views. Rather, she would invite the student to join her in an adventure of learning" (190). Like Woolf, who outlined her suspicion and disdain for pronouncements and the authority of what she referred to as the loudspeaker voice of male lecturers, judges, doctors, and any strident voice of authority in her essays and fiction, Harrison's pedagogy and research was based on invitation, collaboration, and interaction.

Despite Woolf's initial rebelliousness noted above towards Janet Case, in general, her diaries and letters give the impression that although her tutor expected discipline and regular practice, Woolf wanted to live up to her standards of excellence. In another letter to Violet Dickinson in early April 1903, she records a distraction that she valiantly endures lest Miss Case observes her lack of attention to her work. She writes, "A great flea jumped on to my Aeschylus as I read with Case the other day—and now bites large holes in me. I was too polite to catch him with Cases eye on me" (L 1: 72). This is not to say, as Yopie Prins points out, in "Ototoi: Virginia Woolf and the 'Naked Cry' of Cassandra," that Miss Case did not leave "room for Woolf to read Greek with a more pure literary interest, for aesthetic pleasure" (168) as well, but rather to suggest that if she left room for such readings, Woolf's transpersonal encounter with Harrison's work liberated her own intellect and imagination. When Woolf writes in her diary, "I have taken the plunge into tough Greek, and that has so much attraction for me—Heaven knows why—that I don't want to do anything else" (L 1:177), it is the same "plunge," an immersion in thinking and reading and emotion that Jane Harrison assigned her students and that Case tried to replicate in her lessons with Woolf.

Like Harrison, Case started off her students with the challenging *Choephori*. Prins and Robinson praise this method as well, with Prins placing both Case and Harrison as being part of a broader trend at the turn of the century to teach "Ladies' Greek" when women began entering universities and taking on classical study. Harrison, however, did not continue to

CORNER OF MARKET St
MARKET PLACE, CAMBRIDGE.

FIGURE 3. Janet Case as Athena, ca. 1881–1883.
Photo Credit: The Mistress and Fellows, Girton College, Cambridge.

teach "Ladies' Greek" (i.e., without the accent), but from her own teaching philosophy and direct method, and Case's own theories for teaching Virginia Woolf Greek were informed by these strategies. For her two Greek notebooks, "The Libation Bearers Notebook" (1907) and "The Agamemnon Notebook" (1922), Woolf used the A. W. Verrall edition as her guide.[8] This is the same text used by Jane Harrison as an undergraduate at Newnham College, the same edition from which she taught her direct method as an instructor there, and the same edition Janet Case used to teach Woolf her lessons. It is the same edition, years later in 1922, that Woolf uses again when she revisits her Greek study and devises her "Agamemnon Notebook." Curiously, she attaches her earlier 1907 "Libation Bearers Notebook" to the manuscript for *Mrs. Dalloway* while she is working on translating *The Agamemnon* at the same time, a discussion we'll take up in more detail in Chapter Two.

Mentoring Janet Case

Harrison, who was fourteen years older than Janet Case, was also a role model for her during her undergraduate years at Girton College, and Case was well aware of her example as a student and later scholar and teacher at Newnham. Case became the first female lead in a Greek play, Sophocles' *Electra,* at Oxbridge in 1883, while at Girton, but it was Harrison's earlier attempts that made that milestone possible. Harrison was popular and somewhat of a local legend, known for testing the boundaries and restrictions imposed on women studying at the university. The performance of Greek plays at Oxbridge was fraught with controversy, and Jane Harrison, while a student at Newnham, was at the center of the debate. She was often at odds with the college's director, Miss Clough. Robinson writes of Clough that "aesthetic and 'mannish' clothes were

---

8. Arthur Woolgar Verrall was a respected Cambridge classicist, but his translations were considered controversial for being too inventive and original. He was a member of the Society for Psychical Research, a forerunner and early supporter of Freudian psychoanalysis, until the two fields of study broke apart. Verrall was married to Margaret Verrall, a lecturer in classics at Newnham, with whom Harrison collaborated on *Mythology and Monuments,* "The Blue Jane." The SPR was made up of many of the eminent thinkers of the day and included the philosopher, ethicist, and co-founder of Newnham, Henry Sidgwick, among its ranks, as well as, C. G. Jung and William James. The organization's purpose was to study telepathy and thought-transference and "to approach these varied problems without prejudice and prepossession of any kind and in the same spirit of exact and unimpassioned enquiry which has enabled science to solve so many problems" (Grattan-Guinness).

her particular bugaboo. Harrison wore both" (*Life and Work* 45). In one incident, Harrison wore a garish, yellow-checked, plaid ulster, which was later celebrated in the pages of *Punch,* to advertise an exhibition by the painter George Frederick Watts. The lyric read "Here's Sir Frederick robed in scarlet, here's Dean Stanley's thoughtful face/And the lady in the Ulster has a certain kind of grace" (qtd. in Robinson 45). When, in 1877, Harrison and a group of students wanted to put on a Greek play, her reputation as a rebel did not help their cause. The play, Euripides' *Electra,* would have been the first to be performed by women rather than men in drag to play the female roles. Miss Clough soon sabotaged their efforts, however, by ordering inspections of their costumes to make sure they were not revealing too much skin. The students eventually were forced to call off the production.

Janet Case's own work as a scholar was also informed by Harrison's research. Case becomes for Woolf "a noble Athena" who introduces her to Antigone, Electra, and the feminism of Clytemnestra, and Case's writings on these figures are fueled by Harrison's reinterpretations. In her essay "Women in the Plays of Aeschylus" (1914), Janet Case writes that "Aeschylus gives his women brains as well as hearts. He believes in women," especially Clytemnestra, who "strips naked the unjust bias of men's condemnation" (7) (JC Papers). According to Case, Aeschylus is the Greek tragedian to whom we must turn in order to resolve the disparity we find between "the women of the Greek drama [who] seem at first sight a world away from the women of real life in 5th century Athens" (3) and to whom we must look for an alternative perspective on feminism in her own time. She writes:

> The sympathetic emphasis of Euripides, the anti-feminism of Aristo-
> phanes are evidence of the vitality of this question as a topic of contro-
> versy. Sophocles reflects it. Aeschylus expresses it, so that the spirit of
> women is neither that of the epic, nor yet—far from it—that of the com-
> mon voice of his own time, but has in it the freshness of a new ideal.
> ("Women in the Plays of Aeschylus" 5) (JC Papers)

In the margins of the essay, Case acknowledges her debt to Jane Harrison's *Themis* (JC Papers), which articulated the cultic realities behind the myths of the women figures in Greek tragedy. Woolf returns to the subject of the role of women in literature versus their reality in ancient Greek culture, when she echoes both Case and Harrison in *A Room of One's Own,* question-ing why it is that in the case of literary figures such as Clytemnestra and Antigone, Cassandra and Atossa, that "Imaginatively she is of the highest importance; practically she is completely insignificant." She extends their analyses, remarking how it is that a woman in literature "pervades poetry from cover to cover; she is all but absent from history" (AROO 43). She quotes F. L. Lucas in *Tragedy in Relation to Aristotle's Poetics* (1927), who agrees that "It remains a strange and almost inexplicable fact that in Athena's city, where women were kept in almost Oriental suppression as odalisques or drudges, the stage should yet have produced figures like Clytemnestra" and other heroines who dominate the plays of the "'misogynist' Euripides." It's a paradox that has "never been satisfactorily explained" (qtd. in AROO 43), but which Woolf's essay seeks to address when she demonstrates that history as written and put forth by men and the biographies of men is "unreal" and "lop-sided" and in need of a "supplement" (45), as she seeks an alternative past based on Case's "freshness of a new ideal" a philosophy informed by Harrison's research into ancient feminist collectives.

In her other scholarly edition, a tiny, delicate volume of *Prometheus Bound* (1905) designed as a primer for her students, Janet Case cites Harrison's *Prolegomena* extensively, acknowledging her debt to Harrison's scholarship. Case was teaching Woolf Greek while she prepared the volume for publication. In "The Sexual Politics of Translating *Prometheus Bound*," Prins explores the motivations behind three different women's translations of Aeschylus' tragedy, Elizabeth Barrett Browning, Edith Hamilton, and Janet Case, and sees Case's version as turning "to Greek tragedy for the collective performance of women's higher education" (170). She views these translations, not as subversive, but as reenactments of turn-of-the-century gender politics. Nevertheless, a woman translating Greek, especially a play about liberation from tyranny, embodies its own political subversion simply in the act of reading and writing. In both "Women in the Plays of Aeschylus" and *Prometheus Bound,* Case sought parallels between the politics of ancient Athens and her own advocacy of women's suffrage and higher education in order to appeal to a broader, modern audience, and her primer was designed with the amateur or new student in mind. In addition to Harrison's citations, this inexpensive edition "anticipated the great mission of the new Loeb Classical Library" founded in 1911 (Prins, "Sexual Politics" 171), by having the Greek on one side of the page and the English on the other, a practice Woolf replicated in both of her Greek notebooks. Woolf would go on to review the Loeb Library editions "as a gift of freedom" ("The Perfect Language" 114) for their accessibility and acknowledgment of the amateur

FIGURE 4. Jane Harrison as Alcestis, Oxford 1887, Newnham College Album.
Photo Credit: The Jane Harrison Papers, Newnham College Archive,
The Principal and Fellows, Newnham College, Cambridge.

(Prins "Sexual Politics" 171). Janet Case's mentorship and tutoring gave Woolf a similar freedom, the freedom to move on, to refuse to be mastered by an ancient language, but to challenge and revise its stories and ideals, to use Prometheus' gift of the Greek alphabet and pass through the "fire of renewal" ("Women in the Plays of Aeschylus" 23) (JC Papers) to the possibilities in Harrison's research.

Janet Case's role as Woolf's Greek tutor is crucial and functional in delivering Harrison's work to Virginia Woolf, but the portrait we have of her as an intellect and scholar rings at a different decibel for Woolf. Unlike Harrison, Case did not become a professional scholar after leaving Girton. Woolf writes of Case in her obituary that "in her way she was a pioneer; but her way was one that kept her in the background, a counselor rather than a champion [. . .] she wanted no prominence, no publicity" (JC Papers). Harrison's work represented an intellectual passion and excitement for learning and knowledge that Woolf identified with transpersonally and carried forward in her own work as she moved away from the mentorship and "counselor" relationship she had with Janet Case to embrace a different kind of classical conversation.

"Ardent Theories": Greek Text as Dangerous [Sapphic] Lover

Because Virginia Woolf's Greek lessons were begun initially to help an intellectually gifted young girl cope with the loss of her mother and her half-sister, critics have often associated her attraction to Greek literature with a preoccupation with death. In "O Sister Swallow: Sapphic Fragments as English Literature in Virginia Woolf," Anne Fernald argues that what is attractive to Woolf in the women characters in Greek tragedy, namely, Penelope, Antigone, Electra, and Clytemnestra, "is the power of inconsolability, the fidelity and courage of mourning that never ends" (29). Most recently, Theodore Koulouris, in *Hellenism and Loss in the Work of Virginia Woolf* (2010), points to her Greek notebook in particular as demonstrating what he terms "her 'poetics of loss'" (22).[9] While loss, mourning, absence, and death are important themes in Woolf's work, I suggest that what Woolf is looking for in her Greek lessons other than, obviously, the formal education enjoyed by Thoby, but denied her

---

9. It is unclear to which Greek notebook Koulouris refers, "The Libation Bearers Notebook" or "The Agamemnon Notebook."

as a woman, is an alternative to a "poetics of loss," sources for a model that is more suggestive of the vitality and sexual vitality, the regeneration, rebirth, and sensuality posited by Jane Harrison's research read as feminist that declares, as Harrison wrote, "a heroic *society* is almost a contradiction in terms" (AAR 162). Woolf crafts her Greek education seeking out and attracted to the possibilities of counter narratives which would have allowed her mother to break the bonds of "the angel of the house" and live; sources for an alternative social system which would have potentially offered her half-sister Stella another option than sacrifice to the marital bed;[10] and a world conceived upon values of "both/and" thinking, rather than an insistence on hierarchies, competition, and jealousies, which quite possibly could have saved Thoby, and, perhaps, her nephew Julian, but certainly Jacob Flanders, the character, in *Jacob's Room* based upon her brother from a heroic but needless death.

Woolf's desire for Greek is initially linked to her desire for maternal love as represented by Janet Case, but it is set in opposition to her tutor's emphasis on grammar and a perceived conservatism and reserve she resisted and found restrictive. Although she admits that Janet Case "had theories of her own [. . .] ardent theories & she could expound them fluently" (PA 182), she often prefers a more literary reading of the Greek text—Harrison's more direct and emotional "plunge" into a text. Woolf writes that she prefers "a very lovely description of maidenhood in Euripides (?) for instance—how the maiden hangs like ripened fruit within the orchard—but the gates ajar, the passerby spies in—& does not hesitate to pluck. That was the sense of it, & at the end I paused with some literary delight in its beauty. Not so Miss Case" (PA 183). Her tutor points out instead that "'The use of the instrumental genitive in the 3rd line is extremely rare' her comment upon Love!" Woolf sets herself in contrast to Case, as she recognizes the possibilities for intellectual stimulation and eroticism that can be gleaned from the Greek text.

In her diaries and letters, she often writes privately of her Greek text as a dangerous lover she has no intention of relinquishing. We discover that despite the abominations of the rest cure prescribed each time after the death of her mother and then her half-sister, that when "My Dear Dr Seton says I must not do *any* lessons this term" (L 1: 7), she goes to sleep with a Greek grammar Violet Dickinson has given her—"under my pillow (not so improper as it looks)" (L 1: 58), and reveals to her cousin,

---

10. One of the most insightful discussions of Stella Duckworth's death continues to be DeSalvo 61ff.

Emma Vaughn, "I have endless books and *Greek* (tell Marny)—the greatest of comforts to me" (L 1: 30). She has to hide her love for Greek away, keep it secret and safe. She shares this love with her tutor as well, but in a more maternal and somewhat guarded way, as she is able to test the extent to which she both identifies and disidentifies with her mentor. She early on realized that "aesthetic pleasure is so much easier to attain than knowledge of his uses of the genitive" (PA 183) and that she believed that though Case "read with a less purely literary interest in the text than I did; she was not by any means blind to the beauties of Aeschylus and Euripides (her two favourite writers) but she was not happy till she had woven some kind of moral into their plays" (PA 183). Her tutor wins her over ultimately with her methods and pushes Virginia "to think more than I had done hitherto." Case helped her interpret "the relation of Aeschylus towards Fate—or the religious peculiarities of Euripides. This was the side of the thing that most interested her—& to her great credit, she made me, at least, see her point of view." But one senses Woolf's youthful frustrations at being restricted and proscribed by Janet Case's moralizing, as she clings to her Greek grammar and primer, marked up and annotated by Harrison's radical ideas.

Harrison's scholarly explorations into the sensual and erotic aspects of Greek ritual embody Woolf's desire for Greek literature and she reads these as feminist, and, in many cases, as lesbian, or, in using a common usage of her day, Sapphist. Woolf considered Harrison's relationship with Hope Mirrlees, somewhat jealously, as intimate and physically shared, despite the fact that Mirrlees was five years younger than Woolf (Briggs, *Reading* 82). She reviewed Mirrlees's first novel, *Madeleine: One of Love's Jansenists,* which was based on Harrison, as "sapphism so far as I've got—Jane and herself" (L 2: 391). For Woolf, who enjoyed a lesbian affair with Vita Sackville-West, and admitted to the composer Ethel Smyth on 19 August 1930, "that I only want to show off to women. Women alone stir my imagination" (L 4:203), Harrison was a role model of sexual freedom as well. Not only did her work privilege a focus on women, but Harrison was also known as a "Sapphist" in college, who was "prepared to explain to the innocent what was meant by 'Sapphism.'" Deans and former friends warned parents not to send their daughters to Newnham "where Jane Harrison preached free love" (Robinson *Life and Work* 143), lest they be seduced by her teachings and her presence.

Harrison's personal reputation as a rebel held an added attraction to a young Virginia Stephen that only enhanced the example she was already providing by working on the cutting edge of her research.

Harrison's articles and essays, often harshly reviewed by her critics, played out in the pages of the leading journals and reviews on the classics, where the excitement and novelty of her archaeological research would have intrigued the young student studying Greek. It is Jane Harrison who challenges and revises the myth of Pandora, for example, and who discovers that "the box of Pandora is proverbial, and that is the more remarkable as she never had a box at all" ("Pandora's Box" 99), as she explores in exacting detail the nature, shape, and function of the so-called "box," which is in actuality a burial urn. In "Some Fragments of a Vase Presumably by Euphronios," we are let in to the specialist's world of archaeological exploration, when she conveys her excitement at her findings among the débris found in the excavations on the Acropolis in 1888. She writes, "I am not able to offer a complete restoration of the design, nor to explain with certainty all details, but the extant fragments are of such great artistic and archaeological importance that it seems desirable to publish them at once, without waiting either for such explanation or for a detailed examination of the mythography involved" (143). We are then given a meticulous, sensual description of a cylix:

> The necklet and bracelet of the female figure, the head-bands of both, and the other portions in slight relief and now coloured red, once bore gilding. The subject and main outline of the—most important—interior design are happily clear. Orpheus to the right sinks on one knee to the ground; his left hand no doubt supported him. His right arm, of which the turn of the elbow is just visible against the wrist of the female figure, is bent and uplifted, holding a large lyre. In front of him stands the figure of a Thracian woman, her left hand extended, her right hand depressed and apparently holding a bipennis. (144)

And thus begins Harrison's own Orphic song of intellectual discovery as she outlines the role of the bipennis or labrys, a two-headed axe frequently wielded by Thracian women in a Clytemnestra pose, and theorizes the mythography of the subject. "The type," as she notes "is a perfectly familiar one, the fallen foe and the standing victor"(144) which is not specific to Orpheus, but also belonging to Achilles and Penthesilea, Apollo and Tityos, but she makes particular note of the woman. "The Thracian woman has her foot upon his body, but there is no unseemly violence of gesture; the bipennis even is not swung above her head. She is characterized as a barbarian in part by unkempt masses of hair, in striking contrast to the figure of Orpheus. Her hair lies in dank straight folds, something after the fashion of the half-born Pandora on the vase in the British Museum" (145). Her descriptions, her subjects, the angles of her vision teem with vitality and difference. She focuses on the women figures, their roles in myth and ritual, and their stories resonate with a young Virginia Stephen who is acquainting herself with this literature for the first time. Harrison's work offers Woolf alternative sources and the courage to revise and rethink her own plots, her own modernist project, which is distinctive and enriched by Harrison's feminist expansions of myth.

One is reminded here of Woolf's early sensual responses to the physical contours of the Greek landscape, its weather and climate, aspects which find their way into her famous essay "On Not Knowing Greek." She writes that "when we read Chaucer, we are floated up to him insensibly on the current of our ancestors' lives" (ONKG 23), but in order to imagine the Greeks "we must annihilate the smoke and the damp and the thick wet mists" of England.

> With warmth and sunshine and months of brilliant, fine weather, life of course is instantly changed; it is transacted out of doors, with the result [. . .] that small incidents are debated in the street, not in the sitting-room, and become dramatic; make people voluble; inspire in them that sneering, laughing, nimbleness of wit and tongue peculiar to the Southern races, which has nothing in common with the slow reserve, the low half-tones, the brooding introspective melancholy of people accustomed to live more than half the year indoors. (24)

She points out that in order to appreciate Greek literature we must realize its "out-of-doors manner" that the poets and playwrights "were speaking to an enormous audience rayed round them on one of those brilliant southern days when the sun is so hot and yet the air so exciting [. . .] to an audience of seventeen thousand people perhaps, with ears and eyes eager and attentive, with bodies whose muscles would grow stiff if they sat too long without diversion" (25). In her own Greek experience traveling with her sister Vanessa and her brother Thoby to Athens in the fall of 1906, Woolf was attracted to the texture of the landscape, to the material culture emphasized and valued in Harrison's research. Mitchell Leaska in his introduction to Woolf's early diaries in *A Passionate Apprentice* notes the effect Woolf's traveling to Greece had on her writing style. He writes:

> Virginia flourished in the classical world. She was soothed by its order and symmetry, and began to pause longer over what she saw, catching

> the smallest details of people, places, manners, and morals. Something
> new was finding its way into the style in which she conveyed her impres-
> sions: whether she was describing a site rich in ancient history or creating
> a portrait of some fellow guest at the hotel, her writing was becoming
> more suggestive, and more resonant. [...] In Greece [...] Virginia was
> beginning to model her meaning in a way not evident in her earlier jour-
> nals. (xxiii)

Rather than being "soothed by its order and symmetry," I would argue,
during this trip Woolf becomes stimulated and intellectually challenged
by the dramatic landscape, the ruins, the Dionysian underpinnings of the
land and its literature that she has already encountered three years earlier
in *Prolegomena* and Harrison's work on women in Greek ritual. Leaska
calls this "a new prismatic quality in its earliest stages of cultivation" (PA
xxiii). I see this sea-change in Woolf's journal rhetoric and thinking as a
shift away from the ideas of Janet Case, away from a more conservative,
rational, balanced view of the classics and towards the thinking of Jane
Harrison who would write, "Man makes his demons in the image of his
own savage and irrational passions" (P x). I'm imagining, here, too, that
it quite possibly could be Harrison's "Blue Jane," the guidebook *Mythology and Monuments,* that Woolf and her party used as their guide, in a
transpersonal "out of doors" transaction, as they scaled and explored the
ruins of the Acropolis in the "warmth and sunshine" of Greece.

Harrison's "Woman's World" and the Collective as Feminist Network

Virginia Woolf's diaries, correspondence, and work illustrate a woman
whose most intimate, shared relationships were with women and with
her work. She wanted real conversation and to be a part of a fellowship or network of support for women which both Case and Harrison
represented and which Harrison, in particular, spoke about and wrote
about publicly. As the first graduates of the newly founded female colleges at Cambridge, Harrison and Case became part of the debate involving feminist reformers trying to expand job opportunities and educational
opportunities for women. In order to achieve this, 'the woman question'
became part of the discussion of traditional liberal education emphasizing character development versus a "modern" approach favoring professional training and original research.

Women's colleges like Newnham and Girton, which began gradually but courageously against great economic odds, spartan conditions, and appalling cuisine, by the late 1890s were accepted as a part of the university system, but with pervasive inequities and all the attendant biases of being a women's institute for higher learning in a centuries-old, male-dominated academy. As Martha Vicinus writes in *Independent Women: Work and Community for Single Women, 1850–1920,* referring to the early trend of women's colleges to focus on etiquette training and Victorian politesse, "the 1890's saw a shift away from graciousness and bad food toward professionalization and bad food" (132). Woolf also famously commented on the inedible food at Newnham in *A Room of One's Own,* a condition that continued at the college through the 1920s, not to insult the college, but to make a political point about the disparities between women's and men's experiences in higher education.

Both Newnham and Girton struggled to be seen as power bases for learning where women scholars could pursue original research rather than training centers for good manners. In her article "Female Support Networks," Blanche Wiesen Cook writes of the historical tendency "to ignore the crucial role played by the networks of love and support that have been the very sources of strength that enabled political women to function" (276). Harrison found just such a fellowship of support among women when she returned to Cambridge in 1898 as the first woman to hold a research fellowship, funds that were made available and meant to advertise the college as a locus for serious research. She writes nostalgically and poignantly about her attraction and need for just such a sisterhood, a network of intellectual support among women, seeking independence from a prescribed and oppressive domestic ideology:

> Family life never attracted me. At its best it seems to me rather narrow and selfish; at its worst a private hell. [. . .] On the other hand, I have a natural gift for community life. [. . .] If I had been rich I should have founded a learned community for women. (R 88–89)

In her article "The Pictures of Sappho" in *Woman's World* (April 1888) (formerly *Lady's World,* but re-titled by Oscar Wilde when he was editor), Harrison emphasized the importance of the collective and collegiality to a woman's literary life, and tied these to the same "social instincts which had allowed Sappho to flourish in 'a woman's world'" (274) (JH Papers). According to Isobel Hurst, "the reference to the magazine's title suggests that the female readership forms a kind of intellectual community" (91),

and Harrison certainly participated in just such a community by virtue of
her publications, but she yearned for an intellectual sisterhood that would
be on par with the high level of discourse she engaged in mostly with her
peers, formally educated, male colleagues, such as Cornford, her longtime friend and correspondent, Gilbert Murray, and her other Ritualist
male colleagues.

Similarly, in her essays and fiction, Virginia Woolf fantasizes about
bonding with women as she continually tries to envision or recreate circles and networks of feminine support. In "A Society" she creates Harrison's woman's world and learned community out of a gathering of
women engaged in intellectual discourse and inquiry. Jane Marcus traces
these yearnings to her Quaker aunt Caroline Stephen, when she asks:
"With what personal pain and almost erotic longing for escape into a
self-governing world of women does Caroline Stephen argue against the
desire for freedom from family constraints" (*Languages of Patriarchy*
116). The idea of the Quaker pacifist living alone enraged her family.
The desire for community and independence from the restrictive moral
codes and responsibilities of domestic life "haunt the imagination of
[. . .] Virginia Woolf, in her dream of 'a woman's republic," her ideal-
ization of girls' schools and women's colleges because she never experienced this bonding, [and in] her work in women's suffrage, the Women's
Cooperative Guild, and the Women's Service League and Library" (J.
Marcus *Languages of Patriarchy* 116). Furthermore, the female collectives outlined in *A Room of One's Own* and *Three Guineas* each demonstrate Woolf's consistent striving for female-centered companionship,
cooperation, and community, outlined by Harrison in her Greek work,
her memoir, and throughout her writing life.

Janet Case's role in Virginia Woolf's Greek education reveals Case as a
key ally of Harrison, and both women as members of an intellectual community of women Virginia Woolf yearned for and used as a role model
for her fiction and major essays. In *A Room of One's Own*, Woolf's narrator is in awe of Harrison's "bent figure, formidable yet humble, with
her great forehead and her shabby dress" when she emerges "like a great
reality leaping" as if "out of the heart of the spring" (17). Her audience
is emboldened by Harrison's appearance, yet given pause by the clear
disparities of the women's colleges in contrast to the wealth and support enjoyed by the students and faculty at the men's colleges. Woolf
measured the advantages and disadvantages of the formal education she
both desired and resented by her experiences with Harrison and Case.
But Harrison's pedagogical methods, which Case emulated, her work and

example, embody a transpersonal desire for Greek and create a political and theoretical common ground, which Woolf transforms into a writing praxis that frees her from an "ossifying" classicism and allows her to engage the emotional to the intellect and find her own literary and political voice.

CHAPTER 2

The Making and Re-Making of a God(dess)

Re-writing Modernism's War Story— Feminist Ritual Structures as Transpersonal Plots

MYTHOLOGY became an attractive proposition for modernist authors who found very little to support their aesthetic after the carnage of World War I. In the wake of that evitable catastrophe, many writers turned to the narratives of the classics to find a literary method and structure to articulate their alienation. They sought to resist the recent Victorian past and find a way to tolerate the registers of pleasure and pain in the unknowable present. In poetry, Yeats turned to the cult structures of the proto-Celtic hero Cuchulainn, Eliot to a Christianized Tiresias in *The Waste Land,* and Pound ultimately to the rhythms and songs of the East. In the novel, James Joyce pursued "the young God" in the figure of Stephen Daedalus, D. H. Lawrence, "the brotherhood of the Olympians" in *Sons and Lovers,* and E. M. Forster, "the devouring female" in *A Room with a View.* The dominant plot of modernism is the male quest, the hero's journey, essentially a war story, often borrowed from and built upon a romanticized interpretation of the classical world's pantheon of male Olympian gods. Virginia Woolf sought a different story, in a different way, one that she read through the feminist lens of Harrison's revision of the classics, and one that she incorporated transpersonally to craft and inform her own modernist aesthetic and literary project.

Nancy K. Miller notes in "A Feminist Friendship Archive" that women often write themselves out of unremarkable or marginalized circumstances to transform themselves or re-create themselves into remarkable, accomplished human beings, whether into successful poets, novelists, or academic scholars, for example. Referring to the biographer Diane Middlebrook, Miller writes: "She told her story, I think, under the cover of the biography of another. To write my book, I had to become the biographer of a family I had never known [. . .] to become less personal, more transpersonal" (73). Miller writes that to tell her own story, to write her memoir, she "looked for the fictional plot" that would help her. She "joined [Middlebrook] imaginatively" to find and shape her memoir in a process that became a kind of transpersonal self-reinvention.

In order to revise modernism's war narrative, Virginia Woolf had to write a kind of story we've never known, to look for the fictional plot or plots that would help her to articulate her own story by way of her own modern literary project—to become less personal and more transpersonal—and she joins Jane Harrison, often "imaginatively," but also intellectually and politically, to do so. The Harrison–Woolf encounter gives us an alternative modernism based on a model of relations between women founded on work and shared ideologies—the transpersonal. Whether one reads Woolf's counterplot(s) as whole and fully realized (see, e.g., J. Marcus) or as fragmented, uncertain, and incomplete (see, e.g., A. Fernald), her modernism embodies a search for female community and collaboration, and explores especially the possibilities of a life without marriage or children and without war. As Robinson notes, with the publication of *Prolegomena,* Harrison was "pointing enthusiastically to a society where there was (or so she believed) no institution of marriage—connections had taken place at random and people lived in joyful freedom from societal constraint" (*Life and Work* 143), ideas that particularly appealed to Virginia Woolf.

Unlike Woolf's male contemporaries, for example, T. S. Eliot, who favored more popular versions of primitive religion and folkstory, Woolf's quest brought her to Harrison's work to find an aesthetic which privileged balance and favored the female principle, not to dominate, but to regenerate, to resurrect cooperation and collaboration, but outside what Harrison once called the "most dire and deadly of all tyrannies, an oligarchy of old men" (A&O 28–29). Although Yeats, Eliot, Joyce,

Forster, and Lawrence each read and borrowed from Jane Harrison (often without credit), Woolf transforms Harrison's classicism forward, to help write herself transpersonally out of the shadows of the male plot and into the possibilities of a remarkable and revised present.

When traditional norms had broken down after the war and "all human relations [. . .] shifted" (96), as Woolf wrote in "Mr. Bennett and Mrs. Brown" (1923), an early comment on literary practice and aesthetics, her male contemporaries reached for a reaffirmation of masculine hierarchies in mythic structures. As Eliot writes, in "Ulysses, Order, and Myth," also published in 1923, his contemporaries looked towards myth as "a way of controlling, of ordering, of giving shape and a significance to the immense panorama of futility and anarchy which is contemporary history" (177–78). According to Eliot, the prescription for the "futility and anarchy" of the times was to be found in a mythic re-interpretation and re-visioning of classical literature, but one organized around the masculinist principle of "controlling," "ordering" (177). In *The Waste Land,* for example, Eliot's "mythic passages express pity for the suffering male" and the poet "appears to attribute loss of spirituality, order, communal purity, and joy to the influence of women, the masses, and Jews" (J. Marcus, *Languages of Patriarchy* 37). For his "classicism," Eliot claims to find a rationale and justification for his misogyny. Martha C. Carpentier's incisive analysis of Eliot and Joyce's use of classical sources reminds us that "There is no evidence in any of Eliot's anthropological sources from E. B. Tylor to Frazer or Jane Harrison, of sacrificial rituals involving sexual violation" (117), and yet his work repeats and rehearses a brutal misogyny often overlooked by critics until feminist re-readings of his work in the 1980s.[1] Carpentier notes that the classical texts they use as well as their re-working of them speaks to the mythic method Eliot referred to in praising Joyce's *Ulysses* as "manipulating a continuous parallel between contemporaneity and antiquity" ("Ulysses, Order, and Myth" 177), and that they "express the same universal theme: the violent antagonism between the sexes that is, ultimately, an expression of male oedipal conflict" (118). Joyce's *Ulysses* is a re-reading of *The Odyssey* but also along masculinist lines, focusing on the "heroic deeds" of the young god as separate from the mother, in other words, along Apollonian, or Olympian, structures. Virginia

---

1. In addition to Jane Marcus, see Gilbert and Gubar 31–32.

Woolf regarded Joyce as "egotistical," which is for her the worst form of torture and a quality she loathed on a personal level in her "tyrant father—the exacting, the violent, the histrionic, the demonstrative, the self-centered, the self-pitying, the deaf, the appealing, the alternately loved and hated father" (MB 116). She despised this quality in literature as well, when the ego of the author thwarts and destroys story. Woolf not only had very little interest in the heroism of gods, she dreaded the results of their egotism and the effect of their behavior on women, children, and upon the world. She adhered to and welcomed the collective, feminist emphasis of Harrison's scholarship and identified male egotism with a British patriarchy and imperialism that brought about violence and the wars of the twentieth century.

In "Mr. Bennett and Mrs. Brown," which Woolf developed and extended from the earlier essay "Modern Novels" (1919), she pleads with contemporary writers "not to preach doctrines, sing songs, or celebrate the glories of the British empire," but to explore characters, "to steep oneself in her atmosphere" (101), and look at Mrs. Brown on her way to London, "as she is." Woolf insists, "all novels begin with an old lady in the corner opposite" (102), as she outlines the need to turn away from the "artificial" and literary conventions of the Edwardians toward the emotional, toward "reality." As she argues "Mrs. Brown is eternal, Mrs. Brown is human nature [. . .] it is the novelists who get in and out—there she sits and not one of the Edwardian writers has so much as looked at her" but have instead "made tools and established conventions which do their business" (110). She found much to recommend in the modernist experiments of her contemporaries, to whom she refers as Georgians (such as Eliot, Joyce, Forster, and Lawrence), despite the fact that she often did not share their professional direction or literary goals, but saw the devices of conventional fiction as instruments of "ruin" and "tools" of "death" (110) for literature. As she reiterates later in "Modern Fiction" (1925), "For the moderns [. . .] the point of interest lies very likely in the dark places of psychology" (152) and that "the 'proper stuff of fiction' does not exist; everything is the proper stuff of fiction, every feeling, every thought; every quality of brain and spirit is drawn upon; no perception comes amiss" (154). Woolf elevates not the Young god or the hero, but Mrs. Brown to a Themis-like status, who becomes for Woolf the embodiment of "all novels," writing Mrs. Brown out of shadows of the corner opposite and bidding her, speak.

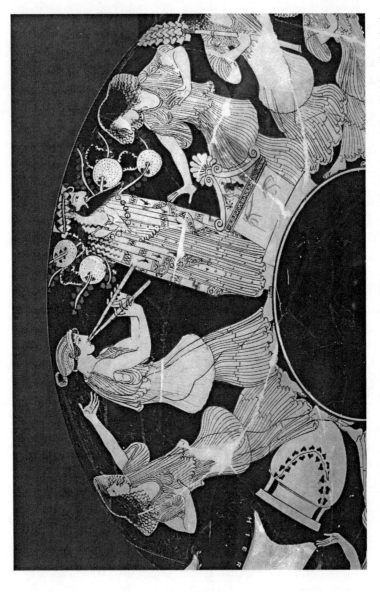

FIGURE 5. A drinking bowl featuring Dionysus and his Thiasos, a relationship Harrison explored at length in both *Prolegomena to the Study of Greek Religion* (1903) and later in *Themis* (1912). (Attic drinking bowl, tone rotfigurig (1st quarter 5th century BCE). Height 12.3 cm, diam. 33 cm. Inv. F2290. Photo Credit: bpk, Berlin, Antikensammlung, Staatliche Museen, Berlin, Germany. Photo by Johannes Laurentius/Art Resource, NY.

Re-writing Zeus as Year-Spirit and "Recurrent Vital Day"

Jane Harrison's published work on Greek literature and ritual essentially and dramatically changed the way Virginia Woolf read the classics. In *Prolegomena to the Study of Greek Religion*, Harrison brought her anthropological approach along with her sociological and psychological theories on religion to the ancient Greeks, an area, which, at the time, focused exclusively on the textual study of the Olympians. In this the first of her "big books," not only did Harrison have the audacity to suggest the pantheon of Olympian gods and Greek myth were derived from ancient rituals, from the *dromenon,* or "the thing done," by primitive local deities, she also identified these ceremonies and social structures as matrifocal, that is, as she pointed out later in her second major work, *Themis* (1912), not matriarchal as in hierarchical and dominant, but as female-centered.

She writes that in "man-fashioned Olympus," Zeus revised the Earth Goddess:

> She who made all things, gods and mortals alike, is become their plaything, their slave, dowered only with physical beauty, and with a slave's tricks and blandishments. (P 285)

Prolegomena disrupted patriarchal norms and challenged gender hierarchies, by privileging not the individual heroic Olympian goddesses and gods, but circles upon circles of women. In it, Harrison challenged the assumptions of academic readings of the classics, which suggested that the patriarchal tenets of the Olympians provided ideal societal role models for the present. In one instance, she cites St. Augustine's reading of the myth of the rivalry between Poseidon and Athena. In order to appease the wrath of Poseidon, who lost the vote between men and women, when women outvoted the men in favor of Athena, "the men inflicted on the women a triple punishment, 'they were to lose their vote, *their children were no longer to be called by their mother's name* and they themselves were no longer to be called after their goddess, Athenians'" (P 261–62) (original italics). The myth recounts a shift in social organization in ancient Athens that Harrison argues has been persistently misread in order to keep patriarchy in place. She links this transition to a change also in marriage laws that saw Cecrops as introducing patriarchal forms of marriage as a contract between a man and a woman. Harrison cites a pupil of Aristotle who wrote that before this shift, "people did not know who their fathers were, on account of the number (of possible parents)" (262). Harrison challenges this notion, writing that "a society that had passed to patriarchy naturally misjudged the marriage-laws of matriarchy and regarded it as a mere state of promiscuity" when such was not the case.

Prolegomena itself is a bit of a shape-shifter, and begins with setting out Harrison's literary objectives, a desire to more fully understand Greek poetry, but aimed at achieving these goals through a study of the development of Greek religion. Its early chapters deal in the main with indigenous cultic rituals and festivals, but the later sections focus more emphatically on Dionysus and Orpheus as the reader is allowed to witness her mental processes and her confidence in using an open, improvisational style to explore her intellectual pursuits. In the introduction to *Prolegomena*, Harrison claims that

> literature is really my goal. I have tried to understand primitive rites, not in love of their archaism, nor yet wholly from a singleminded devotion to science, but with the definite hope that I might come to a better understanding of some forms of Greek poetry. Religious convention compelled the tragic poets to draw their plots from traditional mythology, from stories whose religious content and motive were already in Homer's days obsolete. A knowledge of, a sympathy with, the milieu of this primitive material is one step to the realization of its final form in tragedy. It is then in the temple of literature, if but as a hewer of wood and drawer of water, that I still hope to serve. (viii)

Harrison's love of literature, her gift for writing, and her articulation of the debt she felt towards literature as the springboard for her serious scholarly work on the social origins of Greek religion were also factors that endeared her to Virginia Woolf's imagination. Harrison's topic of reading the Olympians through a feminist lens, as well as her process that allows for the discovery of research as she and the reader seem to go on this journey together, also gave Woolf a model of a kind of scholarly anti-lecture that was collaborationist and conversationalist rather than linear, methodical, and rationalist, a style of rhetoric that she adopted in both *A Room of One's Own* and *Three Guineas* (see Chapters 3 and 4). Harrison's methods, then, also help to allow Woolf to turn her back on conventional plots and devise new forms.

In a letter to her colleague Gilbert Murray, with whose work on Dionysus in Euripides' *Bacchae* she was becoming increasingly familiar, Harrison good-naturedly blames Murray for *Prolegomena's* strange twists and turns. When *Prolegomena*, a book she referred to in her correspondence with Murray as "the fat and comely one," was nearly finished on 10 September 1902, she writes:

> It is rather dreadful, the whole centre of gravity of the book has shifted. It began as a treatise on Keres [daemons] with a supplementary notice on Dionysus. It is ending as a screed on Dionysus with an introductory talk about Keres. Whose fault is that? *Never, never* again will I ask you to lecture when I am writing a book, a nice sound one too, it was, till last autumn. (JH Papers)

One of the great contributions of *Prolegomena* was that it challenged the convention in the classics of treating Greek myth and Greek religion as one and the same thing, and forced classical scholars to look more seriously at the rites behind the myths; in other words, at the myths as more than a collection of intriguing stories. Another was asking the question of how Greek literature, Greek tragedy, in particular, related to the social reality of Greek life, a question Harrison extended and complicated in *Themis*, where Robert Ackerman points out, she "surpasses" Nietzsche's *The Birth of Tragedy* (1871), a work of genius that she credits in *Reminiscences of a Student's Life* as a major influence.[2]

Harrison, who was often quick to acknowledge her work as collaborative, was a self-described "disciple of Nietzsche" (T viii). She built on his work on the origins of Greek tragedy but by way of scientific method and with the benefit of the most recent archaeological evidence. While Nietzsche, as Harrison notes, uncovered the Dionysian principles behind nineteenth-century idealizations and rationalizations of the Olympian, or Apollonian, system, his views were marked by male deities exclusively. Harrison thought it surprising that, for his study of Dionysus, or for any study of Dionysus, for that matter, he discussed neither Euripides' *Bacchae* nor Aeschylus' *Oresteia*, instead favoring Aeschylus' *Prometheus*, the god whom Nietzsche considered the embodiment of a Dionysian hero.

---

2. According to Ackerman, Nietzsche's work forecasts the general hypothesis of the Cambridge Ritualists as well as Harrison's willingness to use nonrational factors as a means to discern human behavior. Nietzsche writes in *The Birth of Tragedy* that there is in Greek tragedy "a Dionysiac condition, tending toward the shattering of the individual and his fusion with the original Oneness. Tragedy is an Apollonian embodiment of Dionysiac insights and powers [. . .] Dionysos *remains* the sole dramatic protagonist and that all the famous characters of the Greek stage, Prometheus, Oedipus, etc., are only masks of the original hero" (qtd. in Ackerman, *Myth and Ritual School* 99–100).

In contrast, Harrison's work pursued Dionysian ritual structures through the primary source materials of both *The Bacchae* and *The Oresteia,* because they were filled with Dionysian rites, and were an obvious place to start. She soon discovered that goddess figures, priestesses, and female archetypes were vital to these early rites, and was struck by Nietzche's omissions. Buffeted further by archaeological evidence and her expertise in analyzing vase fragments, she discovered, too, that even Dionysus was a later manifestation born or merged with earlier matrifocal cults. Ritual for Harrison ultimately becomes the bridge connecting religion and art. Her examination and portraits of the goddesses and priestesses in Greek religion and Greek theater, specifically Greek tragedy, have creative significance in Virginia Woolf's work as she seeks to alter the narratives of modernism.

After the publication of *Prolegomena,* Harrison was called upon to defend her position, which she refused to do, because "it may be impossible," but decided instead to offer an *apologia pro haeresi mea,* or at least to tell how she arrived at her findings. This strategy, far from apologizing, achieved the opposite result in that it furthered her theories and position. In an article in *Proceedings of the Classical Association 5* (1907), which is later reprinted in part in "Alpha and Omega," in *Alpha and Omega* (1915), one gets a sense of the nature of the attacks upon her work as well as her deft and eloquent handling of a hostile intellectual situation:

> My friends have brought against me of late a somewhat serious charge. They tax me with some lack of reverence for the Olympian gods; for Apollo, for Athena, nay even for Father Zeus himself. My interest, I am told, is unduly focused on ghosts, bogies, fetiches, pillar-cults. I pay to them and to such like the attention properly due to the reverend Olympians. Worse still, in matters of ritual I prefer savage disorders, Dionysiac orgies, the tearing of wild bulls, to the ordered and stately ceremonial of Panathenaic processions. In a word, my heart, it would seem, is not in the right place. ("The Pillar and the Maiden" 1)

Indeed, Harrison's work focused on the "savage" rites and ecstatic practices of the Greeks. Her research emphasized the attendant maenads, for example, to the "young Zeus" or "new king" Dionysus. We learn that "Maenads means of course simply 'mad woman,' and the Maenads are the women-worshippers of Dionysus of whatever race, possessed, maddened or, as the ancients would say, inspired by his spirit" (P 388). She points out that they were not merely satyr substitutes, but historic figures, "for no poet or painter ever attempted to give them horses' ears and tails. And yet, so persistent is the dislike to commonplace fact, that we are repeatedly told that the Maenads are purely mythological creations and that the Maenad orgies never appear historically in Greece" (388). She follows the origins of their name that is in fact "almost a cultus-ephithet" as it represents not a tribe, but "a state of mind and body" (388). She describes Dionysian orgies as, "rites of possession and ecstasy" and "the women were possessed, magical and dangerous to handle" (397–98). With the help of archaeological evidence, the vase paintings and fragments she was expert in analyzing, Harrison's approach shocked the discipline, because they feared not only the content of her research but also her process and methods; that the joys of combing the ruins would displace the authority of the texts. Despite the energy and resources required of her to counter the attacks upon her work, with *Prolegomena,* she changed the discourse and the way scholars spoke about Greek religion. Her ideas that the Olympians are late and the stuff of literature rather than religion, and that the Dionysian and Orphic Mysteries embodied Greek religion and culture are now assimilated into the mainstream, with scholars of intellectual history and historians of anthropology, archaeology, and structuralism seeking to re-examine her work.

In the meantime, however, the publication of *Themis: A Study of the Social Origins of Greek Religion* in 1912 would only deepen the divide as its premises continued to challenge the authority of the text. In the Hymn of the Kouretes, Harrison discovers in the "temple of Diktaean Zeus" (T 544) on Crete that even the "Father of Gods and Men," the "archpatriarchal bourgeois" (P 285) Zeus, she identifies in *Prolegomena,* came from matriarchal origins. She had found a text that "embodied this very group-thinking, or rather group-emotion toward life," in which worshippers "sink their own personality and . . . by dancing to a common rhythm, above all by the common excitement, they become emotionally one, a true congregation, not a collection of individuals" (T 45–46). In the Hymn of Kouretes, the young male dancers invoke Zeus as the "greatest Kouros, who was clearly a projection of the thiasos of his worshippers," that is, as a projection of themselves as a group (T 544), and the young God never stands alone or separate from the group, as their relationship is reciprocal and both his and their lives are interdependent.

In *Themis,* Harrison writes:

Nowhere save in this Hymn do we hear of Zeus with attendant daimones. He stands always alone, aloof, approached with awe, utterly

delimited from his worshippers. One god only, Dionysos, and he but a
half-bred Olympian, is attended by daimones. We can scarcely picture
Dionysos without his attendant thiasos, be they holy women, Maenads,
be they the revel rout of Satyrs. We think of this thiasos of daimones as
attendants, inferior persons, pale reflections, emanations as it were from
the god himself. It seems appropriate that he should be surrounded by
attendants [. . .] superior persons, high officials, always are. If this be all,
how strange, how even unseemly is it that Zeus, the supreme god, Father
of Gods and Men, should have no thiasos, no escort. The Hymn brings
us face to face with the fact that Zeus once had a thiasos, once when he
was a young man, a Kouros. When he grew up to be the Father, it seems,
he lost his thiasos and has gone about unattended ever since. (12)

In *Ancient Art and Ritual,* a text that went far to explicate many of the
theories put forth in *Themis,*[3] Harrison writes that the Olympians express
individual heroes and the epic poets celebrate "klea andron, 'glorious
deeds of men,' of individual heroes; and what these heroes themselves
ardently long and pray for is just this glory, this personal distinction, this
deathless fame for their great deeds" (159). Further, "the highly personalized, individualized god is fashioned on the highly personalized, individualized self, and the essence of the sense of self is separateness, or
consciousness of the severance of one self from other selves, and of that
self as subject and distinct from objects" (T 473).

  In contrast to the Olympian pantheon, the more primitive "Year
Daimon" or "mystery god" like Dionysus, "arises out of those instincts,
emotions, desires which attend and express life" and are projections
"rather of the group than of individual consciousness" (T 543). The Year-
Daimon or Year-Spirit embodies the necessary process of regeneration, or
the passing of the old age into the new. Harrison writes that "The divine
figures of Mother and Child reflect the social conditions of a matriarchal
group with its rite of adolescent initiation; its factors are the mother, the
child, and the tribe, the child as babe and later as Kouros [young man]"
(41). This formulary is further supported by Murray in "The Excursus on
the Ritual Forms Preserved in Greek Tragedy," which Harrison included
as a chapter in *Themis,* and to which Murray returns in the *Journal of
Hellenic Studies* 71 in 1951, long after Harrison's death. In his essay, he
explains Harrison's use of the term *eniautos* meaning Year-Spirit and that

---

3. Harrison's colleague and friend Francis Cornford claimed he could not understand
Themis until he had read *Ancient Art and Ritual.*

the word *eniautos* literally translates as "recurrent vital day," that seam or point in time which marks the dawning of an important age as "the arrival of each Eniautos is the beginning of a new Aion or Age" ("Excursus" 120). In the Olympian version, Zeus is the eternal father, but Murray, in alignment with Harrison in *Themis* points to Hesiod, where the myth appears in its oldest form, which speaks of "another, and apparently more original conception, [in which] the series has no conclusion, since the Old Zeus gives way to a New Zeus, and he at the end of the year will pass it on to another new Zeus" (122). Dionysus, whose name means "Young Zeus, or Zeus the Son, the New King" not only is the Young God, he *is* the new age.

It is useful to return to Harrison's concept of ritual then as a *dromenon,* an action that is "not merely a thing done, but a thing re-done, or pre-done with magical intent" (T 545). The *dromenon,* according to Harrison's definition, is "a thing which, like the drama, is collectively performed" and its "basis or kernel is a thiasos [worshippers] or choros" (T 545). As Yopie Prins notes, "the omophagia [eating of raw flesh] is Harrison's most important example of a *dromenon,* enacted by maenads who therefore symbolically give birth to the god they worship" ("Greek Maenads" 67). For Harrison, "Dionysus is but his thiasos incarnate" (T 38) and a product of an earlier matrilineal family dynamic. As Prins explains, "Not only do the maenads take his spirit into the body, but he is the very incarnation of their own spirit and thus projected in song [. . .]. In the collective performance of this cry, as a performative utterance, the god is called into being" ("Greek Maenads 67).

Harrison is unafraid to make the analogy between this ancient paradigm and the structure of her own times, a position that often drew the ire of her critics. It was difficult for her to sustain an academic distance between herself and her research, because she saw these two aspects of her scholarship as intricately entwined. As Robinson notes, "she believed, and made it quite clear she believed, that what we learn from ancient Greek religion has everything to do with the way we live our present day lives" (*Life and Work* 143), a position also adopted by Woolf's tutor, Janet Case, as we have seen, in her article "Women in the Plays of Aeschylus." Harrison often pointed out Victorian hypocrisy and challenged both academia and a public discourse that was intellectually unfair to women and often corrupt, as she was sarcastically termed "an advanced thinker" (Robinson, *Life and Work* 142) as early as 1882 for her radical ideas about these time-honored texts. In another example, in *Themis,* she writes that "The social structure represented by the Olympians is the same as that of the

modern family, it is patrilinear," whereas the "figure of Dionysus, his thiasos, and his relation to his mother and the Maenads, is only to be understood by reference to an early social structure, known as matrilinear" (T
551–52). The thiasos is the group of attendant worshippers, themselves
daimones, such as Dionysus' satyrs and Maenads, from whom he is never
separate. For Harrison, the group marks the matriarchal deity, while the
patriarchal god is essentially solitary.

Patriarchy, Harrison contends, "would fain dominate all things,
would invade even the ancient prerogative of the mother, the right to
rear the child she bore . . . [it] usurps the function of the mother . . . "
(T 495), and goes on to cite as examples the Olympian structure that
narrates the birth of Athena as springing from Zeus' head and Dionysus
from Zeus' thigh, about which Harrison writes, "the motherhood of the
mother is obscured, even denied" (500).

Prins reads Harrison's maenadic ritual as embodying multiple relations. In other words, she digresses from a feminist reading, rejecting
the binary of matriarchy and patriarchy. She argues "Harrison's emphasis on maenadic ritual is often interpreted as part of an argument about
matriarchal culture prior to patriarchal mythology, but the maenad also
destabilizes the binary opposition of patriarchy and matriarchy, by mobi-
lizing relations between women beyond the maternal role: the power of
the thiasos is that it can project and embody multiple relations" ("Greek
Maenads" 67). This position does not negate Harrison's advocacy of a
timeline that casts mother-centered cults as existing before the usurpation
of the patriarchal pantheon of Olympian gods, which is indeed what Harrison was arguing, but leaves out Harrison's own insistence on these early
cultures as "matrilineal" and "matrifocal," and not "matriarchal." Harrison writes:

> It may seem strange that woman, always the weaker, should be thus dom-
> inant and central. But it must always be observed that this primitive form
> of society is matrilinear not matriarchal. Woman is the social centre not
> the dominant force. So long as force is supreme, physical force of the
> individual, society is impossible, because society is by cooperation, by
> mutual concession, not by antagonism. (T 491)

It is a view, as we have seen, she echoed in *Ancient Art and Ritual,* when
she wrote that "a heroic *society* is almost a contradiction in terms" (162).
Harrison's argument places women, the maenads, in Prins, for example,
as crucial functionaries in an inter-dependent relationship that is recipro-

cal and, inclusive of Prins, also, multiple but decidedly, as Harrison theorized, matrifocal, women-centered, women guided. Both Harrison and
Woolf read this process and this relationship as feminist, without declar-
ing it so, as it challenged and revised their understanding of gender relations, gender roles, and power.

Articulating Themis

But what of this matrifocal figure? Who is she? Harrison leaves the figure
of Themis until Chapter XI unformulated, devoting an entire chapter and
the title of her book to an exploration of her significance. In Aeschylus'
Prometheus Bound, the playwright identifies her as "but another form of
Gaia" when Prometheus relates that his mother, "Themis/And Gaia, one
in nature, many-named" has foretold his future, and Harrison points out
that Themis, in Aeschylus, at least, is "envisaged as the oracular power
of Earth" (T 480). She then brings in archaeological evidence, the narrative found on a red-figured cylix from the Berlin catalogue, and her experiences in the Themis sanctuary on the south slope of the Acropolis, as
well as the account by Pausanias of Themis' altar, in order to deepen our
understanding of this complex goddess, a figure whose complete portrait
once filled out by Jane Harrison, Virginia Woolf reanimates throughout
her fiction. In the illustration (see figure 1, we see Themis seated as other
gods come and go, but she with a vial of water in one hand and a sprig
of laurel in another "is below and above all gods" as she "abides there
seated" (480).

Harrison asks, "But if Themis be but the projection, the imperson-
ation of Earth and of the prophetic powers of Earth, why should she be
above and beyond all other gods?" (T 481). She explains that Themis is
the embodiment of prophecy and not prophecy as the Olympians would
have it, but "in the old sense of prophecy, utterance, ordinance, not in the
later sense of a forecast of the future" but even more at ordinance than
utterance. In Homer, she points out Themis has a dual role: "she convenes
and dissolves the assembly; she presides over the feast [. . .] over the banquet. When Hera enters Olympos, the gods rise up to greet her and hold
out their cups in welcome, and she takes the cup of Themis who is first.
[. . .] It is the meed of Themis to convene and dissolve the agora; it is
hers too to preside over the equal, sacramental feast" (482).

This relationship seems at first glance to cast Themis in an inferior or
subordinate role, an impression Harrison is quick to dispense.

FIGURE 6. A kylix featuring Themis, which Jane Harrison studied and reinterpreted. She named her second major work, *Themis: A Study of the Social Origins of Greek Religion* (1912), after the priestess seated here. Kodros Painter (5th century BCE) attributed to: Aegeus receiving the oracle of Delphi from the priestess Themis who is sitting on the tripod. Kylix (drinking cup), from Vulci, c. 440 BCE. Diam. 32 cm. Inv. F2538, Photo Credit: bpk, Berlin, Antikensammlung, Staatliche Museen, Berlin, Germany. Photo by Johannes Laurentius/Art Resource, NY.

We think of Themis as an abstraction, as Law, Justice, Right, and, naturally, we are surprised that she who is above Zeus himself should be set to do the service of a herald, an office surely meter for Hermes or Iris. Why, we ask, with Hermes and Iris at hand, ready to speed over earth and sea with messages and mandates, should Themis have to execute just this one office of convening the assembly? To preside over the banquet may be an honorable function, but to "range about all over," fetching up gods and demigods, is no more a mark of supremacy. (T 483)

In order to solve this dilemma, Harrison turns to linguistics and philology to get to the source of the Greek word Themis, and reveals that both Themis in the Greek and the word Doom in English share a parallel development. "Doom," she writes is the "thing set, fixed, settled; it begins in convention, the stress of public opinion; it ends in statutory judgement. Your private doom is your private opinion [...] but [...] it is the collective doom, public opinion, that, for man's common convenience, crystallizes into Law" (483). Themis, she has shown, was worshipped initially in the plural. In other words,

> [...] out of many dooms, many public opinions, many judgments, arose the figure of the one goddess. Out of many themistes arose Themis. These themistes, these fixed conventions, stood to the Greek for all he held civilized. They were the basis alike of his kingship and of his democracy. These themistes are the ordinances of what must be done, what society compels; they are also, because what must be will be, the prophecies of what shall be in the future; they are also the dues, the rites, the prerogatives of a king, whatever custom assigns to him or any official. (483)

Themis, in the beginning as a part of the tribe, "was all powerful," but as her status is diluted by migrations, invasions, and disruptions, she becomes from "the debris of the shattered group-system" the polis, adapted from primitive impulses, associated with Earth-worship and kinship. Harrison points out that Themis, like Antigone, another figure who held special significance for Virginia Woolf, "stands for kinship and the dues of Earth, Creon for patriarchalism incarnate in the Tyrant and for the Zeus religion that by that time had become its expression" (T 484). Themis "is the very spirit of the assembly incarnate," a figure barely discernible from the actual agora who is "trembling on the very verge of godhead." And as Harrison portrays her, "She is the force that brings and binds men together, she is 'herd instinct,' the collective conscience, the social sanction [...] the social imperative" who exists "before the particular shapes of gods; she is not religion, but she is the stuff of which religion is made. It is the emphasis and representation of herd instinct, of the collective conscience, that constitutes religion" (485). It is important to point out here that when we discuss Themis, or any of the goddess figures in Harrison's mythography as Earth Mother, this is not the journalistic, sentimentalized, New Age, Earth Mother, conjured during the spiritual supermarket of the 1970s and 1980s, as an eternal nurturer. Far from it. With etymological affinities with the English word "Doom," Themis, as Harrison outlines, is both "behind" and "above," both Mother and Father, in contemporary terms, perhaps akin, metaphorically, to science's "theory of everything," not making order out of chaos, but holding chaos within the fabric and folds of her raiment and representation. She presides over the assembly and embodies plurality, public opinion, public judgment, and public law, as she constructs and binds civilization together.

Harrison's emphasis and theories on group dynamics in relation to Greek myth and ritual find their way into Woolf's fiction and her own exploration of family rituals and group dynamics in relation to social mores and group pathology. The narrative structures in Woolf's work refuse to give us heroes, and often point instead to the consequences of a society based upon the glorification of the individual in service to a patriarchal and imperialistic ideal. In revising Zeus and outlining and adding dimension to Themis, Harrison's work offers Woolf the possibility of changing modernism's war story, questioning its cultural and political values and challenging its assumptions about gender and women's roles in relation to families and the state.

Harrisonian Ritual Structures in Virginia Woolf's Fiction

Reading Harrison's revisions of Greek literature transpersonally, Virginia Woolf is able to envision a world where Antigone survives and thrives. Anne Fernald, however, suggests that Woolf's "emphasis on ancient Greece [. . .] in no way tempts Woolf to concoct her own counter narratives refuting the dominant ones," theorizing instead that Woolf uses fragments to disassociate Greek literature from nation and empire building (19). She admits that Woolf "recognized Greek literature's part in the patriarchal and martial past" and despite being aware of a culture of "violent death," which "relegated women to the role of weeping for and burying their men," she "still always loved Greek literature" (19). But it is Harrison's work, indeed her work in re-interpreting the narratives on vase fragments, which allow Woolf to engage in Greek literature from an alternative perspective, and challenge the sexist, violent, heroic, imperialist, and deeply entrenched bias of the classics as translated and presented by a Victorian classical education.

While critics often link Woolf's "Greekness" to loss and Fernald to a theory of distance and a fragmentary aesthetic also bound to loss and grief and lamentation, I see every aspect of Woolf's connection to Greece and Greek literature as directed by Harrison's scholarship, as circumventing classical literature's *klea andron* and positing, if not a revised narrative, then certainly the possibility of one. When Fernald argues that "it becomes possible for Woolf to imagine that emphasizing the fragmentary nature of our understanding might shift the resonance of Greek literature" and "if others could share her sense of Greek as fragmented, they might not so confidently link it to England and British Empire" (18), we can easily see points of contact with Harrison's work with fragments, reading transpersonally, and feeding Woolf's imagination, as we also see that Woolf's critique of empire is informed and fueled by Harrison's research, which relentlessly denies the English their war heroes. Vassiliki Kolocotroni agrees that Woolf is not simply using her knowledge of Greek as what Fernald terms "cultural capital" (17), but "to apply what the difficulty of access to Greek taught her to the forging of a new aesthetic: to the creation of meaning 'on the far side of language,'" as Woolf writes in "On Not Knowing Greek" (322). This new aesthetic, this attraction to the "fragment" are linked to the transpersonal sharing between Harrison and Woolf and to Harrison's own insistence on revision and alternative possibilities, ways of seeing, of expression, and in very real terms, ways of being.

If we explore Woolf's novels, each one is an attempt to re-create "a society," as defined by Jane Harrison. Both *The Voyage Out* (1915) (in its earlier version given the Greek-sounding title *Melymbrosia*) and *Night and Day* (1919) can be read as a condemnation of and re-thinking of marriage; in *Jacob's Room* (1922), the young god or hero is killed, uncharacteristically off-text. There is no regeneration under patriarchy, and it's even worse for men. In *Mrs. Dalloway* (1925), Septimus, too, is a war hero, but I read him as a martyr to the cause of pacifism, because he refuses to reproduce. Mrs. Dalloway also suffers under patriarchy, and seems to be arguing, that, yes, fine, I'll have one child, but now leave me alone. No more children for wars. In *To the Lighthouse* (1927), Mrs. Ramsey, whom critics frame as the Angel in the House, represents to Woolf that overwhelming force and pressure on women to nurture that the woman artist has to kill in order to succeed. Woolf outlines the fissures and hypocrisies of this false construction by revealing to us that Mrs. Ramsey often despises her role and sometimes her children. At many points in the novel, she seems to be saying, I truly hate patriarchy, because it has only brought hardship and misery to me, until the requirements under it to "be good" and to be the Angel in the House literally kill her. *Orlando* (1928) exists in a world or many worlds, which throb between two genders, and *The Waves* (1931) has no characters at all. *Flush* (1933) is preoccupied with a dog's world, and *The Years* (1937), titled in manuscript *The Pargiters,* was initially a hybrid form of Woolf's own creation, a novel-essay, but a novel with no plot linked to essay fragments, many of which would later be published in her pacifist polemic *Three Guineas* (1938). Her last novel, *Between the Acts,* published posthumously in 1941, ends with an insistence and plea from the muddy and eluvial Miss La Trobe to invent new plots.

In the following readings, I've focused on a representative sample of Woolf's novels, which have received little or no attention in relation to Harrison's scholarship. Themis figures pervade Woolf's work, and perhaps, Mrs. Ramsey, in Woolf's masterpiece, *To the Lighthouse,* is one of the more obvious examples, but the novel has already been discussed in relation to Harrison in an essay by Martha C. Carpentier.[4] Here, I explore Woolf's second novel, *Night and Day,* as an example of her early work; *Jacob's Room* and *Mrs. Dalloway* from the height of her literary career; and lastly *The Waves,* considered her most innovative effort and a text whose publication in 1931 marked the beginning of the last full decade of her life. Woolf's two Greek notebooks, collectively "The Libation Bearers Notebook" and "The Agamemnon Notebook," are also discussed here as her efforts to learn and translate Greek, as we've seen, inspired by both Case and Harrison, become relevant to her fiction and her search for new forms and new questions.

Themis and Greek Ritual in *Night and Day*

In Woolf's second novel, *Night and Day,* ritual dictates the unfolding of the book's narrative structure. Indeed, the writing of the novel itself was

---

4. See Carpentier's chapter on Themis and Mrs. Ramsey in *To the Lighthouse;* for other critical attention given to Woolf and Harrison in relation to *The Voyage Out,* see Kolocotroni; for *The Years,* see Jane Marcus' chapter in *Languages of Patriarchy;* for *Between the Acts,* see Patricia Maika; and for a reading of *Orlando,* see Beer, who sees Orlando as living between genders "without guilt or Tiresian pangs" (57).

completed within a ritual of one half hour's worth of writing a day, during an enforced "rest cure" while recovering from an earlier illness. Beginning the novel in late 1914 or early 1915, Woolf wrote the book to prove her own sanity, but she fretted over the prospect "of finishing a book on this method—I write one sentence—the clock strikes—Leonard appears with a glass of milk" (L 2: 107). The "method," however, worked and she finished late in 1918, and published October 1919 under her half-brother George Duckworth's imprint.

Night and Day has been discussed as Woolf's "traditional" discourse on marriage and frequently read as a comparatively unsuccessful update of the marriage plot from novels of the nineteenth century which critics have often claimed it is trying to imitate. Missing the Harrisonian markers, E. M. Forster dismissed the novel as "an exercise in classical realism, and contains all that has characterized English fiction, for good and evil, during the last two hundred years: faith in personal relations, recourse to humorous side-shows, geographical exactitude, insistence on petty social differences" (Virginia Woolf). It has been read as Shakespearean comedy (Rachel Wetzsteon) and Mozartian opera (Jane Marcus), but if we explore the novel through a Harrisonian understanding of ritual, which the text invokes, an alternative reading emerges. Night and Day is a ritual of courtship, but not one performed along traditional mores or conventions of the nineteenth-century novel, as it is essentially a marriage plot about a woman who does not want to get married, but who wants instead to be alone with her work. she breaks off her engagement with the poet and government clerk William Rodney by summoning ritualistic power and courage after she has "fixed her eyes upon a lightning-splintered ash-tree, and, almost as if she were reading a writing fixed to the trunk." She then begins her declaration: "She did not want to marry any one. She wanted to go away by herself, preferably to some bleak northern moor, and there study mathematics and the science of astronomy" (ND 242). And by the novel's end, the "marriage" she agrees to with the solicitor and would-be writer Ralph Denham is one based on an unspoken agreement to allow each other the space and time to work, as "books were to be written, and since books must be written in rooms [. . .] they sketched a habitation for themselves" (507), this after Katharine has gazed longingly and lovingly up at the feminist, political activist, Mary Datchett's window from the sidewalk where "[t]hey stood for some moments, looking at the illuminated blinds, an expression to them both of something impersonal and serene in the spirit of the woman within, working out her plans far into the night" (506). The tacit agreement to allow each other the space to work and think exists alongside an underlying ambiguity, anxiety, and transpersonal yearning for intellectual intimacy, a kind of Harrisonian holopsychosis, as Katharine tries to convey that she wishes "Ralph to understand that she followed the track of his thought." Even though "she felt him trying to piece together in a laborious and elementary fashion fragments of belief, unsoldered and separate, lacking the unity of phrases fashioned by the old believers," she realizes that "together they groped in this difficult region, where the unfinished, the unfulfilled, the unwritten, the unreturned, came together in their ghostly way and wore the semblance of the complete and the satisfactory" (506). The novel ends with the uncertain couple "in their ghostly way" riding the bus, as Katharine continues to wonder "What woman did he see?" before they dismount and part upon the threshold of a "door half open" and "loosed their hands" (508).

This is not a description of requited love, nor has the unfolding of the plot thus far been a quest for love in the conventional sense of "marriage plots" that have come before, but is instead, an examination of the process of a woman's decision to marry with no clear-cut goal that has been reached. Indeed, she misses Denham completely, in a micro-version of Clarissa Dalloway and Septimus Smith in *Mrs. Dalloway* who never lock eyes, as she walks on The Strand repeating over and over in her head a ritualistic chant, "some lines which had stuck to her memory: 'it's life that matters, nothing but life—the process of discovery—the everlasting and perpetual process, not the discovery itself at all'" (130), lines that invoke Bergson's durée, as critics have pointed out, but also a concept shared by Jane Harrison, who wrote about their shared credo in her memoir: *nox est perpetua una dormienda* (literally, "an eternal night must be slept." Hence live now, since death is forever). The novel, in terms of form, then, is in a sense a meta-marriage plot, a privileging of process over outcome, an examination as it were of the ribs of a ship, rather than the relationship itself.

The novel is further distinguished from its Victorian predecessors, because it is dominated by the central figure of Themis as embodied in Katharine Hilbery, a character, despite its many associations with Woolf herself, based on her sister, Vanessa, arguably one of the more Themislike, Great Mother, Doom figures in Virginia's own life. Indeed, *Night and Day* is dedicated to Vanessa. To dispel any doubt about who Hilberty represented, Woolf enjoined to Janet Case on 19 November 1919 to "try thinking of Katharine as Vanessa, not me" (L 2: 400).

Reading transpersonally through a Harrisonian lens, we see once again circles upon circles of women, where the sacred dance of the group generates a collective energy that subsumes the development of the individual and is presided over by Themis. I would also argue that *Night and Day* is not a *bildungsroman,* or novel of education, in the least, as neither Katharine nor Denham's characters crystallize into a defined new stage of development. Rather the transformations that do take place are for the good of the group, for the development and growth of the tribe, the society, of civilization itself.

Katharine, as one Themis character among many,[5] is not so much a character as an omnipresent feminine force that does not impose on the masculine, but seeks, not without difficulty, to integrate Denham into the circle.

In the opening scene, Katharine is "mistress of a situation," presiding before the assembled guests over the ritual of afternoon tea, when the door is flung open and we are introduced to the Young God, Ralph Denham, who "muttered something, which was indeed all that was required of him" (ND 10). For Harrison, rituals reveal insight into the values and beliefs of the group, "what a people does, social custom, convention, collective action" (T 546). Throughout the novel, Woolf deploys character and plot through ritual as Katharine Hilbery directs the choreography and is established as Themis from the outset. As such, she is responsible for completing the circle, maintaining harmony, and bringing the Young God into the center of her community. Woolf writes:

> Katharine stirred her tea, and seemed to speculate, so Denham thought, upon the duty of filling somebody else's cup, but she was really wondering how she was going to keep this strange young man in harmony with the rest. She observed that he was compressing his teacup, so that there was danger lest the thin china might cave inwards [. . .] anyhow, he would not be easily combined with the rest. (ND 11)

---

5. Others are Mrs. Hilbery, who "made her house a meeting place for her own relations, to whom she would lament the passing of the great days of the nineteenth century [. . .] and weaved round them romances which had generally no likeness to the truth" (ND 37–38); the suffragist Sally Seal, that "odd little priestess of humanity [. . .]who thought of nothing but her vision" (170); Mary Datchett, who relishes the single life, despite its consequences, whose pace quickens on her way to work, "so as to get her typewriter to take its place in competition with the rest" (80), and who seeks "to draw Katharine into the community" at her office over tea despite Katharine's "unlikeness to the rest of them" (86–88); and Joan Denham, Ralph's older sister, who gives her brother "ancient sympathy" (35) and who presides over the women's circles of their own home, the drawing-room where Denham "heard low voices [. . .] saw women's figures, [. . .] and could even smell the scent of the cedar log which flamed in the grate" (28).

In Harrison's mythos, the individual has but a slight conscious awareness of himself as distinct from his group. In *Themis,* she argues that to disconnect from the thiasos, or worshippers, is death for the god. Olympians are "the last product of rationalism, of individualistic thinking" and "cut off from the very source of their life and being, the emotion of the thiasos, they desiccate and die" (48), whereas in matrifocal systems, the "mystery-god" is an expression of emotion and of group unity, "the impulse of life through all things, perennial, indivisible" (476). The Olympians are a celebration and privileging of rationality, of the individual as distinct from the group, unlike the more primitive "mystery-god," "Year-Daimon," the "recurrent vital day," who "arises out of those instincts, emotions, desires which attend and express life" and are projections "rather of the group than of individual consciousness" (T 546). In other words, "Broadly speaking, these Olympians represent that tendency in thought which is towards reflection, differentiation, clearness, while the Eniautos-Daimon represents that other tendency in religion towards emotion, union, indivisibility" (551). In an Olympian construct, the ritual dance is overpowered by an individual or masculine god, but here the emphasis privileges circles, community, and the collective as presided over by a female principle.

Other characters in the novel also have an awareness of Katharine as a Themis figure. William Rodney, Katharine's fiancé, describes her as "the mistress of her little section of the world; but more than that, she was the person of all others who seemed to him the arbitress of life, the woman whose judgment was naturally right and steady, as his had never been in spite of all his culture" (ND 240). He cannot imagine her entering a room, a sacred space, "without a sense of the flowing of robes, of the flowering of blossoms, of the purple waves of the sea, of all things that are lovely and mutable on the surface but still and passionate in their heart" (240). Katharine is clearly a goddess, but not an Olympian Athena or a Judeo-Christian Eve; she is Themis, "arbitress of life," who presides over each and every communal gathering, in the drawing room at tea, but also, over the past "her time was spent in imagination with the dead" (240) and future, as she, along with her mother, Mrs. Hilbery, who thinks in circles (she can write only about fifteen minutes at a stretch), is in charge of her grandfather's legacy, the relics of the past and his reputation in the future. She also presides over literature and art, at the reading of Rodney's essay in Mary Datchett's rooms, over the family gathering of her aunts, and ultimately over tea at Denham's family home. There, she is at first disgusted at their unrefined tastes, but she eventually increases her understanding of Ralph when she assures him, "I thought you more wonderful than ever" (380), because she believes now that she has found, not someone to love in a physical sense, but someone she can talk to about her work. As Themis, Katharine desires to share and encourage the flow of creativity from Denham, as she also embodies public opinion, power, and social capital as an "arbitress" and protectress of civilization.

Curiously, and another distinctive Harrisonian aspect of this unusual book, as Ralph Denham and Katharine Hilbery's relationship unfolds, neither robs the other of power. Separate spheres are united into a larger whole, represented by their ritual encounter in Kew Gardens.

> Soon a look of the deepest satisfaction filled them, though, for a moment, he did not move. He watched a lady who came rapidly, and yet with a trace of hesitation, down the broad grass-walk towards him. She did not see him. Distance lent her figure an indescribably height, and romance seemed to surround her from the floating of a purple veil which the light air filled and curved from her shoulders.
>
> "Here she comes, like a ship in full sail," he said to himself, half remembering some line from a play or poem where the heroine bore down thus with feathers flying and airs saluting her. The greenery and the high presences of the trees surrounded her as if they stood forth at her coming. He rose, and she saw him; her little exclamation proved that she was glad to find him, and then that she blamed herself for being late. (ND 329)

She marvels at the beauty of their surroundings: "the lake, the broad green space, the vista of trees, with the ruffled gold of the Thames in the distance and the Ducal castle standing in the meadows" and she pays "tribute" to the Ducal lion's tail with her "incredulous laughter." The idea of a distinctive, individualistic character, however, is lost. Katharine commands salutation, but she also merges with her surroundings, as the two characters are romanced by one another through their surroundings, in a seductive ritual that leaves the reader desiring a physical closeness that never completely materializes. Ralph finally secures an attachment to Katharine by novel's end, one that satisfies his ego, as it enhances his position, but not one that alters her status or catapults her into paroxysms of joy at having finally found true love.

That moment of physical closeness and emotional intensity is reserved for another creatively significant Themis figure, Mary Datchett, the feminist New Woman, in whom Katharine recognizes an aspect of herself. In a scene charged with primal eroticism and connection, Katharine loses her sense of alienation and loneliness when she meets with Mary. At the reading of Rodney's paper, Katharine feels so close to Mary that she has no need to even speak to her verbally. As Denham is left "as if he were tearing handfuls of grass up by the roots from the carpet" (ND 57), Katharine is joined by Mary at a seat upon the windowsill, from which vantage point, "the two young women could thus survey the whole party" (57). "She was conscious of Mary's body beside her, but, at the same time, the consciousness of being both of them women made it unnecessary to speak to her" (57). But they do speak, about professions for women, a topic that feels alien to Katharine "as if feeling her way among the phantoms of an unknown world" (58). She yearns to have a voice, to be able to assert herself knowledgably and politically. Her conversation with Mary is intimate, but also based on respect and illustrates an interaction from which they each learn and profit, as they become progressively closer. "Katharine drew back the curtain in order perhaps, to conceal the momentary flush of pleasure which is caused by coming perceptibly nearer to another person" (58) as they decide upon calling each other by their first names and gaze together at the moon and clouds and rooftops of London. Their "pleasure" and the transpersonal connection they enjoy is "destroyed" by a joke made by a man in the room behind them.

The novel is filled with Greek references, from the Greek lexicon Katharine hides her math studies in, to the Aeschylean bird imagery which reappears throughout several of Woolf's novels. In *Night and Day*, Denham has a trained rook, "a wretched bird, with half its feathers out and one leg lamed by a cat" (27), Mary Datchett doodle-draws a picture of suffragist committee head Mr. Clacton as a "bald-headed cock-sparrow" (166). Katharine's circle of "My aunts!" are filled with large-bird imagery as they lead an "incarnadined existence" with their "high-pitched, cooing note[s]" (144) and function as attendant themistes to the Young God as they reveal the cultural and social beliefs of the tribe.

Jacob's Room, Mrs. Dalloway, and *The Waves* as Greek Trilogy

Harrison's concepts of the Dionysian mystery God, or the Eniautos-Daimon and Year-Spirit are helpful to Woolf in crafting her own plots and metaphors. Her literary style becomes more fully realized and mature, when she writes, with greater political implications, the three novels *Jacob's Room, Mrs. Dalloway,* and *The Waves.* I read each of the heroes or anti-heroes in these texts, in the figures of Jacob, Septimus, and Percival, respectively, as Dionysian Young Gods, or as Harrisonian "Year-Spirits," tragically trapped in an Olympian, hero-worshipping world, and the novels themselves as a trilogy for Woolf, her three-volume social protest against violence and war.

There are many parallels to be drawn between them and what I characterize as Woolf's transpersonal reading of Aeschylus' *Oresteia* from a Harrisonian perspective. Aeschylus' *The Agamemnon, The Libation Bearers* (or *The Choephori*), and *The Furies* (or *The Eumenides*) chronicle a moment of cataclysmic change, the moment of transition away from the collective towards the individual, away from matrifocal groups to the patriarchal Olympians and Greek democracy. But this happens not without a significant caveat, which makes Aeschylus' work, read through Harrison, especially attractive to Woolf—that "freshness of a new ideal" articulated by Janet Case in "Women in the Plays of Aeschylus" and supported by Harrison's research in *Prolegomena* and *Themis,* namely, that communities of women from the past existed, make up a matrifocal history, and constituted the stuff of ancient Greek religion.

As we follow the cycle of violence from *The Agamemnon* through *The Furies,* the *klea andron,* or heroic deeds of men, are countered by the complexity of Clytemnestra's motivations in killing Agamemnon in the first place, among other women-centered constructs he deploys throughout the *Oresteia.* In her reading of Aeschylus' trilogy, it is no accident that Virginia Woolf's "sympathies [. . .] lie almost entirely with Clytemnestra" and that she can write in "On Not Knowing Greek," that "Clytemnestra is no unmitigated villainess [. . .] she says—'there is a strange power in motherhood.' It is no murderess, violent and unredeemed, whom Orestes kills within the house" (26–27). This is because she is reading the plays through the feminism and political radicalism of Harrison, whose own "sympathies" defended Clytemnestra and many of Aeschylus' women as feminist-activist role models for her own contemporary times. For Woolf, Clytemnestra is not only avenging the death of her daughter Iphigenia, sacrificed by Agamemnon in order to speed his way to war; she is also behaving as she must, for the good of the family, the community, and civilization, itself, as she has known it. As if the murder of their daughter were not enough to condemn him, Agamemnon also returns home with his mistress, the nightingale-prophetess Cassandra, notably another slave woman, and enters Clytemnestra's sacred space, the home, walking upon the carpets in a transgressive act equal to the pollution of her "temple."

Reading through Harrison, Woolf notes that Aeschylus makes a gesture in *The Furies* to integrate women's history into his current society. He not only names the entire play after this terrifying group of women, he satisfies their desires for justice and peace by the end of the play. It is significant that only Athena can look upon The Furies, the monster-goddess women from the ancient cults explored by Harrison's research. Orestes, under the aegis of Apollo, is helpless and unable to face them, unable to face even himself. But Aeschylus does not allow "the noble Athena" to decide everyone's fate, for to do so would appease only The Furies, and would be an implicit validation of the old ways over the new. Nor does he give the task to the Olympian Apollo, Orestes' mentor and protector. Instead, he has Athena set up the areopagus, an impartial committee that ultimately allows all parties to come away from the table at least partially satisfied in their dispute, and which also plays into the hands of the "new ways" he was both theatrically and politically responsible to affirm to his contemporary Greek audience.

Woolf's three novels also document a profound shift in ritual systems, but at a different point in human history, poised on the brink of catastrophic change. Like Aeschylus' trilogy, these three texts often seek to act as a corrective to a world that has gone too far in the direction of *klea andron,* and she composes as a woman trying to write herself out of the bell jar of a fully realized patriarchal world. For Woolf to argue for the potential in a society as a collective, group energy that seeks to integrate and strengthen the individual in a formulary that has no end, because it is and must be regenerative, is a radical and politically important act. To position the Young God, our "recurring vital day," in decades of death, mechanized warfare, cataclysmic loss of life, displacement, fragmentation, disease, and levels of unspeakable grief and horror that had exceeded thus far any other era in human history, is an attack on the patriarchal establishment and its cultural control of our lives. Woolf is in essence writing herself both into and against Greek literary tradition, in my view, as it is a revised classical tradition that she engages with transpersonally.

With *Jacob's Room, Mrs. Dalloway,* and *The Waves,* Woolf, invoking Harrison's work and politics, exposes the violence, bloodshed, and war that this hero-worshipping "society" has wrought. Woolf's novels not only diagnose the problem, but also seek answers along Harrisonian lines, insisting that we reconsider how we integrate the individual into the community and learn how to balance conflict through conversation, dialogue, and cooperation. As Carpentier writes, both Harrison's and Woolf's "feminist visions reassert the transcendence of the female principle. Both associated merger and sensibility with femaleness, with the mother. Both associated individualism and rationalism with maleness, with the father. Both sought in their work to resurrect the primacy of mother over father, of mysticism over rationalism, of merger over separation, of collectivity over individuality" (173), statements with which I agree. The only exception is "the primacy of mother over father," which does not quite accurately convey Harrison's idea of matrifocal community versus matriarchy, a distinction Harrison labors to make clear in *Themis*, and one, I argue, to which Virginia Woolf singularly adheres. Woolf is seeking not to resurrect an exact replica of Harrison's pre-Olympian goddess circles, but to use these models to provoke deeper questions, to challenge the patriarchal status quo, and to offer possible revisions of the political and economic inequities of her own times.

"The Agamemnon Notebook"

Indeed, in 1922, at the age of forty, the year that *Jacob's Room* was published, Woolf, like Harrison at nearly the same age, who was about to begin her research fellowship at Newnham, was re-evaluating her approach to her Greek studies. She had kept a number of notebooks on her readings in Greek drama and poetry, and had begun her "Libation Bearers Notebook" in 1907 as she worked with Janet Case. Nearly twenty-five years later, on 4 October 1922, she decides to "read Greek now steadily," and declares "I shall read the Trilogy" (D 2: 205). "The Agamemnon Notebook," Woolf's own crib translation of Aeschylus' play, was begun in a daily ritual because "at forty I am beginning to learn the mechanism of my own brain" (D 2: 206), as she was beginning to work on *Mrs. Dalloway,* but enjoying the fruits of her labor with the publication of *Jacob's Room.* On the same day she decides to commit herself to Aeschylus' play, she writes, referring to *Jacob's Room,* "At last, I like reading my own writing" (D 2: 205). To make the notebook, which was at one time catalogued simply as "the little black book," she took shears to an 1831 edition of the play in Greek and then used Verrall's 1904 translation, which had both the Greek and English to guide her own transcriptions by hand. As noted in Chapter One, Verrall's is the same edition she used to make her earlier "Libation Bearers Notebook" and the same edition used by Harrison, who was Verrall's former student, to teach Greek.

In her essay, "Otototoi: Virginia Woolf and the 'Naked Cry' of Cassandra," Yopie Prins does a thorough textual analysis and reading of Woolf's "Agamemnon Notebook" in terms of its creating an "interlingual space that allows us to read in multiple directions," not merely horizontally or in a linear motion between text and crib translation. Prins usefully characterizes Woolf's notebook as "a theatrical spectacle in its own right" (165) and her "unauthorized glossolalia of Ladies' Greek" (173), assessments with which I agree, although I object to the overuse of the diminutive, dismissive term "Ladies' Greek" when discussing Woolf's, but especially Harrison's Greek aptitude and ability. Indeed, Jane Marcus suggests in a note in *Virginia Woolf: Languages of Patriarchy* that Woolf may have contributed to the classicist Walter Headlam's *Agamemnon of Aeschylus with Verse Translation, Introduction, and Notes* whom she was dating at the time before his sudden death, and, according to Prins, Headlam also "may have intended to dedicate his translation to her" ("Otototoi" 173). Furthermore, Harrison, who was somewhat of a linguistic genius, to say the least, although insecure about her philological knowledge of Greek, did not study "Ladies' Greek" with Verrall and her other instructors while at Newnham College, and used her own innovative methods to teach from as well (see Chapter One). Prins also reads "The Agamemnon Notebook" as part of a tradition that "reflects back on a long history of translating Greek tragedy for the page and not for the stage" ("Otototoi" 165), which connects it to an earlier classical tradition, rather than the more innovative approach practiced by Jane Harrison and conveyed to Woolf via Janet Case.

I see Woolf's "Agamemnon Notebook" (and her "Libation Bearers Notebook") as an artifact embodying Harrison and Woolf's transpersonal relationship and demonstrating the vitality of an autodidactic female scholar's mind. The lively dance upon the page back and forth, between English and Greek, above and below, inside and outside the margins, marked by her changes and notations, false starts, and revisions seem to me more connected to a "performance" by Jane Harrison—to her colorful, charismatic, and vigorous approach to the classics than to the classical tradition Harrison challenged that would prefer to parse a sentence rather than understand the meaning behind it.

One of the most intriguing sections of "The Agamemnon Notebook," as Yopie Prins points out, is the Cassandra scene translated by Virginia

Woolf as "the naked cry" in her essay "On Not Knowing Greek." The "barbaric" speech of the kidnapped prophetess Cassandra is linked to the myth of the sisters Procne and Philomela and the plaintive cry of the nightingale, which, as Harrison notes, "is as old as Homer" (*Mythology and Monuments* lxxxv), but which "as would be expected in a Homeric myth, [has] nothing whatever to do with Athens" (lxxxvi). Athenians took Procne and Philomela as ancestors, yet they were purely poetic constructions, sprung from earlier nature myths that were "complicated by contamination and accretion" (lxxxiv), but they in later versions were sisters, one of whom was raped by her brother-in-law, Tereus, and whose tongue was cut out so she could not tell her story. She is able to sing, however, of her violation, when she is transformed in later versions into a nightingale and in earlier versions a swallow. In her commentary in the guidebook *Mythology and Monuments* Harrison writes:

> We are accustomed, burdened as we are with Ovidian association, to think of Philomela as the nightingale. Such was not the version of Apollodorus, nor, so far as I know, of any earlier Greek writer. According to Apollodorus, Procne became the nightingale and Philomela the swallow. It was Philomela who had her tongue cut out, a tale that would never have been told of the nightingale, but which fitted well with the short restless chirp of the swallow. To speak a barbarian tongue was "to mutter like a swallow." [. . .] (lxxxix)

This is why Clytemnestra refers to Cassandra's strange speech in her "naked cry" as a barbarian speaking in a "swallow's twitter." The nightingale association comes through the Chorus's mention of Procne's son, Itys or Itylus, from an earlier version. Tereus, the rapist, who as punishment is also turned into a bird, the hoopoe, is a later addition, although he, unlike Procne and Philomela, did have an historical basis, although a "somewhat ironical ritual" (lxxxiv). He was a leader driven to suicide due to the contempt of his citizens, who "made him a grave, and offered him yearly sacrifice using pebbles instead of barley" (lxxxiv). In any case, Tereus has been wrongly attributed to Aeschylus and is not earlier than Sophocles, although he does bear "one genuine Aeshylean mention of the Tereus story, and here the nightingale is 'hawk-pursued'" (xc). Sophocles, however, played with the truth in making Tereus, a colorful bird, royal and martial in appearance who comes in the winter to pursue the swallow, when in fact, according to Harrison, "he shows his total ignorance of the hoopoe's character" because he is not a colorful bird, nor royal in bearing and "instead of pursuing the swallow, "a passing swallow frightens him" (xc).

For Woolf, nightingales and swallows have profound resonance as prophets, as illustrations of the paradoxes and boundaries of speech, and of the ceaseless struggle for the truth to be heard, all associations she has drawn from the many versions of the tales she has encountered in Harrison's work and in her study of Greek and Greek plays. We see this Greek voice in the disembodied radio voice prophesying war in *Jacob's Room*, in the "Greek voices" that haunt the shell-shocked Septimus Smith in *Mrs. Dalloway*, and in the "phrasemakers," the six choral voices in *The Waves*. Harrison's revisions and research into the translations of Greek myth change the emphasis of the story, as in the case of the hoopoe, from one of martial brilliance to a foregrounding of the song of the more common swallow, as Woolf gives voice to the narratives of the voiceless, from Mrs. Brown in the corner opposite to the seemingly indistinct Marys in *A Room of One's Own*.

Jacob's Lost Thiasos

Jacob's Room, the first in Woolf's trilogy, is a critique and condemnation of the individual and family structure as instruments of a militarized, war hero-worshipping state, and shares many parallels with Harrison's "Year-Spirit" or *eniautos daimon* and Woolf's understanding of Aeschylus' project in *The Agamemnon* as read via Harrison. Jacob is the anti-hero, who is undermined by an epic wave of violence. The imminent destruction is of Olympic proportions, sometimes insidiously, at other times blatantly, grown upon patriarchal values, and it is about to swallow him up and doom humanity—but from outside the edges of the book. Like Orestes in *The Agamemnon*, Jacob is disconnected, undrawn as a character, absent, out of sync, and a pawn in the larger machine of war, violence, and death. Jacob's aimless, ordinary life plays out center stage on the page in the theater of life while the violence and bloodshed, the theater of war, happens off-text. In *The Agamemnon*, we know very little of Orestes, who has been sent away for protection by his mother, Clytemnestra, who kills his murderer father, Agamemnon, and his kidnapped mistress in the central action of the play. In *Jacob's Room*, Woolf refuses to write directly about the war, but focuses instead on the gift of Jacob's ordinary life. His violent and abrupt death is a fact we understand only through the final scene in the book when his mother is left with the task of cleaning out her son's lifeless, but ghost-filled room. "Listless is the air in an empty room, just swelling the curtain; the flowers in the jar shift. One fibre in the wicker arm-chair creaks, though no one sits there" (JR 39), she writes in a passage foreshadowing Jacob's death in her first description of his room when he initially goes up to Cambridge. His friend, Bonamy, is dumb-struck by the fact that Jacob has left everything as it was and seems dis-gusted that he could not see the consequences that were in store for him by going off to war. He asks of the air and of the things in the room, "What did he expect? Did he think he would come back?" (176). His mother, who should be able to feel deeply the loss of her son, but who, as a Themis-figure cut off from the Young God and trapped as well in a patriarchal construct, is only able to burst into the room, ready to also do her duty, her domestic duty—to clean. She has unwittingly already per-formed her duty to the state—sacrificed a son she hardly knew, and now is left holding his empty pair of shoes, as she asks Bonamy "What am I to do with these?" (176). The disconnect between mother and son has been carefully orchestrated by the state from Jacob's childhood onwards as he is encouraged to shed his thiasos, his support, and dismiss any emotional tie he may experience or long for.

Throughout the novel, Jacob seems to operate within Harrison's holophrasis or a desire for intimacy that takes place as Woolf writes of Greek "on the far side of language" (ONKG 31), as he yearns to con-nect to Themis, to his mother, to women in general, but without success, as he is in lock-step with the clock of the state, but out of step with his mythic time as articulated by Harrison in her work. This is a motif Woolf consistently disrupts with the blending, foreshadowing, and reversals of narrative time throughout the book. His name, Jacob Flanders, associ-ates him from the beginning with both his introspection and position as a Young God but also with his imminent death on the battlefield. Jacob is the third biblical patriarch, who holds onto his brother Esau's heel on the way out of his mother's womb, and whose name is associated with "struggle with God." In the Bible, of the two boys, Jacob is the more reserved and studious one, and his Ladder in the Book of Genesis rep-resents the struggle between Heaven and Earth as angels tread up and down this bridge between two worlds between two time-projects. Flan-ders, echoing Flanders Fields, the battle fields in Belgium for hundreds of thousands of dead soldiers, joins the other place names throughout the novel with military resonations: Scarborough, bombed by the Ger-man navy in a series of raids and the site of the first civilian casualties of the war; Gibraltar, site of a British Naval base; the 20th Hussars, a British cavalry regiment; Marathon, the first major battle between the Greeks and Persians, and Salamis, in 480 BCE, the site of a navy battle between same.

In the opening scene, Jacob is lost on the beach, separated from his mother, as both she and his brother, Archer, search for him. In addition to disconnection and dislocation, he is immediately tied to death even as a young boy. He tries to compose himself in the face of his circumstances when he discovers a skull on the beach, "perhaps a cow's skull, a skull, perhaps with the teeth in it" which sets him to "sobbing, but absentmindedly" while he runs "farther and farther away" holding the skull in his arms" (JR 20). The skull later shape-shifts into a sheep's skull, the jaw of which Jacob retains, but a symbol of death his widowed mother, Betty Flanders, insists he drop. Jacob refuses. At night, the sheep's jaw lies at his feet while Jacob is "fast asleep, profoundly unconscious." Outside, his "child's bucket was half-full of rainwater; and the opal-shelled crab slowly circled round the bottom, trying with its weakly legs to climb the steep side; trying again and falling back, and trying again and again" (14), suggesting Jacob's own entrapment and the absurdity of his life as he is held prisoner and used for corrupt purposes by a value system from which he is estranged.

As a boy, Jacob enjoys nature studies. He likes animals and birds, the natural sciences, but he is not an exceptional academic student, often falls asleep over unfinished books, and has never read a Shakespearean play all the way through (JR 47). Indeed, it is Shakespeare and not the Greeks who is knocked overboard during the erotically charged nude bathing scene between him and his schoolmate, Timmy Durant, as they boat together off the Cornish coast, while Jacob fantasizes about the classical landscape of Italy and Greece. Jacob is unworldly and not intellectually curious, a fact that is drawn into sharp relief when Woolf juxtaposes him beside her portrait of a woman student, "the feminist," Julia Hedge, self-consciously trying to study at the British Museum. His unfinished essay, languishing back in his room, asks "Does History consist of the Biographies of Great Men?" a question Virginia Woolf returns to more seriously in her tribute to Harrison's scholarly achievements in *A Room of One's Own* and an issue that preoccupied Woolf throughout her life as the daughter of Leslie Stephen, the editor of Britain's *Dictionary of National Biography,* documenting the lives of Britain's "great men." "Jacob's mind continues alone, onwards, into the darkness," as he, too, is a cog in the wheel of a larger machine, until he becomes distracted by the common, everyday arguments of the street instead. He ultimately ends up in a friend's rooms where "they were saying something that was far, far too intimate to be said outright" (JR 110), when he walks in.

There is a sense of entitlement to Jacob's life that has political reso-nance for Woolf, but also an ordinariness and banality that her entire novel laments losing, because for all his flaws, distinguished but nonde-script, he was alive, vital, a Jacob "who sat astride a chair and ate dates from a long box, [who] burst out laughing" (JR 44). He is stubborn and uncommunicative with his mother, but, Captain Barfoot, one of Betty Flanders regular suitors, "who was lame and wanted two fingers on the left hand, having served his country" (25), counts Jacob as his favorite, though he is not sure why, and Bonamy, his friend, thinks Jacob stupid and ridiculous, and yet "'there is something—something'—he sighed, for he was fonder of Jacob than of any one in the world" (140).

The difficulty of reaching Jacob is what is simultaneously appealing and lamentable about his character, and speaks to a fundamental human desire, evoked, fostered, and encouraged in Harrison's matrifocal soci-ety, to connect. Woolf discusses the great gulf that exists between one human being and another, moored in a society that privileged competi-tion to absurd extremes. She characterizes this gap as that "something which can never be conveyed to a second person save by Jacob himself," a quality that "is always impelling one to hum vibrating, like the hawk moth, at the mouth of the cavern of mystery, endowing Jacob Flanders with all sorts of qualities he had not at all [. . .]. Yet over him we hang vibrating" (JR 73). He was a boy and then a young man, representa-tive of an entire generation, communities of young men, about whom Woolf writes with the most bitter irony and overt condemnation of war: They were "simple young men, these, who would—but there is no need to think of them grown old." She then moves on to mundane details of how others in his circle of Cambridge friends were "eating sweets; here they boxed" [. . .] as they gathered together in common rooms with "legs, perhaps, over the arms of chairs; smoking; sprawling over tables, writing while their heads went round in a circle as the pen moved" (43).

In *Jacob's Room,* unlike in her previous novels, the circles of men and of women do not cross or overlap, a motif of sterility Woolf carries through in different ways in *Mrs. Dalloway* and *The Waves.* Jacob is not only disconnected from his mother, he is unable to be integrated into any women's circle. He is awkward in social settings, uncomfortably reticent, "his hymn-book open at the wrong place" (32), Clara Durant, whom he "honours the most," has the ankles of a stag and her "letters were those of a child" (94). He is unashamed of his misogyny, compares women to dogs, and is vehemently against having women at college, because they are distracting: "why allow women to take part in it? [. . .] No one would think of bringing a dog into church [. . .] a dog destroys the service completely. So do these women" and besides "they're as ugly as sin" (JR 33). Florinda, whom he considers as somewhat promiscuous, "entirely at the beck and call of life" (79), has the instincts of an animal, but is "brainless." Nevertheless, "Jacob was restless when she left him" (79), and meets with her again, because "after all it was none of her fault. But the thought saddened him" and he protests a headache when they are meant to have sex, for "in spite of defending indecency, Jacob doubted whether he liked it in the raw" (82). According to Jacob, the feeling of disconnection is profound and "the problem is insoluble" (82), leading him to conclude that "It's not catastrophes, murders, deaths, diseases, that age and kill us; it's the way people look and laugh, and run up the steps of omnibuses" (82)—in other words, the way we interact on a daily basis, the lack of communication between the sexes, between generations, between one human being and another.

Reading transpersonally, in Harrisonian terms, Jacob is the Young God unattended by his thiasos, frustrated, angry, and unmoved by the women in his circles, which leads methodically, rationalistically, inevitably to his Olympian proscribed death. The procession of women who hover near him, but with whom he never connects continues mid-novel when he leaves Fanny Elmer for his tour of Greece, with his guidebook (perhaps the Blue Jane?) in his pocket. In Greece, he is pestered by the circles of tourist women he finds there: "Damn these women—damn these women!" (JR 151). He bemoans their existence and their behavior, "without any trace of bitterness, but rather with sadness and disappointment that what might have been should never be" as he presses his guidebook to his hip, moves away from them, and, exploring the Erechtheon, "looked rather furtively at the goddess on the left-hand side holding the roof on her head" (151). Woolf does not leave Jacob's own behavior, however, without comment, as she interjects the parenthetical "(This violent disillusionment is generally to be expected in young men in the prime of life, sound of wind and limb, who will soon become fathers of families and directors of banks)" (151), thus perpetuating the cycle of family dominance, power, and capital in terms of egotism and the elevation of the male principle. The only woman he becomes frustratingly and fleetingly attracted to is Sandra Wentworth Williams, who is married and ultimately unavailable.

Alongside or perhaps above this anxiety, the most intimate moments of bonding occur whenever members of the same sex gather together, and this moment of self-actualization and fulfillment often crystallizes for Woolf into one of humanity's greatest losses, our inability to communicate on an intimate level. When the group of male students breaks up, Jacob is left in his Trinity rooms with Simeon, who murmurs something partially inaudible about Julian the Apostate. Julian the Apostate was called "The Philosopher," and was, not coincidentally, the last pagan Roman emperor to reject Christianity. It is midnight and Woolf gives a ghostly goddess figure a walk-on, but dozing part. Around that hour "there sometimes rises, like a veiled figure suddenly woken, a heavy wind; and this now flapping through Trinity lifted unseen leaves and blurred everything" as Simeon murmurs the words "Julian the Apostate"; "[s]o, if the veiled lady stepped through the Courts of Trinity, she now drowsed once more, all her draperies about her, her head against a pillar" (JR 46), when Simeon says of this figure, "Somehow it seems to matter":

> The voice was even lower that answered him. The sharp tap of a pipe on the mantelpiece cancelled the words. And perhaps Jacob only said "hum," or said nothing at all. True, the words were inaudible. It was the intimacy, a sort of spiritual suppleness when mind prints upon mind indelibly. [. . . Jacob] swayed a little. He appeared extraordinarily happy, as if his pleasure would brim and spill down the sides if Simeon spoke.
>
> Simeon said nothing. Jacob remained standing. But intimacy—the room was full of it, still, deep, like a pool. Without need of movement or speech it rose softly and washed over everything, mollifying, kindling, and coating the mind with the luster of pearl, so that if you talk of a light, of Cambridge burning, it's not languages only. It's Julian the Apostate. (46)

But Jacob does move. He murmurs good-bye and leaves the room as his footsteps tap out a chant-like rhythm across the quadrangle as he returns to his rooms. They "echoed with magisterial authority: "The young man—the young man—the young man—" (46).

Jacob is also "the silent young man" (JR 59), but in contrast to his brother growing up, he was "the handful," as well, introspective, reserved, like his biblical namesake, but stubborn and often remote from his surroundings. At one point, he gets excited about a censorship issue raised by the garrulous Bonamy concerning an edition by Wycherly that excised the "indecent phrases" (70), but as he writes letters to the various magazines "he knew that no one would ever print them; and sure enough back they came from the *Fortnightly*, the *Contemporary*, the *Nineteenth Century*" (70). He tosses them into a black wooden box, like a Harrisonian Pandora's box, because that is the place "where he kept his mother's letters," and "The lid shut upon the truth" (70). The truth, the regenerative powers of Themis, is embodied in his mother's letters, but they are trapped inside the box. Harrison read the Pandora myth as containing not the ills and destruction of all the world, but the secrets of recreation. Jacob keeps the box on his desk, but the lid is shut tight. Without Themis, Dionysus has no means of access to the wine and fruits of life, to a connection to women and to men. When Jacob, as a boy, is asked to choose a going-away gift from his Latin tutor, Mr. Floyd, he chooses a volume of Byron's complete works, a gift which associates him appropriately with both the historical Byron and the fictional Childe Harold outlaw. Byron's anti-hero is an outcast, a brooding refugee, unable to connect to his generation as he surveys the devastation of the Napoleonic wars. He is forever questing, but never arriving, a figure which privileges the process, the struggle, rather than the destination, the attainment of the vision. Like Byron himself, perhaps, but unlike the Byronic hero of his work, Jacob's process, his eternal quest as a Year-Spirit, is sickeningly truncated by war.

His mother, Betty Flanders, as a Themis figure also confined in a hero-worshipping world, doubts herself, her instincts, her "mother wit," despite the fact that she consistently reveals these qualities to the reader. As she pulls the two boys along she takes note of her natural surroundings:

> [. . .]looking with uneasy emotion at the earth displayed so luridly, with sudden sparks of light from greenhouses in gardens, with a sort of yellow and black mutability, against this blazing sunset, this astonishing agitation and vitality of colour, which stirred Betty Flanders and made her think of responsibility and danger. (JR 11)

She is deeply connected to her world, but also fearful and suspicious of it and not completely in control of it. She asks her son, Archer, what she had asked him to remember, but the boy cannot recall what it was. "'Well, I don't either,' said Betty, humorously and simply," leading Woolf to comment:

> Who shall deny that this blankness of mind, when combined with profusion, mother wit, old wives' tales, haphazard ways, moments of aston-

ishing daring, humour, and sentimentality—who shall deny that in these respects every woman is nicer than any man?

Well, Betty Flanders, to begin with. (11)

Betty Flanders possesses all these qualities, but not majestically or authoritatively, unless she is presiding over the sacred space of her home or connecting with another woman. She questions herself, her abilities, and her perceptions. She is also, notably, not completely fond of Jacob, who is out of step with his mother at nearly every turn. She is "unreasonably irritated by [his] clumsiness in the house" (71), a factor Woolf attributes to one's inability to perceive the intractable impermanence of the human condition.

> It seems then that men and women are equally at fault. It seems that a profound, impartial, and absolutely just opinion of our fellow-creatures is utterly unknown. Either we are men, or we are women. Either we are cold, or we are sentimental. Either we are young, or growing old. In any case, life is but a procession of shadows, and God knows why it is that we embrace them so eagerly, and see them depart with such anguish, being shadows. And why, if this and much more than this is true, why are we yet surprised in the window corner by a sudden vision that the young man in the chair is of all things in the world the most real, the most solid, the best known to us—why indeed? For the moment after we know nothing about him.
>
> Such is the manner of our seeing. Such the conditions of our love.
> (72)

In addition to this shadowy procession of people that the old woman Julia Eliot, in the final pages of the book, sees "passing tragically to destruction" (168) in her mind's eye after a riderless horse passes her by, the novel is filled with the ghostly figures of women as priestesses struggling to keep the Young God alive in a world that has no place for them or him. She lulls her children to sleep with fairy stories and images of mother birds feeding her children in their nest before checking on her younger son being cared for by an attendant *themistes*,[6] Rebecca. Woolf writes, "The two

---

6. Harrison writes that Themis "was worshipped in the plural [. . .] out of many dooms, many public opinions, many judgments, arose the figure of the one goddess. Out of many *themistes* arose Themis. These *themistes*, these fixed conventions stood to the Greek for all he held civilized" (T 483).

women murmured over the spirit-lamp, plotting the eternal conspiracy of hush and clean bottles while the wind raged and gave a sudden wrench at the cheap fastenings," an image of priestess figures tending to the ritual preservation of life she repeats, chant-like, five lines down: "Rebecca called her ma'm, though they were conspirators plotting the eternal conspiracy of hush and clean bottles" (13).

Mrs. Jarvis is another ghostly woman, at forty-five years of age, a walker between the worlds, as she restlessly paces the moors at night:

> Mrs. Jarvis was just the sort of woman to lose her faith upon the moors—to confound her God with the universal that is—but she did not lose her faith, did not leave her husband, never read her poem through, and went on walking the moors, looking at the moon behind the elm trees and feeling as she sat on the grass high above Scarborough. . . . [. . .] "If only some one could give me . . . if I could give some one . . . " But she does not know what she wants to give, nor who could give it her. (JR 27)

Later on in the novel, Mrs. Jarvis reappears to comment on Jacob's letters and on death as she encourages Betty Flanders to come walk with her on the moor. The two women bond over a discussion of death as "they had climbed the dark hill and reached the Roman camp": "The rampart rose at their feet—the smooth circle surrounding the camp or grave. How many needles Betty Flanders had lost there! And her garnet brooch" (132). It is an ordinary garnet brooch that Jacob gave her, Betty Flanders's sacrifice to the Earth—ordinary things and the life of her son. Mrs. Jarvis tells her that she does not pity the dead, for "they are at rest" and "we spend our days doing foolish unnecessary things without knowing why" (131). But Mrs. Flanders murmurs and is uncertain as she turns over the turf with her toe:

> Did the bones stir, or the rusty swords? Was Mrs. Flander's twopenny-halfpenny brooch for ever part of the rich accumulation? And if all the ghosts flocked thick and rubbed shoulders with Mrs. Flanders in the circle, would she not have seemed perfectly in her place [. . .]. (132)

Their voices float above them, as "The moonlight destroyed nothing. The moor accepted everything" (134). But Betty Flanders feels suddenly that it is "foolish to vex the moor with questions—what? And why?" (134), and so, out of step with her own world and lost to her son, she is forced to change the subject.

Mrs. Dalloway and "The Libation Bearers Notebook"

The Harrisonian Young God tragically imprisoned inside an Olympian *weltanschauung* is fully realized in Woolf's second post-war novel, *Mrs. Dalloway*. But here the consequences of his position are manifested not in the aimless life in-text and subsequent death off-text on the battle-field of the anti-hero as in *Jacob's Room,* but in his psychological ruin and the abrupt shock, the anathema of the Young God's suicide. And how extraordinary, I think, "What a lark! What a plunge!" that Woolf attached her 1907 notebook with her crib translation of Aeschylus' *The Libation Bearers* to early draft pages (from 9 November 1922 to 2 August 1923) of *Mrs. Dalloway,* as it seems to me Aeschylus' problem in *The Libation Bearers* is the same problem Woolf poses in *Mrs. Dalloway.* What do we as a society do now with all of these dead bodies? It is as if the texts of both "The Libation Bearers Notebook" and *Mrs. Dalloway* perform a kind of ritual, regardless of intention, with the manuscript asking the translation, how do I perform this task? How do I write this novel? And how does the content of that novel unfold, tap out the rhythm, bang the drum, pour out the libations over the sacrifice? And who, after all, is being sacrificed and why?

In *The Libation Bearers,* Electra has been asked by Clytemnestra to perform a ritual over the grave of her father, Agamemnon. Clytemnes-tra has, according to the ancient law of her soul, killed Agamemnon in a bid to set right her family and her home. She has been plagued by a nightmare, in which her son, Orestes, while suckling at her breast, is turned into a serpent that viciously bites her. She asks Electra to perform the ritual to appease the gods, but when Electra goes to the graveside of her father, she has no idea how to begin. In order to perform the ritual, she must ask The Libation Bearers, who are essentially slave women of a lower class brought to Argos as spoils of The Trojan War. Just as he will name his third play, *The Furies,* after a group of monster goddesses responsible for maintaining balance in the world, he names the second drama after a group of slave women (this is Greek democracy in action) responsible for the legacy and reputation of the dead. In each case, these groups of women function as the Greek chorus, "the undifferentiated voices who sing like birds in the pauses in the wind" (ONKG 29), whose prophecies, although sometimes accurate and sometimes flawed, guide the actions of the drama and the fabric of the characters' lives. For them, "life beats on" but "we nurse our lives with tears" (Aeschylus *Libation Bearers* Act 1, ll 31–32), after "they led us here as slaves" (Act 1, l 76). The high-

born Electra must ask the servants for assistance in executing the ritual
(just as Clarissa Dalloway asks her servants to help her perform the ritual
of her party), when she says, "I'll need your help with this, / What to say
when I pour the cup of sorrow?" (Act 1, ll 85–86). So too Woolf seems
to be asking Aeschylus, but an Aeschylus she has read and understood
transpersonally through Jane Harrison: How do I write this book?

Woolf's translation of *The Libation Bearers* text uses the A. W. Verrall
edition as her guide, the same text used by Jane Harrison as an undergraduate at Newnham College, the same edition from which she taught
as an instructor there, and the same edition Woolf used as her guide for
"The Agamemnon Notebook" (see above and Chapter 1), which she
began in 1922. Comparing her version to more contemporary translations today, specifically those by R. D. Lattimore and Robert Fagles,[7] it
becomes clear that while Woolf is following along, using Verrall as her
guide, her translations are not taken down as dictation from Janet Case,
but rather a product that relies on a great deal of refreshing accident and
lively improvisation as she writes in her notebook about Greek that "in
the obscurity of the language lies its dramatic merit" (LBN).

When Orestes is about to unwind the robes shrouding the bodies of
his mother and Aegisthus on the funeral bier, just as Clytemnestra had
exposed Agamemnon and Cassandra to the chorus at the altar in *The
Agamemnon,* he shouts "Behold the double tyranny of our land! They
killed my father, stormed my fathers' house," (Aeschylus, Act 1, ll 964–
65), it is a passage which a young Virginia Stephen translates as "Look
now upon the twofold tyranny of the land murderer of my father, waster
of my house" (LBN). Her translations reveal that she is looking more at
the context of the scenes, at the literariness rather than at a literal translation. Earlier, when Orestes is about to kill his mother, Woolf writes:

> Here, Clytemnestra comes out, asks for a manslaying axe; "this evil has
> now reached such a point" one can only kill or be killed. Does she mean
> the whole tragedy in the house, in which case she is a passive instrument
> or her own private act, in which she is active and responsible?
>
> "There is a cryptic chorus while the murder axe (is?) being done off
> or on? The stage. When Orestes comes on bearing an olive bough and
> speaks over the bodies of Ae. & Cly. (LBN)

---

7. I wish to thank classicist Dr. Elias Theodoracopoulos for his help in translating
both of Woolf's Greek Notebooks at the Berg Collection of the New York Public Library.

In her youthful notebook, Woolf is grappling with the same complex questions she faces in the *Mrs. Dalloway* manuscript she has attached to it, from the vantage point of a woman writing in her early forties after the devastation wrought by world war. Who is responsible for the violence? And where do we draw the lines and set the levels of our moral compass in terms of responsibility? How do we disentangle ourselves from this accursed net of violence and bloodshed?

Aeschylus and Virginia Woolf ask similar questions, and yearn for a social system that will help us cope with our decisions and our answers. But Woolf's Aeschylus is introduced to her by Case and Harrison, and is a text she revises as a mature woman artist and intellectual through Harrison's feminism and pacifism. In *Mrs. Dalloway*, we open in a post-war world, a world that "has raised its whip" and asks a second time, in a sadistic portent of yet another conflagration, "where will it descend?" (14). Clarissa Dalloway, as a Themis figure, embodies both mother and sister, Clytemnestra and Electra. Her character runs parallel alongside, but never locks eyes with, the returned war hero, the shell-shocked and psychologically maimed *eniautos-daimon*, Septimus Smith, as they each try to navigate the remnants of their lives in a single day after somehow having survived that "little shindy of schoolboys with gunpowder" (94). In contrast, in *The Libation Bearers*, Electra places her footsteps inside the footprints of her returned brother, Orestes, in one of the most memorable scenes of recognition in all of literature. When she comes across a lock of Orestes' hair that he has given as an offering to his dead father, Electra now must teach the Chorus, as she immediately identifies the lock as her brother's:

ELECTRA: Look at the texture, just like—
LEADER: Whose? I want to know.
ELECTRA: Like mine, identical, / can't you see?
LEADER: Orestes . . . he brought a gift / in secret?
ELECTRA: It's *his*—I can see his curls.
[. . .]
Look, tracks. / A new sign to tell us more. / Footmarks . . . pairs of
    them, like mine. / Two outlines, two prints, his own, and there, a
    fellow traveller's.
Putting her foot into Orestes' *print.*
    The heel, the curve of the arch /
Like twins.

While Orestes *emerges from behind the grave, she follows cautiously in
    his steps until they come together.*
    Step by step, my step in his . . .
                    We meet—
(Aeschylus ll 174–210)

Electra and Orestes unite in their grief, but also run parallel to each
other in the sense that Electra's emotions over the death of her father,
her outrage at her mother are unwieldy and ineffectually extreme, while
Orestes is left with weighing his circumstances more carefully. He is not
so quick to commit matricide, but is compelled to by Apollo and by the
Chorus, who misinform him about the true nature of the consequences of
his actions. In "On Not Knowing Greek," Woolf looks at the nature of
the women characters in Greek plays in particular, gives more dimension
to the impossibility of their position as well. She writes of Electra that
although "her words in crisis are, as a matter of fact, bare; mere cries of
despair, joy, hate" [. . .] it is not so easy to decide what it is that gives
these cries of Electra in her anguish their power to cut and wound and
excite" (ONKG 26). It is, Woolf argues, at least in part, that we know her
as she knows herself, "blunted and debased by the horror of her position,
an unwed girl made to witness her mother's vileness and denounce it in
loud, almost vulgar, clamour to the world at large" (26). The Greeks, for
Woolf, gave us the emotions, the complete, "original human being" (27),
and to the Greek audience sitting on the hillside in the sunlight, the artist had to make sure that "every sentence had to explode on striking the
ear, however slowly and beautifully the words might then descend, and
however enigmatic might their final purport be" (31), a fact not lost on
Woolf, especially as she embodies the Greek choral voices she creates in
the third part of her trilogy, *The Waves,* as we will see later in this section.

Here, in *Mrs. Dalloway,* Septimus, like Orestes, is plagued by doubt
and guilt and shame at being asked, forced to kill. Septimus is haunted
by Greek voices, Greek words mediated through the wind and birdsong,
mysteriously, ghostlike, because, as Virginia Woolf frequently reminds the
readers of her essays, we, none of us, know what Greek really sounds like.
Septimus's role and function as the Young God comes to him in a Greek
choral chant, from the birds, as he espies his dead friend, Evans, a hidden
shape behind the veil of his perception:

Change the world. No one kills from hatred. Make it known (he wrote it
down). He waited. He listened. A sparrow perched on the railing oppo-

site chirped Septimus, Septimus, four or five times over and went on, drawing its notes out, to sing freshly and piercingly in Greek words how there is no crime and, joined by another sparrow, they sang in voices prolonged and piercing in Greek words, from trees in the meadow of life beyond the river where the dead walk, how there is no death. (MD 24)

The ghost of Evans continues to haunt him, his conscience, "Evans was speaking. The dead were with him," just as the servant calls out in the corridors of the House of Argos, "the dead are killing the living," as Orestes reluctantly takes his cog-like position in the cycle of violence and war and kills his mother, Clytemnestra, and her lover. Septimus, as a Young God positioned upon the irrational circle of the state, takes on the mantel of his role uneasily, with great torment and resentment, with none of the emotions he would have experienced had he been connected and integrated into a Dionysian matrifocal Unbounded Whole as articulated by Harrison. Here, the "unseen bade him":

Look [. . .] Septimus, lately taken from life to death, the Lord who had come to renew society, who lay like a coverlet, a snow blanket smitten only by the sun, for ever unwasted, suffering for ever, the scapegoat, the eternal sufferer, but he did not want it, he moaned, putting from him with a wave of his hand that eternal suffering, that eternal loneliness. (25)

Septimus struggles to maintain the boundaries of his identity, to hold onto himself by repeating, or rather muttering, the chant "Communication is health; communication is happiness, communication—" (91), but this is overridden by the more regular and daunting rhythm Woolf repeatedly intones throughout the novel, that "once you stumble [. . .] human nature is on you" (90) and by the leaden circles of time dictated by the state in the form of the patriarchal Big Ben, pushing him forward towards death.

Each of the characters struggles to navigate this shift in relations and conflict between the individual and the group or family and the harsh realities and demands of the state. "The communal spirit of London" is regarded as "one of the triumphs of civilization" by Peter Walsh, one of Clarissa's thwarted suitors from her youth, who returns for Clarissa's gathering of souls at her party. But this is countered by Sally Seton's question and assessment of their position amidst the realities of the world they actually do live in: "what can one know even of the people one lives with every day? [. . .] Are we not all prisoners? [. . .] Despairing of human relationships (people were so difficult), she often went into her garden and got from her flowers a peace which men and women never gave her" (MD 188). Sally Seton also draws her energy, her life's blood, from nature, from the earth, and it is she who speaks the Harrisonian credo at the end of the novel, privileging emotion over reason, asking before she says good-night, "What does the brain matter [. . .] compared with the heart?" (188).

As in *Jacob's Room,* prophetesses and priestesses haunt the pages of the entire day. When Peter Walsh arrives at a crossroads walking through London, opening and closing his pocketknife, as he bemoans Clarissa's coldness towards him, he is interrupted by a disembodied voice with ritualistic and Greek choral functionality. It was

> [. . .] a quivering sound, a voice bubbling up without direction, vigour, beginning or end, running weakly and shrilly and with an absence of all human meaning into
>
>>ee um fah um so
>>foo swee too eem oo—
>
> the voice of no age or sex, the voice of an ancient spring spouting from the earth; which issued [. . .] from a tall quivering shape, like a funnel, like a rusty pump, like a wind-beaten tree for ever barren of leaves which lets the wind run up and down its branches singing
>
>>ee um fah um so
>>foo swee too eem oo
>
> and rocks and creaks and moans in the eternal breeze. (MD 79)

This disembodied voice shape shifts into an ancient wailing woman and finally into her manifestation in her own hero-worshipping times as a "poor old woman!" (80), a wretch. Harrison's Themis and the Year-Spirit, the eternal Greek cultic formulary, "the tragic rhythm of regeneration" found in *Prolegomena, Themis,* and later *Ancient Art and Ritual* help Woolf craft her modernism, her response to patriarchy and ultimately war, by privileging and foregrounding the voice of a goddess figure as she transitions through the centuries from maiden to crone. Out of the ashes of war, her voice emerges:

> Through all ages—when the pavement was grass, when it was swamp, through the age of tusk and mammoth, through the age of silent sunrise, the battered woman—for she wore a skirt—with her right hand

exposed, her left clutching at her side, stood singing of love—love which has lasted a million years, she sang, love which prevails, and millions of years ago, her lover, who had been dead these centuries, had walked, she crooned, with her in May; but in the course of ages, long as summer days, and flaming, she remembered, with nothing but red asters, he had gone; death's enormous sickle had swept those tremendous hills, and when at last she laid her hoary and immensely aged head on the earth, now become a mere cinder of ice, she implored the Gods to lay by her side a bunch of purple heather, there on her high burial place which the last rays of the last sun caressed; for then the pageant of the universe would be over. (MD 79–80)

The ancient song emerges from the earth, the young maiden, now "old wretch," the battered beggar is the archetypal Mother goddess, timeless, a three-fold, Demeter-Persephone, another of Woolf's working-class priestesses, another singer in an Aeschylean Greek chorus found on the modern streets of London begging for coins, members of the lower classes empowered with the voice of prophesy.

In contrast to these female voices, in her blistering condemnation of the medical profession, she places the doctor, Sir William Bradshaw, in the realm of egotism, individualistic rationalism, and maleness. Bradshaw, along with Dr. Holmes, denies Septimus's emotions, reducing his "madness" to "merely a question of rest," a matter of "not having a sense of proportion" and "a question of law" (MD 94). The war provides Bradshaw with a "stream of patients [. . .] so incessant" (93) that she names him a "ghostly helper, the priest of science" (92).

Clarissa Dalloway's position as a Themis figure is consistently drawn from the beginning of the day to its end. The party upon which the entire structure of the novel turns is indeed her offering and bid for the preservation of life:

"That's what I do it for," she said, speaking aloud, to life.
[. . .] all she could say was (and nobody could be expected to understand): They're an offering; [. . .] she felt if only they could be brought together; so she did it. And it was an offering; to combine, to create; but to whom?
An offering for the sake of offering [. . .] that one day should follow another; Wednesday, Thursday, Friday, Saturday; that one should wake up in the morning; see the sky; walk in the park [. . .] After that, how unbelievable death was!—that it must end [. . .]. (MD 118–19)

Richard Dalloway, her husband, assesses Clarissa as possessing "something maternal" about her, as "He admired her courage; her social instinct," her "power of carrying things through" (60), but he has a feeling "that they were all gathered together in a conspiracy against him" (61). But Woolf writes of Clarissa, "She must assemble" (182).

Clarissa is a Themis figure who, having a parasol, "handled it like a sacred weapon which a Goddess, having acquitted herself honourably in the field of battle"(29), files it into an umbrella stand, but she is operating without her full powers, trapped and circumscribed by the demands of a patriarchal, militaristic state. After repaying in her daily rituals with servants, family members, pets, and husband, what she calls "this secret deposit of exquisite moments" (29), her libations to her day, Clarissa ascends the stairs to her room feeling "alone, a single figure against the appalling night" and as she pauses on the landing, she experiences herself as "suddenly shriveled, aged, breastless," unable to "dispel a virginity preserved through childbirth which clung to her like a sheet" (30). She feels disconnected from her husband as if she has failed him, a pervasive warmth "which broke up surfaces and rippled the cold contact of man and woman, or of women together" (31), and feels the greatest moments of bonding and community with women. She confirms that "she could not resist sometimes yielding to the charm of a woman, not a girl, of a woman confessing, as to her they often did, some scrape, some folly" (31). She feels "undoubtedly [. . .] what men felt" towards women, which she describes as follows:

> Only for a moment; but it was enough. It was a sudden revelation, a tinge like a blush which one tried to check and then, as it spread, one yielded to its expansion, and rushed to the farthest verge and there quivered and felt the world come closer, swollen with some astonishing significance, some pressure of rapture, which split its thin skin and gushed and poured with an extraordinary alleviation over the cracks and sores! (31)

Her relationship with her girlhood friend Sally Seton is the most profound of her life, and the kiss between them recorded as "the religious feeling!" (35). Clarissa's experience with women consists of moments of happiness in a world where "the secret signal which one generation passes, under disguise, to the next is loathing, hatred, despair," a signal passed along by all of the great authors, "Aeschylus (translated) the same" (86). In a continuation of, but variation on, the corruption of the Themis/ *Eniautos-Daimon* formulary from *Jacob's Room*, Clarissa and Septimus never meet, never connect, although their parallel experience conjoins in a single sentence when at "twelve o'clock [. . .] Clarissa Dalloway laid her green dress on her bed, the Warren Smiths walked down Harley Street" as "Twelve was the hour of their appointment" (MD 92). Without her abilities in full sail as they are in Katharine Hilbery in *Night and Day,* for example, she does not experience his existence until his suicide, after he has jumped out of the window and impaled himself on the spikes of "Mrs. Filmer's area railings" (MD 146). The doctor, notably, brings the perversion of his death, the news of Septimus's suicide, into Clarissa's party, her bid for the preservation of life. It is not until this point, that Clarissa, aware of the Young God, processes his suicide as if it were her own:

> Always her body went through it first, when she was told, suddenly, of an accident; her dress flamed, her body burnt. He had thrown himself from a window. Up had flashed the ground; through him, blundering, bruising, went the rusty spikes. There he lay with a thud, thud, thud in his brain, and then a suffocation of blackness. So she saw it. (181)

As a goddess figure, she tries to explain his death, but as one trapped in a construct that does not respect her wishes or her abilities, she struggles with the way in which he dies, and questions if he has killed himself, "had he plunged holding his treasure?" (180). She strives to perceive his suicide as a "defiance. Death was an attempt to communicate; people feeling the impossibility of reaching the centre which, mystically, evaded them; closeness drew apart; rapture faded, one was alone. There was an embrace in death" (180). She experiences an awful fear and terror, the dreaded idea posited at the beginning of the novel "that it was very, very dangerous to live even one day" (8) especially in a post-war world "when millions of things had utterly vanished" (4); and now here she is at the end of the day, at the end of the novel, with a feeling of the "overwhelming incapacity, one's parents giving it into one's hands, this life, to be lived to the end, to be walked with serenely" (180). In a final bid of recognition, in her step toward fulfilling her function as Themis in full power, she tries to integrate the Young God's suicide into her experience at the party, that "somehow it was her disaster—her disgrace" (181). His death has been a perversion of the sacrifice of the Young God in the ritual preservation of life, because it has happened too soon and without purpose, but it is a wrong she at least attempts to correct by ingesting him, into her own identity, in Harrison's ritual, symbolic, *omophagia:* "She felt somehow very like him—the young man who had killed himself. She felt glad that he had

done it; thrown it away" (182), as this will hopefully be the end of the
cycle of violence, and she will be able to return to her party. She refuses to
pity him, as "he made her feel the beauty; made her feel the fun" (182).
But as Themis, Woolf knows, Clarissa "must go back," "She must" after
all "assemble" (182).

The Waves, the Furies, and the Unbounded Whole

In the last of Woolf's trilogy, her "abstract, mystical, eyeless" (D 3: 203)
book, written as she claimed, "to a rhythm and not to a plot" (D 3: 316;
L 4: 204) as a kind of "playpoem" (D 3: 203), *The Waves* is made up
of six choral voices, or "verbal exposures," who have assembled festi-
val-like to reanimate the Young God, Percival, and defeat Death. As in
Aeschylus' *The Furies* (or *The Eumenides*), where the Furies take on the
role of chorus and sing for nearly the entire drama in pursuit of Orestes,
the six sound-pieces here lament the Year-Spirit's passing, but celebrate
this young and beautiful god through their assemblage as his thiasos, his
worshippers, who have a ritual dinner to honor him and to make him
"known." As Woolf writes, "Now is our festival; now we are together.
But without Percival there is no solidity" (W 122).

   The Waves has been read as a creation myth linked by Gillian Beer to
Woolf's Quaker aunt Caroline Emilia Stephen's religious tract, *Light Arising: Thoughts on the Central Radiance* (Cambridge: W. Heffer, 1908),
but this Christianized model, though instructive, is not as useful in understanding Woolf's broader canvas, the way in which, when she sits down
to write, she thinks in Greek proportions and is, in my view, positioning
herself among them but via a distinctly feminist rewriting of the classics.
Reading Woolf's bold experiment in *The Waves* through a Harrisonian
understanding of Greek ritual reveals a transpersonal sharing of ideas
that creates a radically innovative modernist experiment unlike any of her
male contemporaries. When Woolf writes in *The Waves: The Two Holo-
graph Drafts,* "I am telling myself the story of the world from the beginning. I am not concerned with the single life, but with lives together"
(6), it is the ghost of J—H— writ large that we must conjure, re-animate,
before us, "vibrating at the mouth of the cave," and the place where we
must look for Woolf's sources, her political and intellectual role models,
for the literary blood in her veins. For the depth and length of the shadow
of the Greeks enfolds, encompasses, includes, and out-darkens the important but much smaller intellectual shelters cast by Shakespeare and the

Elizabethans, Milton and the Romantics, Wagnerian and Mozartian operas, Bloomsbury, the eighteenth and nineteenth centuries, and Quaker aunts. As an artist, for Woolf, it is the Greeks, as interpreted through Jane Harrison, that hold the structure, the backbone, ribs, heart, and brain, of the entire breathing, vital, living organism of her creative production, Harrison's "world soul" as outlined in *Ancient Art and Ritual.*

The choral voices assembled in *The Waves,* however, have not come together without a struggle or without an understanding, each in his or her own way, of the importance of their task, to reanimate the Year-Spirit, through speech and as a disparate community, together. The indomitable and first feminist critic of Virginia Woolf's work, Ruth Gruber, writes significantly of the two "characters" Neville and Bernard as representing two poles of literary traditions and styles, seeing Neville as a "humanist" who "detests all vagueness and fitful connotations" and as a "lover of Roman ratiocination," whereas Bernard is "counterbalanced" by his "more feminine aesthetics and aspect of life" by "the irrational, chaotic experiences of life" (67). Reading transpersonally through Harrison, Neville represents order, tradition, rational Olympian values, while Bernard embodies Dionysian emotion, sensation, and the passions, but they each participate in the *dromenon* as a collective, when Neville says, "With infinite time before us [. . .] we ask what shall we do?" (102).

But with *The Waves,* Woolf is herself functioning as Athena, setting up the areopagus in *The Furies* with a committee of voices who must interact as a collective energy, a consensus, as "lives together," who will convene to preserve life and continue civilization. In addition to Neville and Bernard, she has brought together Louis, who is associated with ancient history and "the impulse to pull together the disparate facts of the past" (Hite "Introduction and Notes" 223). Jinny, also Virginia Woolf's childhood nickname, is tied to the social and the sensual. Rhoda is linked to the Romantic Shelley (Hite xli–xlii), but fantasizes about Greek settings ("white petals" (28), marble columns" (76) and embodies the choric "I sink, I fall; I faint, I fail," (18, 40), and Susan, whose voice captures the torment and eternal conflict between her chant elements, from the Catullan *odi et amo* ("I hate and I love") (9), is steadfast, concentrated, but limited in her understanding beyond that of her chant. They are each flawed, but in need of one another as they struggle towards connection to the Young God. In their articulation of his spirit, they strive to chant him into existence via their voices, creating a kind of collective holophrase of vibrating sound. For sound, the sound of the human voice, the sound of the waves, the sound of the universe, was crucial to Woolf's project, as, after reading a review in the *Times Literary Supplement* commending her "characters," she wrote in her diary in an 8 October 1931 entry, "Odd, that they [. . .] shd. praise my characters when I meant to have none" (D 4: 47).

Louis becomes part of Harrison's larger "Unbounded whole," as she writes in *Alpha and Omega* (1915) in relation to religion. He speaks of "himself" as transcending time and identities:

> I have lived a thousand lives already. Every day I unbury—I dig up. I find relics of myself in the sand that women made thousands of years ago, when I heard songs by the Nile and the chained beast stamping. What you see beside you, this man, this Louis, is only the cinders and refuse of something once splendid. (W 127)

Louis tries to keep the pieces of history together, but it is the Dionysian Bernard to whom Woolf gives the final speech to "sum up" (176) all the others. Bernard is referred to by Woolf as being in the habit of "phrase making," a line that has been connected to a reference much earlier in 1908 when Woolf writes that "This is what Adrian calls 'phrase making'" (L 1: 335), but which has curious resonance with Harrison's "holophrases." It is Bernard who articulates the principles at work in Harrison's linguistic theory, of sounds, whole-concepts, that occur pre-language, before the divisive 'parts of speech.'" Bernard is a visionary who knows about the perils of extreme individualism:

> "But soon, too soon," said Bernard, "this egotistic exultation fails. Too soon the moment of ravenous identity is over, and the appetite for happiness, and happiness, and still more happiness is glutted. The stone is sunk; the moment is over. Round me there spreads a wide margin of indifference. Now open in my eyes a thousand eyes of curiosity [. . .] I can see a dozen pictures. But what are stories? Toys I twist, bubbles I blow, one ring passing through another. And sometimes I begin to doubt if there are stories. What is my story? What is Rhoda's? What is Neville's? There are facts [. . .]. That is the truth; that is the fact, but beyond it all is darkness and conjecture." (W 143)

Each of the other voices struggle to preside over the different realms of land, animals, planets, ordinary objects, plants, time, past, and present, as they try to "hold" the vision of Percival, of what Jinny calls "youth and beauty, and something so deep sunk within us that we shall perhaps never make this moment out of one man again" (W 145). Rhoda sees "forests and far countries [. . .] seas and jungles [. . .] moonlight." Neville sees "happiness [. . .] the quiet of ordinary things [. . .] the petal falling from the rose." Susan sees "Week-days [. . .] whether it is April, whether it is November" (146). But Bernard sees the future:

> We are creators. We too have made something that will join the innumerable congregations of past time. We, too, as we put on our hats and push open the door, stride not into chaos, but into a world that our own force can subjugate and make part of the illumined and everlasting road. (146)

But what of Percival, the Young God who is spoken about, but who never speaks for himself? His name has been pointed to by critics as connected to Arthurian legend, as Percival, the "holy fool" or "the perfect fool," who finds the Holy Grail, which, in later versions, becomes the cup from which Christ drinks at the Last Supper, and to the Wagnerian opera *Parsifal*, which Virginia Woolf saw in 1909 at the Bayreuth Wagner Festival. He is also, like Jacob in *Jacob's Room*, modeled on Woolf's beloved older brother, Thoby, dead from an illness contracted after their trip abroad to Greece in 1906. But Percival also finds his roots in the earlier proto-Celtic figure of Peredur, the young son, who saves his sister, Blanchefleur, from being raped. In later versions, she becomes his lover, until, in even later incarnations, a Christianized Peredur becomes a virgin and Blanchefleur recedes into the background. *The Waves* in some respects can be read as a corrective to the alienated war hero separated from his social group.

Not despite, but through their own inarticulation, from their own infirmities, the communal six voices will recover what was lost to them, for holophrasis, far from being impersonal, indifferent, is speech at its most intimate, "man entangled as it were in his own activities, he and his environment utterly involved," as Harrison writes (T 474). The sacrifice, "if sacrifice he performs, will be a sacrament partaken of, not a gift offered to a person" or to a state, for "man felt himself at first not as a personality separate from other persons, but as the warm excited centre of a group [. . .] the collective daimon is before the individual ghost, and still more he is before the Olympian god" (475). The Young God we have seen perversely separated from his thiasos in *Jacob's Room* and *Mrs. Dalloway*, is here regenerated by his thiasos, re-introduced to Themis, who is Gaia, the Great Mother, the "collective conscience" of the community, "the social fact and focus" (T 494), the life-blood of civilization, the universe, paid homage here by the gathering of voices, by the heart-sound that is *The Waves*.

Each of Woolf's novels is informed by Harrison's "world soul," communities united and revised by emotions and art. Joining Harrison transpersonally in her goddess-making research, Woolf, in her fiction, remakes these figures, seeking to offer counter narratives to established modernist forms. Through Harrison, she is constantly providing us with a new way of seeing, asking us to renew our art, but also our way of living, our society, and our way of expressing ourselves, and she demands, like the *themistes* before her, that we assemble, unify, cooperate, or disperse.

CHAPTER 3

Reading Transpersonally I—
"Next Comes the Wife's Room . . . "

A Room of One's Own
and "Scientiae Sacra Fames"

IN ORDER TO WRITE *A Room of One's Own*, Virginia Woolf invoked not only the spirit of "J—H—" the ghost of the professional woman scholar haunting the grounds of her fictional Fernham College, but also, Jane Harrison's essay "Scientiae Sacra Fames," on women's access to knowledge, their "soul hunger" for *scientiae sacra*, sacred knowledge, sacred in the sense of "oath" or "that which binds." *A Room of One's Own*, Woolf's feminist manifesto, is often considered a posthumous tribute to Harrison, and classicist Annabel Robinson wrote briefly of Woolf's concentration on "a room" as being a "covert acknowledgement" of Harrison ("Something Odd at Work" 215). This chapter argues that both *A Room of One's Own* and "Scientiae Sacra Fames" perform a lateral, transpersonal sharing of ideas and experiences as it explores the ways in which these two essays speak to one another about feminism, politics, women's education, and women's writing as helping to form women's social identity and cultural production.

In "Getting Transpersonal: The Cost of an Academic Life," Nancy K. Miller refers in her endnotes to *A Room of One's Own* as Virginia Woolf's "academic autobiography" (178) as she explores how "the personal [. . .] negotiates the transpersonal," which she understands as "the links to others that we establish with generations past and present" (166). Miller's focus in her article is on the struggles and difficult passages, "the academic cost," experienced by "women, minorities, ethnically marked Americans, and global transplants" as she explores contemporary memoir and autobiographical writings by Edward Said, Jane Tompkins, and Michael Awkward, among others. Applying Miller's notions of the transpersonal to Harrison and Woolf's essays on women's access to education allows us to read them both as illustrating plots of transformation, about women who were either denied, as in Woolf's case, or thwarted, as in Harrison's, in their respective academic goals and aspirations.

Both *A Room of One's Own* and "Scientiae Sacra Fames" were given as lectures before becoming essays in their final forms. *A Room of One's Own* began as two lectures, or rather, talks ("I give you my thoughts as they come to me"; AROO 6), that Woolf gave for the Arts Society at Newnham College on 20 October 1928, accompanied by Leonard Woolf, her sister Vanessa Bell, and Vanessa's daughter Angelica, and for the student organization ODTAA (which stood for "One Damn Thing After Another") on 26 October 1928 at Girton College, accompanied by her lover, Vita Sackville-West. "Scientiae Sacra Fames" was given as a lecture, originally entitled "Women and Knowledge," before The London Sociological Society on 28 October 1913 and on 8 November for the Cambridge Branch of the National Union of Suffrage Societies, and appeared in print in the *Newnham College Letter* of 1913. It was reprinted as "Scientiae Sacra Fames" in the *New Statesman* on 1 November 1913 as a supplement to "The Awakening of Women," a feature edited by Beatrice (Mrs. Sidney) Webb, and also appeared in *The Times*, 29 October 1913, and in the *Cambridge Review*, 30 October 1913. It was later collected as "Scientiae Sacra Fames" in Harrison's *Alpha and Omega* in 1915, a copy of which Virginia Woolf owned and read. Woolf had visited Harrison in April 1928 as Harrison lay on her deathbed in Bloomsbury. Following the meeting, Woolf wrote in her diary of her seventy-eight-year-old friend and intellectual mentor that she looked "exalted, satisfied, exhausted" (D 3: 180).

Harrison's "Scientiae Sacra Fames" remains one of the earliest articulations of Woolf's position that if a woman is to be able to write, create, and think, she must have financial support and a room of her own. In outlining the physical contours of the home and their proscription of behavior based on gender, Harrison writes, "Next comes the wife's room, the drawing-room: not a room to withdraw into, by yourself, but essentially the room into which "visitors are shown"—a room in which you can't possibly settle down to think, because anyone may come in at any moment [. . .]. One of the most ominous signs of the times is that woman is beginning to demand a study" (SSF 128).

Strategies of Subversion

Both *A Room of One's Own* and "Scientiae Sacra Fames" adopt similar rhetorical strategies that undermine conventional notions of authority and argument, refusing the lecture-voice of the credentialed academic in favor of more collaborative and cooperative techniques. Both sought to challenge a conventional, patriarchal "first duty of a lecturer—to hand you after an hour's discourse a nugget of pure truth to wrap up between the pages of your notebooks and keep on the mantel-piece for ever" (AROO 4). Woolf and Harrison are each careful to acknowledge her own "prejudices" and to side-step the argumentative pitfalls of being accused of having "an axe to grind." Their rhetorical approaches also reveal the genius behind their mutual strategies. Harrison, as the university-educated scholar, demonstrates her intellectual passion and openness to new ideas. Woolf, feeling both concerned about women's education as well as alienated from her academic audience, employs "all the liberties and licenses of a novelist" (AROO 4), playing to her strengths. She wrote later, on 8 June 1933, in a letter to her friend the composer Ethel Smyth, that she used fiction as her medium for her presentations, because she feared that "If I had said, Look here am I uneducated, because my brothers used all the family funds which is the fact—Well theyd have said; she has an axe to grind; and no one would have taken me seriously" (L 5: 195). As Jane Marcus speculates in her essay "Virginia Woolf, Cambridge, and *A Room of One's Own*: 'The Proper Upkeep of Names,'" which also originated as a talk at Newnham and Girton Colleges in October 1993 on the sixty-fifth anniversary of Woolf's visits there, "Imagine Virginia Woolf, the autodidact intellectual, asked to speak at a university, feeling inadequate and even envious of those who study here" (11), as she identifies Woolf's "grudge" against the university and its neglect of the scholarly achievements of Jane Harrison as "ressentiment," which "many brilliant and successful people of colour and women spend a great deal of energy smothering [. . .] in exactly the same way that Woolf's narrator had to fling inkpots at the Angel in the House" (9). "Ressentiment," from the French, implies indirect resentment, and is often expressed by demeaning the values held by the hated individual. Elisions in the early drafts of *A Room of One's Own* in relation to the passage on "J—H—" also bear out Woolf's sense of isolation from her academic audience as well as the deeply felt insistence about her project to implore women to sustain the legacies of their female intellectual role models. Marcus writes of these early drafts that "the words 'I have no right to talk openly,' crossed out [are] the poignant reminder that she is just as much a stranger at the women's college as at the men's" ("'The Proper Upkeep of Names'" 12). She continues that "crossed out also is her description of 'the sort of mocking derision which women, when they have ceased to be young, & yet have won a great name; as Jane Harrison had . . . and never spend a penny on the proper upkeep of their name . . . '—endure" (12). The persistent distortion or elision of Harrison's reputation is an example of Woolf's fear that women writers and thinkers would continue to be written out of the record, by a discourse dominated by men, but also by one in which women neglect or deny their own intellectual role models.

In contrast to Woolf's sense of alienation, Harrison wrote "Scientiae Sacra Fames" from the vantage point of one of the first generation of Cambridge-educated women. But she, too, was keenly aware of the inequities, consequences, and personal costs of being a woman pushing the boundaries of a centuries-old discipline and promoting a feminist position, in a male-dominated, hostile academic world. In addition to the grim and uninviting conditions of the women's colleges, female students enjoyed no official status until they were admitted as late as 1948 and it was "a standard joke to tell of the dons who began their lectures with 'Gentlemen,' even during the two wars when almost all of their audiences were female" (J. Marcus, "'The Proper Upkeep of Names'" 7). And yet, in the face of the profoundly bitter opposition to women's education at Cambridge, Harrison, addressing the nature of prejudice in general, wrote with the intellectual curiosity of an educator, seeking to unveil and discern truth using not fiction, but a scholarly approach wed to her belief and practice that from profound feelings we arrive at fact:

> But still there remains in the minds of many thinking persons a prejudice to the effect that only certain kinds of knowledge are appropriate to women. I have the greatest possible respect for honest prejudices; they are the stuff out of which right opinion is ultimately, if slowly, moulded, they are the genuine growth of a living emotion [. . .] our most enlightened views grow out of unreasoning prejudices. (SSF 119)

Adopting a collaborative argumentative stance, Harrison meets biased opinion head-on as fertile ground for new ideas, and her essay is one of the best examples of Harrison's ability to balance the emotional with the rational demands of study. Woolf also provides a caveat to her audience, a rhetorical disclaimer which paradoxically achieves her argumentative ends.

> One can only give one's audience the chance of drawing their own conclusions as they observe the limitations, the prejudices, the idiosyncrasies of the speaker. Fiction here is likely to contain more truth than fact. [. . .] Oxbridge is an invention; so is Fernham; "I" is only a convenient term for somebody who has no real being. Lies will flow from my lips, but there may perhaps be some truth mixed up with them; it is for you to seek out this truth and to decide whether any part of it is worth keeping. (AROO 4)

In addition to avoiding a critique of her position as developing from "an axe to grind," Woolf uses a fictitious voice in order to find her own. Her extensive "allusiveness" to figures and entities both real and imagined or a composite of both, as Susan Gubar writes, "allowed Woolf to eschew tendentious didacticism, for throughout her life she found repugnant what she mocked as the loudspeaker voice, which was inhospitable to her temperament" (Introduction, AROO xxxvii). Hence, Woolf begins her essay, "But, you may say, we asked you to speak about women and fiction— what has that got to do with a room of one's own?" (AROO 3), as an anti-lecture in the midst of a conversation, a question with a potential answer, engaging her audience in a dialogue we seem to be creating along with her.

Jane Harrison also preferred learning to lecturing and employed unconventional methods at both the podium and in the classroom, using interactive, dialogical methods ahead of their time that included slides, conversation, anecdote, and essays. Not only were her theories excessively attacked for elevating the role and function of women in Greek ritual and myth, demonstrating women's use of agricultural and horticultural tools in ritual as significant, for example, or in re-interpreting Pandora not as a catalyst for disaster, but as an Earth Goddess and "bringer of all gifts" ("Pandora's Box 101"). She was also criticized for her "florid" style, an imaginative literary flair that was praised by her female readership and disparaged by male reviewers. With the publication of *Themis,* she was marked by the following descriptions from male readers as "subjective," as displaying "excessive sympathy," being "propagandistic," "willful," "too dogmatic and cocksure" (qtd. in Arlen, "'For Love of an Idea'" 172). When Harrison would respond to her critics, her behavior was deemed inappropriate and unladylike. Her responses to a particularly virulent critic, Lewis Farnell, for example, who "projected his antagonism to Harrison's atheism and feminism onto his critique of her work" (Arlen 173), were counterattacked by several of Farnell's friends who wielded a great deal of power and influence in the Classics at Cambridge and Oxford.

Similarly creating and embracing "the broken sequence," "the female sentence," Woolf employed distinctly unconventional rhetorical methods. Gubar points out that "it is precisely because she refused to hammer home her points or deliver prescriptions like a doctor would drugs or a pedant rules or a judge pronouncements or a preacher sermons that *A Room of One's Own* evinces a tone many readers find whimsically playful, others cloyingly coy or frustratingly evasive" (Introduction, AROO xxxvii). Like Jane Harrison before her, Woolf changes our readerly experience. She questions everything, challenges her and others' assumptions, and insists we take part and interact with the text. She gives up her own authority as author, as lecturer, and gives us an alternative, shape-shifting rhetorical strategy (is it fiction or non-fiction?), which Harrison also employed as she pursued her research without dismissing her emotions, indeed by putting them to practical use. Both Harrison and Woolf gave us strategies of subversion, which continue to challenge the way we know and understand anything.

Audience as Feminine Collective: Using Ritual to Revise

Their strategies, while radically feminist, were also, however, risks that required effort, both intellectual and financial, on the part of their largely female audiences at the time. A look at the demographics of Harrison's popular lectures on Greek religion provided her with insight into the nature and politics of learning, and how gender issues fall along economic and class lines as well. This is a theme that Woolf picks up and reveals in *A Room of One's Own* (and later in *Three Guineas*) as she explores at length the money, "an unending stream of gold and silver" (AROO 10), and lavish surroundings of the men's college: "[P]ainters brought their glass for the windows, and the masons were busy for centuries up on that roof with putty and cement, spade and trowel" (11). She famously

remarks upon the delicious food enjoyed at the men's colleges, while the
women's colleges are overrun by rats and the students have to learn in
dingy surroundings, eating dry biscuits and stringy prunes, "stringy as a
miser's heart and exuding a fluid such as might run in misers' veins" (18).
As Woolf points out, "One cannot think well, love well, sleep well, if one
has not dined well" (18).

In an interview of Harrison in *The Pall Mall Gazette* in 1891, we also
gain a sense of who had access to which types of knowledge and why.
Harrison was asked in the interview about the make-up of her audiences,
to which she responded that they came

> from all the educated classes. A few men are interested, but the major-
> ity are women. Of these the mothers of young children are the most
> eager attendants. They have boys and girls growing up, and they want
> to share the interests of their children; they want to be able to talk to
> their boys, during the school holidays, about these things, or they want to
> assist them in their studies. Other mothers, again, come to learn so that
> they themselves may teach their children at home. This, however, applies
> chiefly to the London mother. In the provinces I have scarcely been able
> to watch the after-results of lectures sufficiently to formulate my impres-
> sions. (2) (JH Papers)

Harrison's experiences as a lecturer exposed her to the singular plight
of women as so burdened by domestic responsibilities that the purpose
of their attendance was not for themselves, but to help others at home.
She also makes note of the lack of intellectual curiosity among the leisure
classes and the utter uselessness women, Woolf's "daughters of educated
men," experience on a daily basis. It is an existence, Woolf contends in
Three Guineas, that may be more onerous and oppressive than the experience of women in the working classes. Writing from her experience as
a woman whose life was often cruelly circumscribed by Victorian mores
and a frequently enforced infantilization, Woolf felt, somewhat enviously,
if also a bit naively, that at least working class women had a function,
a use, a purpose, a job. In an interview, Harrison also raises and recognizes the intellectually disturbing plight of women in the leisure classes
and their resulting psychological debilitation:

> Then another large section of the audience is formed by the well-to-do
> women who have a good deal of leisure. They have nothing to do in
> the afternoon; their lives are somewhat dull and empty; they want some

outside interest, and have not the energy to create one. To them the lectures come as a new amusement. They do not require very much, and the
lecturer has to make the subject as light and as varied as possible. Also
he or she must be prepared to generalize a good deal, which is apt to
result in much personal demoralization—the hunger for generalization in
half-educated women is a fact I have observed without quite understanding. The popular lecturer on Greek art often must feel that his attitude
towards his subject and his audience is intellectually a somewhat squalid
one, but he will have his good moments too when the flame he has tried
to light for others brings its after-glow for himself. (2) (JH Papers)

Harrison strengthens and extends her views of women's economic and
class positions in relation to knowledge in "Scientiae Sacra Fames," tying
her argument into the hierarchy of a paternalistic ritual system, in this
case one from the "oriental gods" where there are usually two types, a
"head-god" and an "under-god." Women play the same role, she con-
tended, as the under-god plays: she does not think, she does. The head-
god, Harrison tells us, "thinks and plans and wills; he sits aloof, supreme,
inert." By contrast, the secondary under-god "originates nothing himself,
but carries out the thoughts and behests of the head-god. Although "gods
among Orientals are usually male," women in British society embody all
the characteristics of the oriental under-god in relation to knowledge.
Illustrating the inferior position of women as helpmeets to husbands
and fathers, educators to intellectually indolent sons and brothers, Harrison lists the female under-god's duties: "A woman learns a little medi-
cine that she may carry out the instructions of a doctor and soothe a
patient; she learns modern languages that she may help out a linguistically dumb brother or husband when he takes his walks abroad [. . .]
she becomes generally "well informed" that she may partly understand
or—much more important—appear to sympathize with and admire
man's conversation" (SSF 116).

Harrison and Woolf both upend this hierarchical structure. Each
offers alternative possibilities for a woman's role and function in relation
to learning, which are deeply rooted in reinterpreting ancient ritual. Harrison uses the ritual of the "under-god" in order to further her political
objectives in service to women's desire for knowledge and education. Furthermore, it is no accident that "J—H—"'s appearance on the grounds
of Fernham is connected to the seasons, to Jane Harrison's research and
theory casting Dionysus as a Year-Spirit and harbinger of a new day, a
new idea. Woolf famously makes note of this change in the weather, when
"all was dim, yet intense too, as if the scarf which the dusk had flung over

FIGURE 7. Jane Harrison, seated with (standing, L-R) members of her Cambridge Ritualist circle, H. F. Stewart, Gilbert Murray, and Francis Cornford, in Malting House Garden, Cambridge, ca. 1904, the year she was introduced to a young Virginia Stephen by Janet Case. Photo credit: The Jane Harrison Papers, Newnham College Archive, The Principal and Fellows, Newnham College, Cambridge.

the garden were torn asunder by star or sword—the flash of some terrible reality leaping, as its way is, out of the heart of the spring" (AROO 17), just as we espy Harrison's ghost. Both Harrison's and Woolf's talks were given in October; October marks the beginning of the new year in pagan ritual, and, as Jane Marcus points out, "It is Michaelmas Term in Cambridge, the birth of the academic year" ("'The Proper Upkeep of Names'" 3). Woolf's disruptions of the conventional lecture with her disruptions and interruptions in the text share a mutual bond of outsidership with her mentor and friend's work, disrupting the ritual of scholarship and challenging a more conventional, masculinist reading of ritualist research.

"The Gates of the Temple of Learning Clang as They Closed"

In addition to her lecturing in London and in the provinces, Harrison's own experiences, as a precocious young girl growing up in a household that vigorously resisted and curtailed her ambition to become educated, allowed her to apply personal resonance in "Scientiae Sacra Fames." Just as Miller writes, as a feminist, in her essay on contemporary academic autobiography and memoir that she "can't speak for the descendants of Henry Adams, the men, some of whom still exist, who enjoy their lives in the well-appointed rooms of the ivory tower," and that the cost of an academic life for the marginalized "tends to be particularly high" ("Getting Transpersonal" 178), Harrison and Woolf write from their own personal and transpersonal experience in order to navigate, articulate, and negotiate their views on education. Harrison remembers that soul-killing moment when she discovered for the first time as a young girl that learning for the sake of learning was not expected nor required of girls. The objective for a girl was not to find "a room of one's own" in which to work, but to acquire "a home of her own" through marriage, in order to serve and manage for another, to "keep house." Harrison writes, similarly to Woolf, of having to hide her desire for Greek, for learning:

> Some half-century ago a very happy little girl secretly possessed herself of a Greek grammar. A much-adored aunt swiftly stripped the gilt from the gingerbread with these chill, cutting words: "I do not see how Greek grammar is to help little Jane to keep house when she has a home of her own." A "home of her own" was as near as the essentially decent aunt of those days might get to an address on sex and marriage, but the child

understood: she was a little girl, and thereby damned to eternal domesticity; she heard the gates of the temple of Learning clang as they closed. (SSF 117)

Indeed, we hear "the gates of the temple of Learning clang as they closed" echo with the closing of the university's library doors upon Virginia Woolf. Indeed, Harrison's position speaks to Woolf's own experiences and lack of a university education in deference to her brothers. Writing transpersonally, Woolf famously recounts being chased off the grass to the gravel path by the gesticulating beadle in *A Room of One's Own* because as a woman she was "only admitted to the library if accompanied by a Fellow of the College or furnished with a letter of introduction" (6). Woolf writes indignantly at first about the experience:

That a famous library has been cursed by a woman is a matter of complete indifference to a famous library. Venerable and calm, with all its treasures safe locked within its breast, it sleeps complacently and will, so far as I am concerned, so sleep for ever. Never will I wake those echoes, never will I ask for that hospitality again, I vowed as I descended the steps in anger. (AROO 8)

But she then extends Harrison's position on the consequences of exclusion in one of her most memorable instances of defiance from a daughter of an educated man, a bubbling up of Marcus' "ressentiment" by wondering (ironically?) if it might perhaps not be "worse to be locked in" (AROO 24).

Indeed, Woolf must animate, conjure up from the cauldron of her imagination, a fictional sister, Judith Shakespeare, as Harrisonian "under-god," to illustrate the intellectual abuse and secondary status of women denied opportunity and resources to realize their potential. The doomed life of Judith Shakespeare, who must hide her intellectual passions as Woolf and Harrison had to hide, reads like a Greek tragedy, as the young girl schooled to "not moon about with books and papers" suffers beatings, mockery, humiliation, rape, pregnancy, and inevitably suicide at the crossroads of the Elephant and Castle bus stop.

It is a formulary that is the antithesis of Harrison's Year-Spirit, for as an intellectual genius, who happens to be a woman, Judith Shakespeare, in a patriarchal societal construct, must die—not for the good of the community or for the advancement of humanity—but because she is irrationally feared and relentlessly oppressed by a system of societal norms, by "England [which] is under a patriarchy" (AROO 33). Denied access to knowledge, Judith Shakespeare's intellectual potential withers and her ability to create becomes corrupted, distorted, and ultimately destroyed.

The "Binocular Brain" and Gendered Ways of Knowing

But "what is it lies behind the Golden Gates? What is the nature of this air too pure and rare for a woman to breathe?" (SSF 118) Harrison asks. Women are barred from "the dear delight of learning for learning's sake a 'dead' language for sheer love of the beauty of its words and the delicacy of its syntactical relations, the joy of tracking out the secret springs of the human body irrespective of patient or doctor, the rapture of reconstructing for the first time in imagination a bit of the historical past" because to do so is considered unwomanly, and Harrison wants to know "Why?" Why, she asks, was "the Peri [. . .] ever excluded from Paradise" (SSF 118) and what are the sources of these prejudices against women's access to knowledge, the sources of the fear of women's knowledge? Harrison considers what types of knowledge popular prejudice (she also calls it "herd-opinion") allows women to possess and cautions us to be aware that whenever such questions are raised about "whether women should or should not know this or that, the ghosts of these delicious old schoolmen gather round" (SSF 118).

Certain types of knowledge were allowed, as "it is not that any particular knowledge or information is denied as unsuitable," and Harrison points out that "Men only came to learn Latin and Greek by the accident of medieval tradition" (SSF 118). But what truly rankles societal norms is a woman possessed of "unstinted knowledge." "Between feeling and knowing there is a certain antithesis; the province of women was to feel: therefore they had better not know. There is, as in all the most poisonous falsehoods, some grain of muddled truth" (SSF 118). According to Harrison in her interview, and making a point reiterated by Woolf in *A Room of One's Own,* the importance of intellectual stimulation for women was that it should take them out of themselves, to become less personal, more transpersonal. Harrison states:

> I believe the great good is that lectures on Greek art create for these ladies an interest that is *non-personal.* You want to be a woman to know what the rest of that is. People talk of the good that lectures do by bringing people and classes together. I should like to talk of the good they do—for

women, at least—by sending them away from each other into a desert place, to think where you only can think—alone; and the more remote the subject, the more averse from modern association—as Greek art is— the better. And then, I am glad to say, there are some to whom these lectures are the beginning of serious study and of lifelong interest. (2)

Harrison elaborates on this idea of the "impersonal" in "Scientiae Sacra Fames" in her argument for using the "binocular" brain. She writes, "There is I believe between man and woman an intellectual difference which makes their co-operation desirable, because fruitful." It is not a difference of "faculty," but rather "a difference of focus—of focus of attention [. . .]. No manly strength or womanly tact will make them otherwise" as "Intellect is never wholly and separately intellectual. It is a thing charged with, dependent on, arising out of, emotional desire" (SSF 140). Harrison, in an illustration of her own undying passion for learning, writes of the process of intellectual discovery that "Anyone who makes even a very small mental discovery can note how, at the moment of the making, there is a sudden sense of warmth, an uprush of emotion, often a hot blush, and sometimes tears in the eyes. Who can say that a process so sensuous and emotional, or at least attended by concomitants so sensuous, is insulated from a thing as interpenetrating as sex?" (140– 41). In other words, "To face the facts and the problems of life is characteristic of to-day. To see them clearly we need the binocular vision of the two sexes" (141).

These passages resonate with Woolf's own desire for women to have a room in which to create, and to be able to create employing both the male and female sides of their brains. She writes, "it is fatal for anyone who writes to think of their sex. It is fatal to be a man or woman pure and simple; one must be woman-manly or man-womanly. It is fatal for a woman to lay the least stress on any grievance; to plead even with justice any cause; in any way to speak consciously as a woman" (AROO 103). Woolf offers her detailed analysis of the second-rate Mary Carmichael's *Life's Adventure* as the work of a novelist who nearly gets it right, holding the reader's interest, because "Chloe liked Olivia perhaps for the first time in literature" (AROO 81). The unknown Mary Carmichael is made known by Virginia Woolf, because as one of the four Marys, she tried to do something new and original in *Life's Adventure,* even if the finished novel was not of the caliber of a Proust or a Shakespeare. As Woolf points out, her great achievement was in mastering the "first lesson": "she wrote as a woman, but as a woman who has forgotten that she is a woman, so that her pages were full of that curious sexual quality which comes only when sex is unconscious of itself" (AROO 91).

Harrison writes of the two aspects of intellect brought forward by both men and women as a man's "insularity" and a woman's sense of "tact," by which she means touch or contact. She realizes that "there is still a feeling in many minds that disinterested knowledge in a woman endangers exclusive family devotion" (SSF 122)—a point she concedes. It is true, but this, Harrison argues, "is clear gain," as she contrasts excessive male egotism as a pitfall to the objectives of science and knowledge. "A man would not say: 'I must not devote myself to science; it might endanger my exclusive devotion to myself.' But without self-contempt he might say, and his wife agree with him, she had better not devote herself to art or science, lest the dinner and the children be neglected" (122). She casts aside the argument that women are not necessary for advancing knowledge, "though Sappho and Jane Austen may give us pause" (122), but we do not have to worry too much about this either because "our present age is an age of co-operation, marked not so much by individual emergence as by interdependent, collective advance, and for this pre-eminent genius is not essential" (123). Harrison is writing here before the outbreak of the Great War, and on the crest of the wave of an anthropological movement and as part of a community of scholars who worked creatively and collaboratively in trying to effect change. As she notes, "We must always remember that freedom to know has but recently been won for men. Almost as soon as they realized their prize they were willing to share it. Even about men the old, semimagical question is still asked, What *use* is this or that subject in education—that is, what immediate relation has it to action?" (123). Education at the turn of the nineteenth century and the desire to include women was very much in the forefront of contemporary and popular debate.

Harrison broadens the question: "We used to be told that 'a man does not want a learned wife,' 'men do not want to talk to learned ladies.' The hopeful thing now is that thinking men and women nowadays do not ask what 'a man wants,' but in what direction humanity is moving" (SSF 124–25). Harrison concedes that though "specialization is intenser than ever," it is "conscious of its unity, its interrelations" (SSF 136). She uses her own and her Ritualist colleagues as examples of how feminine principles helped reinvigorate the Classics; that through female "tact" or rather connection to both emotion and action, the disciplines were saved, the intellect and the intellectual community were enriched and enhanced:

My own subject, classics, which used to be a garden enclosed, and well-nigh a *hortus siccus,* is now saved. Thanks to archaeology, to anthropology, it is now open to all the winds of heaven; its half-stifled life breathes afresh. By contacts we are saved. (136–37).

She also identifies psychology and sociology as fields whose life-blood depends upon the female attributes of the intellect: "And what is psychology, but the science of human behavior, of human reaction, of *contacts,* not insulations. Our whole morality is looked upon now, not as a system of heaven-sent virtues—truth, purity, constancy, obedience, what not—but as a balance maintained between the interests of the individual and the interests of the race, the better relating of the two" (137; emphasis in original).

But, Harrison wonders, playing devil's advocate, is it necessary biologically for women to be more given to "imaginative altruism" and are they capable of impersonal detachment? Women are more open to the social current. Men are more insulated, but is that an advantage? Is it a part of our nature or is it socially constructed? Here, she seeks an answer by exploring the architectural construction and layout of the home, "which are to me deeply depressing" (SSF 128), as she outlines the women's province as restricted to the social setting of the drawing room in comparison to the man's "study," his room of his own that Woolf writes into her essay. Of the man's study, Harrison writes:

Then, at the back of the house, there is a hole or den, called a "study"— a place inviolate, guarded by immemorial taboos. There man thinks, and learns, and knows. I am aware that sometimes the study contains more pipes, fishing-rods, foxes' brushes, and golf-clubs, than books or scientific apparatus. Still, it is called the "study" or the "library," and the wife does not sit there. There are rarely two chairs—there is always one— possibly for a human being to sit on. Well, that study stands for man's insularity; he wants to be by himself. The house where you don't and mustn't sit in the study is to me no home. But then, I have long known that I am no "true woman." (128)

The man expects his wife to keep him in touch with the world, because otherwise, he would go off to his room of his own forever, "and lose himself in his own specialism." The physical layout of the home emphasizes separate spheres, one that grooms and encourages a man to think,

to learn, to know, and another that grooms and encourages a woman to
serve and renounce the self.

Harrison and Woolf both look on the ideal as being able to create
from both the male and female aspects of the mind, Harrison's "binocular" vision, Woolf's androgynous creative brain: "Some collaboration has
to take place in the mind between the woman and the man before the act
of creation can be accomplished. Some marriage of opposites has to be
consummated" (AROO 103). Like Woolf, Harrison writes of how difficult the ideal is to achieve. They both explore the impossible, insoluble
bridge between the sexes, Harrison when she notes that "Each sex is conservative and irrational about the other. The reason is, of course, clear.
From a centre of personal emotion it is hard to get far enough back to
see clearly and judge sanely" (SSF 124). Like Woolf, Harrison recognizes
the difficulties for women to embrace both action and emotion, insularity
and contact, and that she often feels as if she were "writing in the dark"
(139), because "It is hard to shake oneself loose from these fossil virtues;
they are bone of our bone, and the old skeleton still rattles" (138). However, "one thing is clear: we must avoid dogmatism; we must adopt the
method of experiment," and she repeats, "we must experiment" (139).

Reading Harrison transpersonally, Woolf talks of the similar difficulties of one sex being able to re-create on the page the experience of the
other. "Even so it remains obvious, even in the writing of Proust, that
a man is terribly hampered and partial in his knowledge of women, as
a woman in her knowledge of men" (AROO 82). Even writers with the
reputation of, for example, Shakespeare, suffer from their lack of understanding of women, a state of affairs Woolf attributes to women's oppression by society in general, and by their exclusion from knowledge and
formal education. "[L]iterature would be incredibly impoverished, as
indeed literature is impoverished beyond our counting by the doors that
have been shut upon women" (82). Woolf suggests that there is no language, no words for what it is that happens when a woman walks into
a room. "How" Woolf asks, "should it be otherwise? For women have
sat indoors all these millions of years, so that by this time the very walls
are permeated by their creative force, which has, indeed, so overcharged
the capacity of bricks and mortar that it must needs harness itself to pens
and brushes and business and politics. But this creative power differs
greatly from the creative power of men" (86). She then uses a Harrisonian
"ancient lady" to further illustrate her point of the generational connection that occurs between women and how that "very ancient lady cross-
ing the street on the arm of a middle-aged woman, her daughter, perhaps,

both so respectably booted and furred that their dressing in the afternoon must be a ritual," represents a life, a story that has disappeared. "No biography or history has a word to say about it. And the novels, without meaning to, inevitably lie" (87–88).

Knowledge as Collective Will: Chanting Together in "the Four-Eyed" World

Like Woolf, who was atheistic in her belief that it is possible to pursue a moral life without an institutional interpretation of God, Harrison feared the specter of an uninformed understanding of religion. She warns, speaking somewhat prophetically about our own times, that the greatest damage that can be done to civilization is to misperceive and misinterpret religion. Relating religion to knowledge, Harrison discusses her own controversial atheism and what she means by her use of the word "God" and of "religion," when she invokes Bernard Shaw and her colleague Gilbert Murray's views in his *Four Stages of Greek Religion*:

> I think it was Mr. Bernard Shaw who said somewhere that, if the great congregations of cowards, known as the Human Race, were to be made courageous, they must be made religious, and by religious he meant, if I remember rightly, the sense of being part of something bigger and stronger than yourself. Religion has never been denied to women. But the emotion of religion, this sense of being part of God, may be the deadliest danger unless informed and directed by a knowledge of the ways of God—i.e., the nature of the universe and that part of it which is man. A religious woman without knowledge is like a lunatic armed with an explosive. Moreover, imparted information avails little. She must have within her the scientific spirit, what the Greeks called *sophrosyne,* which knows and is quiet, which *saves* and is saved. (SSF 123; emphasis in original)

Ultimately, Harrison points out the importance of men and women working together, communally, on an intellectual or creative project. "Your thoughts are—for what they are worth—self-begotten by some process of parthenogenesis" (130), but then there comes a time when you want to separate and "disentangle" them from yourself and your emotions in order to bring them to fruition. "To talk a thing over with a competent man friend is to me like coming out of a seething caldron of suggestion into a spacious, well-ordered room" and what she seeks within herself, as well as, outside of herself, "the male element in the mind [. . .] its power of insulation" (131). Women, although possessive of "inferior insularity," have "superior 'tact'" (132), by which she suggests that women are more closely tied to social currents, to family and communal settings, to the furtherance of the human race, which is of vital importance to the intellect as well, and appallingly underappreciated and undervalued. She goes on to argue, "It is intellectually useful to be able to insulate yourself" (133), but "it is also intellectually fruitful to turn on your searchlight," to be "in touch" with your emotions and connections to the world, to others, outside of yourself. Furthermore, women "*can* detach themselves—they *are* individuals." What is of crucial importance, however, is to use both of these qualities. Because science and politics are "co-operative, more democratic" (136), women are poised at an important moment in history to exercise greater freedom and influence on the world because, according to Harrison:

> the present day is [. . .] marked by an emergence, unparalleled in history, of the *racial* conscience. This shows itself in politics. The only human will to which we bow nowadays is the collective will of the people of which we are ourselves a part. It shows itself in religion, which of course embodies and reflects social fact. The only god we believe in now is immanent, not imminent; few people are satisfied now with the conception of God as King or even Emperor, as Lawgiver, or as External Creator—all conceptions that have served their turn as the expression of primitive states of society. (136)

Harrison proclaims, "Let man and woman both learn to know, to think dispassionately, to recreate imaginatively, to feel impersonal emotion, and then let them look and act together," and she insists that "the holy hunger after knowledge [. . .] is but the latest, rarest utterance of the Will to Live" (41). Whether a people make their religion based on "a woman, a mother with a subordinate child, a son or lover as attribute of womanhood" or make their god "a man, or, the better to strengthen his manhood and emphasize the exclusion of woman—three men," she advocates that we remember instead "a sect in antiquity, small, despised, persecuted, who made their god in the image of neither man nor female, but a thing bisexed, immaculate, winged, and—this is the interesting thing for us—looking out on the world *four-eyed*" (142). This is an Orphic Hymn Harrison posits as an ideal for which to strive, a social collective where "we would worship knowledge" (142) chanting together "men and women—to-day and to-morrow" (142).

Cross-reading Harrison with Woolf illustrates both the vertical axis of mentoring that brought them together initially as well as the transpersonal, lateral axis of their friendship and shared political ideology. The two essays converse intimately and successfully not only as "feminist friends" who share both strategies and thematics, but also because Woolf's essay can be read as her own attempt "to think back through our mothers" (AROO 75); to write down the voices of unknown women, "all these infinitely obscure lives [that] remain to be recorded" (88); and to outline the historical progression of women writers, like Jane Harrison, to whom she is indebted. A Room of One's Own acts as a corrective to the neglect of Harrison's legacy and the importance of women friends and women mentors for women students. But women writers also need more time, according to Woolf, before their work will bear results, and she asks for at least "another hundred years [. . .] give her a room of her own and five hundred a year, let her speak her mind and leave out half that she now puts in, and she will write a better book one of these days" (93). In A Room of One's Own, Woolf reanimates the ghosts and goddesses of Harrison's life and work. She has taken Harrison's "home of her own," an example of servitude and oppression and that pain of her academic journey as a woman, and transformed it into an image of intellectual freedom, confidence, and defiance, a plot of transformation, as she proclaims: "Lock up your libraries if you like, but there is no gate, no lock, no bolt that you can set upon the freedom of my mind" (75), which will continue to interact transpersonally between women friends and their work across time.

CHAPTER 4

Reading Transpersonally II— Women Building Peace

Three Guineas *and "Epilogue on the War: Peace with Patriotism"*

BOTH JANE HARRISON and Virginia Woolf sought alternatives to the patriarchal language of the state and to the imperialism and militarism they saw as responsible for war, Woolf by way of her fiction and essays, and Harrison by her revisions and reinterpretations of the Olympian gods as well as by her essays, lectures, and speeches as an international scholar and public intellectual.

By cross-reading Virginia Woolf's pacifist manifesto, *Three Guineas,* with Jane Harrison's response to World War I, "Epilogue on the War: Peace with Patriotism," reprinted in her collection of essays *Alpha and Omega* (1915), we not only recover Harrison's important work on peace, but see Woolf revising and extending a politics of peace she recognized in Harrison in a transpersonal relationship, a lateral connection, Chloe and Olivia's "shared laboratory of ideas." Each essay investigates the causes of violence and war, and grapples with issues such as disparities in rights, institutions, and the distribution of wealth, constituting what the discipline of Peace and Conflict Resolution Studies today would term *positive peace.* Reading their essays transpersonally, this chapter locates Woolf's and Harrison's pacifism as part of the women's international peace movement, identifies it as a specifically feminist undertaking, and also sees their contributions as formative in helping to establish an intellectual climate in which the discipline of Peace Studies and peace research have prospered today.

Although we are often well versed in definitions of war, and certainly *Three Guineas* has been read as Woolf's exploration of the root causes of war (see M. Hussey, J. Marcus, B. Silver, et al.), we, somewhat irrationally, it may be argued, are less prepared or comfortable with contending with conceptions of peace. Though present in the discourse as early as Kant, if not in the political theories of the late medieval proto-feminist, Christine de Pizan, Peace Studies, as an academic discipline and area of scholarly research, did not become formalized as part of college curricula in the West until 1948. This, despite the presence and significant advancements made on behalf of peace by Peace churches and by organizations such as Millicent Fawcett's National Union of Women Suffrage Societies (NUWSS), which, unlike the more militant Women's Suffrage and Political Union (WSPU) led by the Pankhursts, refused to support the war, and by the Women's League for International Peace and Freedom (WILPF) led by pacifists, such as Jane Addams, Lillian Wald, and Auletta Jacobs, among others, who pressured neutral countries to offer continuous mediation during the war. Begun on the initiative of the Women's Peace Party at the Hague in April 1915, by 1919, the coalition that would become the WILPF made their committee permanent, and, in concert with Woolf's friend, the economist, Maynard Keynes, denounced the final terms of the peace treaty ending World War I as a vengeful peace that would lead to yet another war. Harrison and Woolf's two essays each investigate definitions of peace and peace-related concepts. Both explore the sources of war, examine the function and excessive use and misuse of the concept of "patriotism," and seek out radical social alternatives founded on feminist principles of cooperation, resistance, and communal outsidership.

In a transpersonal sharing, both texts help to create a vocabulary and a language for discussing peace, which in turn lays an early foundation for the theories and methodologies of global pacifism, peace studies, and peace research. The terms negative and positive peace, for example, were created in an effort to establish normative aims for pedagogical and research methodologies in the discipline of Peace Studies, and are attributed to Johan Galtung and John Burton, who founded the International Peace Research Institute in Oslo in 1959. Essentially, negative peace refers to the absence of direct violence, and places an emphasis on approaches for conflict management, such as peace-keeping, whereas, peace-building is an example of positive peace. By the mid-1990s, Peace Studies curricula in the West had shifted "from research and teaching about negative peace, the cessation of violence, to positive peace, the conditions that eliminate the causes of violence" (Harris, Fisk, and Rank). It is to this conception of peace as positive, with an emphasis on analyses of the conditions necessary for peace, such as conflict transformation and conflict resolution via such mechanisms as peace-building, peace-making, mediation, and conflict resolution, that Harrison's and Woolf's essays attend.

In writing "Epilogue on the War: Peace with Patriotism" and *Three Guineas,* Jane Harrison and Virginia Woolf wanted to change the world. Together, their essays comprise and construct the possibility of a counternarrative to the myth of war experience given new life with the outbreak of World War I, as they theorize and envision a world we've yet to create. Just as Harrison revised Greek mythology, Woolf used the plot of the Greek tragedy *Antigone* to posit a different world view, one that explores the causes of war, dismantles patriarchy, and revises culture. Harrison's radical pacifism in "Epilogue on the War" is a position heralded and extended by Woolf in *Three Guineas,* documenting the rise of fascism in 1938 and calling for a social re-creation, a Harrisonian "unity out of multiplicity" and "world citizen," and is a proclamation that echoes with Woolf's own defiant, and transpersonal, plea for peace that "as a woman I have no country. As a woman I want no country. As a woman my country is the whole world" (TG 129). In these two texts, both Harrison and Woolf undermine the politics of nations, of states, and raise important challenges to the ways in which gender, education, religion, culture, and law interact with and negotiate the borders drawn by patriarchal constructs that deny women a voice. Ultimately, "Epilogue on the War" and *Three Guineas* translate their deeper feminisms into radical pacifist positions, and illustrate a shared ideology about the nature of violence and the individual in relation to the state, as they mutually insist on positive peace, peace-making, and peace-building themes.

"Rage, Sheer Red-Hot Rage": Rhetorical Violence and Searching for the Root Causes of War

"Epilogue on the War" opens with Jane Harrison's shock and disbelief that "all these dons are enlisting." She immediately experiences a violent personal reaction when "Rage, sheer red-hot rage, choked me and held me speechless" (EOW 221). She could not believe that her colleagues, the group of male geniuses with whom she had worked and collaborated, "these men, whose passion it was to know the truth and teach it [. . .] these men, to me the pick of their country's manhood" would support the war, when they had insisted only moments earlier that they had "despise[d] the war"! (221). She notably begins her essay with a Greek epitaph, a line from Euripides' *Alcestis* (which Euripides borrows from Aeschylus), and translates as "many are the shapes of divine beings" to express the changing tides, intellectual aspirations, and hypocritical politics of her esteemed friends. Their decision to fight rocked the foundations of Harrison's values and ideals as an educator and scholar, as she pleaded with them to let us grieve together, but let us not be stupid together, too, especially "when the lust of conquest was maddening half Europe, when every human value hung in the balance, and all that made life worth the living was threatened" (221). In opposition to her colleagues, she adopted a pacifist stance that fantasized about an army of martyrs to the cause of peace rather than an army of soldiers perpetuating war, when she claimed, "In the depths of my fanatical heart I dream of a day when our army will go out, not to war, but, if need be, to martyrdom, and when that army will consist of every man and woman in England" (222). War, according to Harrison, crushed values and diminished and destroyed learning. Her essay is a defiant clarification of her stance as a public intellectual: "It is because, with every fibre of body and mind, I stand for Peace that I want to try and understand this ancient animosity" (223), as she begins her exploration of the conditions which brought about war.

As Harrison tries to disentangle how it came about that "the don has turned soldier, and proudly, if a little shamefacedly, parades the uniform which, ten years ago, would have been to him *anathema,*" Woolf comments on the glorification of war displayed in the uniforms, ribbons, and bows of patriarchy's heads of state, and asks, "What connection is there between the sartorial splendours of the educated man" and the corpses found strewn about a battlefield or landscape devastated by war's destructive force?" She explores the use of military dress "to impress the beholder with the majesty of military office, partly in order through their vanity to induce young men to become soldiers" (TG 26–27), connecting the memorialization and celebration of war to its perpetuation. She discourages pageantry and display and points to the potential dangers in valorizing war and the legacy of war through dress and rituals that honor the destruction of life.

Woolf goes on to unpack and grapple with the motivations behind women's support of war in the public sphere on behalf of a nation that so vigorously curtailed their freedom in the private sector. Harrison also amplifies her discussion from matters "parochial," the inexplicable advocacy of the dons of war, to "questions international" and "on those momentous issues of War and Peace on which our whole being is now exclusively focused" (EOW 223). Woolf expresses her incredulity at women's involvement in the ready, aim, fire formulary to the Great War, two decades earlier, which she carefully investigates in 1938 while trying to answer her male correspondent's provocative question: "How do we prevent war?" When she confronts one of the more controversial aspects of her argument, exposing women's complicity in patriarchy and thereby their "consent" to fascism, she does so by sending us back and forth between endnotes, text, and her notebook archive, which become creatively and politically significant as Woolf's rhetorical structure again challenges so many of our readerly assumptions about what a conventional argument looks like. *Three Guineas,* stylistically, vibrates and chants its argument into existence, much like the circular structure of a Harrisonian Greek chant. In connecting the many strands of her *thiasos,* attendant but critical sub-points, if you will, to the more central point of "how do we prevent war," she begins with a discussion of women's education, their position and function in the home, and the use of their bodies in sex and marriage. "It was with a view to marriage that her body was educated; a maid was provided for her; that the streets were shut to her; that the fields were shut to her; that solitude was denied her—all this was enforced upon her in order that she might preserve her body intact for her husband" (TG 48). Woolf's notations in her scrapbooks reference this section with a clipping "Marriage service. Savages in tail coats." with Woolf's typed note, about the institution of marriage, in general, "The woman has no worldly goods must therefore give her body [. . .]. A solemn moment, really marriage" (Silver 269). She extends the discussion in the endnote in terms of "the duplicity of delicacy" (TG 186) and marriage as the only profession open to women, which, if we delve further into Woolf's scrapbooks, reveal her notations on "The Professions:/ Lady Lovelace the Siren. The bird in the cage" (Silver 255). Returning to the text, Woolf connects the private hierarchy of patriarchy in the home with the public needs of the state. She quotes Lady Lovelace, who wrote that women's efforts are consciously in favor of "'our splendid Empire . . . , the price of which,' she added, 'is mainly paid by women.' And who can doubt her, or that the price was heavy?" (TG 49). While

Woolf sympathizes with the powerlessness of women's position in the home, she labels the dependency demonic when she links its relationship to the state. She is gravely concerned with women's unconscious efforts as well, on behalf of war.

> How else can we explain that amazing outburst in August 1914, when the daughters of educated men who had been educated thus rushed into hospitals, some still attended by their maids, drove lorries, worked in fields and munition factories, and used all their immense stores of charm, of sympathy, to persuade young men that to fight was heroic, and that the wounded in battle deserved all her care and all her praise? The reason lies in that same education. So profound was her unconscious loathing for the education of the private house with its cruelty, its poverty, its hypocrisy, its immorality, its inanity that she would undertake any task however menial, exercise any fascination however fatal that enabled her to escape. Thus consciously she desired "our splendid Empire"; unconsciously she desired our splendid war. (58)

Like Harrison more than a decade earlier, who tried to understand the dons' rush to war, Woolf reflects on these earlier motivations in an attempt to understand similar trends in her own times. *Three Guineas* is a call to cast off the shackles of dependency, reclaim our sexuality, and start anew. In her analysis of the dialectical relationship between women and fascism, in particular the fascism of Mussolini, Hitler, and Franco, "Female Sexuality in Fascist Ideology," Maria-Antonietta Macciocchi cautions against keeping silent about women's roles in the political, social, and economic realities of tyranny. By keeping silent, dismissing, exonerating, or absolving, Macciocchi writes that we create "another way of sending women into a vacuum, or, on the contrary, of creating a theology of women (which in any case runs into the same historical void)." "This vacuum is all the more serious in that, on the reverse side, fascism lay solidly like a huge disturbing carcass, on the politico-intellectual landscape" (67), wherein women become instruments and enactors of a script Woolf identifies as both patriarchal and fascist. In *Three Guineas*, Woolf aligns the tenets of patriarchy, for example, with a Brechtian sense of fascism, which compared the relationship to "that between a protector, or pimp, and his whores [. . . whereby] the state acts as procurer and women become the prostitutes of capital" (Macciocchi 69). As she sends us back and forth among text, notes, and archive, Woolf connects the dots of the oppression of women's sexuality in the home with her larger concern, women as whores for the state. Woolf writes of the pimp/whore dynamic in the private home in terms of marriage, the dependent relationship between husband and wife, but the coinage also works seamlessly in the familial structure of an incestuous household as well, a dynamic with which Woolf was personally familiar.[1]

Interestingly, both *Three Guineas* and "Epilogue on the War," essays on radical pacifism, are marked by a rhetorical violence based on personal experiences of injustice and marginalization. Harrison, in her "rage, sheer red-hot rage," tries to use her reaction as a means for "fruitful analysis." She cannot believe that it is now de rigeur and "possible [. . .] to utter the word *duty* unabashed" and "not even the youngest eyebrow is uplifted to mark the anachronism" (EOW 222). She tries to quell her indignation and violent reaction and reports that "as I went home rage died down, and it is rage, just as it dies down, that 'gives, most furiously, to think,'" for she, as an intellectual, recognizes that "behind our shining armour of righteous indignation lurks a convicted and only half-repentant sinner [. . .] if the charge rankles, we may be almost sure some sharp and bitter grain of truth lurks within it" (222). It is out of this betrayal and angry reaction that she solidifies her pacifist position and exposes a deeper analysis of the conditions necessary to build peace.

Virginia Woolf also possessed a deeply felt understanding of violence and injustice. In "A Sketch of the Past," a section of her memoir *Moments of Being,* she describes how a childhood tussle changes into a beating she took at the hands of her "good" brother, her beloved brother, Thoby:

> As a child then, my days, just as they do now, contained a large proportion of this cotton wool, this non-being. Week after week passed [. . .]. Then, for no reason that I know about, there was a sudden violent shock; something happened so violently that I have remembered it all my life [. . .]. I was fighting with Thoby on the lawn. We were pommelling each other with our fists. Just as I raised my fist to hit him, I felt: why hurt another person? I dropped my hand instantly, and stood there, and let him beat me. I remember the feeling. It was a feeling of hopeless sadness. It was as if I became aware of something terrible; and of my own powerlessness. I slunk off alone, feeling horribly depressed. (71)

The scene resonates with her asking repeatedly, chantlike, throughout *Three Guineas,* "Why fight?" (9). *Three Guineas* is often crafted as

---

1. See DeSalvo.

a rhetorically violent response, written as a mature woman using her pen transpersonally, as weapon, to re-create her personal narrative, her response to the past, present, and the future she strives to re-create. Contrary to the criticism that *Three Guineas* "did not deal with [. . .] women's capacity for martial belligerence" (Lee 670), Woolf rhetorically sympathizes and even participates in militaristic desires as she condemns them as "hollow" and instructs us to be "disinterested" (Pawlowsky 3), neither to "incite [our] brothers to fight, or to dissuade them, but to maintain an attitude of complete indifference" (TG 163). Furthermore, to deny the pervasiveness of Woolf's rhetorical violence not only robs *Three Guineas* of its subversiveness in both the content and style, but also silences Woolf's history—the accidents in her own life of gender, social class, historical moment, cultural context, and familial dysfunction—and by extension the history of all women.

In *Three Guineas,* Woolf is at one and the same time pacifist and militant anti-fascist. She seeks to expose patriarchy's links to fascism, to give primacy to peace, but she also rejects an "enforced pacifism" or an "enforced feminism" (TG 269) and remains unfaltering in her position against force of any kind—what Jane Harrison calls in "Epilogue on the War" *sich imponiren,* imposing one's will onto another human being. Paying tribute to Woolf too narrowly as a parochial pacifist, rather than as advocate for an internationalist pacifism she shared with Jane Harrison, to my mind makes her increasingly easy for critics to dismiss and ironically plays into the hands of the fascist agenda she sought to destroy, when in fact her work is a significant contribution to the women's peace movement, and to a peace vocabulary in general, as well as an incisive exploration of the conditions necessary for building peace.

Transpersonal Sharing: Transforming the Spectacle of War

In addition to the links she made between the public sphere of war and the woman's body in the private sphere of the home and in the marriage bed, Woolf's pacifist project is uniquely tied to the visual evidence of war, the realities of war on the body, rendering it often unrecognizable. The packet of photos of war dead she receives twice a week from the Spanish Republicans fighting Franco's fascist takeover of the government in the midst of the Spanish Civil War in 1936 that she describes but does not display in the text of *Three Guineas* share a tandem, one might argue,

gruesomely transpersonal, relationship with the photographs of the patriarchal figures she does display. The initial mention of photos of war-dead
speaks to Woolf's use of the violent text image to focus our eye and to
make sure we see both the absent image on the page and the photographs
of the patriarchs in the way she wants us to. In contrast to Helen Wussow,
who characterizes Woolf's selection of the patriarchal figures as "whimsi-
cal" (2), I argue that the placement of the photographs in the text as well
as the dialectical tension between the photos and the word pictures on the
page are crucial to Woolf's argument linking patriarchy to fascism and
war. In the original edition, the photographs of heads of state are carefully
laid out intercut with the undisplayed photographs of the children who
are victims of war. Succeeding editions, however, often either displayed
the photographs in a cluster in the center of the text or left them out
entirely.[2] In the initial mention of the photographs of the dead children
she points out the unrecognizability of the bodies as human.

> They are not pleasant photographs to look upon. They are photographs
> of dead bodies for the most part. This morning's collection contains the
> photograph of what might be a man's body, or a woman's; it is so muti-
> lated that it might, on the other hand, be the body of a pig. But those cer-
> tainly are dead children, and that undoubtedly is the section of a house.
> A bomb has torn open the side; there is still a birdcage hanging in what
> was presumably the sitting-room, but the rest of the house looks like
> nothing so much as a bunch of spilikins suspended in mid-air. (TG 14–15)

The ghosts of the dead children continue to haunt the text until they are
ultimately blended at the end with the image of Man. In *Frames of War:
When Is Life Grievable?* Judith Butler, in concert with Woolf, challenges
the nature of recognizability as she explores the effects of war on the
body and the politics and ethics of war photography. She questions how
norms of recognition "operate to produce certain subjects as 'recognizable' persons and to make others decidedly more difficult to recognize."
"The problem," Butler states, "is not merely how to include more people
within existing norms, but to consider how existing norms allocate recognition differentially" (6). In *Three Guineas*, the photograph as transcript
of reality is challenged when the photographs are of dead bodies, because

---

2. See Black for the Shakespeare Head Press (2001) for a detailed account of the differences between the English and American editions of *Three Guineas*. For further insight
into the publication history of *Three Guineas*, see also the introduction and annotations
by Jane Marcus for the edition published by Harcourt in 2006; and Wisor.

the violence inflicted on the photograph's subject is so massive that the subject becomes unrecognizable, unreal, yet its use as a foil for Woolf's argument is effective and crucial, as she uses these word pictures to inform the displayed photos. Woolf's plea that "A common interest unites us; it is one world, one life" (TG 217) is connected to our shared response and responsibility to the undisplayed photos of the victims of war, but also to the recognizability of the male heads of state making the war.

While the figure of Il Duce or the Führer may stand before the photograph of the Spanish dead children, we stand before the photograph of all dead children, whether they are from Spain, Germany, Britain, or any other nation. As Woolf writes, "It suggests that the tyrannies and servilities of the one are the tyrannies and servilities of the other [. . .] we cannot dissociate ourselves from that figure but are ourselves that figure" (TG 217).

Woolf transforms the spectacle of war (the violence, but also the glorification of that violence in the form of finery, medals, ceremonies, processions, and memorials) into the specular (of I see). For the figures she represents in the photographs, unlike the dead bodies, are instantly recognizable or would have been to readers of her time, for each one of them was a public figure, alive during the time of publication and frequently in the press (Staveley 295). In *Regarding the Pain of Others*, Susan Sontag gives a reading of Woolf's discussion of the photographs of the dead children, relying on an edition of *Three Guineas*, which was published without the displayed photographs of the patriarchs Woolf points to as being not only responsible, but recognizable. This oversight makes for a baffling and somewhat simplistic interpretation of Woolf's argument. Says Sontag: "To read in the pictures, as Woolf does, only what confirms a general abhorrence of war [. . .] is to dismiss politics" (9). Without the images of the captionless photos of the male heads of state, Sontag is party to only half of Woolf's argument, as the displayed photos share a specific and complex political and transpersonal critique of the undisplayed photos of the dead children from the Spanish Civil War, which she then connects to education, religion, culture, the professions, and law. Woolf decides not to include a caption on each, other than the generic references in the List of Illustrations to "A General," "Heralds," "A University Procession," "A Judge," and "An Archbishop," transferring power not to the photographic image, but to the reader, who can look at the photographs as if at a lineup of criminals and say, "we know who you are" and not only that we know where you live. Contemporary audiences would have recognized the highly decorated and adorned military hero from the Boer War, founder of the Boy Scouts and Girl Guides, Baden Powell; the former Prime Minister then Chancellor of Cambridge, Stanley Baldwin; the conservative, Gordon Hewart, Lord Chief Justice, author of *The New Despotism* in 1929; and William Cosmo Gordon Lang, the Archbishop of Canterbury, who conspired to bring about the abdication of Edward VIII for marrying Wallis Simpson in 1936. The captionless photos and Woolf's refusal to display the photos of the dead bodies both undermines and serves the credo that "a picture is worth a thousand words" as she denies the viewer and the reader any notion of war as spectacle, something we watch or observe in a photograph of war horror, but from which we feel distant and safe, and points instead to the very real and powerful male heads of state who run the war.

Her position, however, does not refuse or deny women's or the reader's complicity in the war formulary, but instructs us to understand how we become connected to and function in the patriarchal system she is struggling to revise. By not providing captions to the photos she also paradoxically identifies and disidentifies the subject, which both demands we pay attention, as it also suggests an implacable remoteness to the horrors of war, that sense of unrecognizability, which terrifies Woolf. It is a fear and sense of powerlessness she associates with the business of war, and a sensibility she shares with Jane Harrison.

In "Epilogue on the War," Harrison discusses the same disconnection at work in any path to war:

> We do not personally wage war; even the generals sit, not upon their chargers leading the attack, but secluded in their bureaus; even the men lie in their trenches, often unseen by and unseeing those other men they kill. There is horror enough, God knows! But not for us the personal horror of doing your own killing. Everything—war, commerce, politics—is nowadays huge, abstracted, remote. (256)

In her research and scholarship, Harrison was suspicious of "abstraction," especially the ways in which intellectual abstraction can dangerously lead us away from reality. Sontag, in this respect, would agree, as she warns of becoming victims to "fancy rhetoric" that "seems to be something of a French specialty" that views the world we live in as a 'society of spectacle'" (109), citing Guy Debord and Jean Baudrillard, among others. Sontag attributes this discourse specifically to modernity and "the modern," where a sense of reality is lost, that situations have to be transformed into

Figure 8. Virginia Woolf, center, with Lytton Strachey, left, and the pacifist Goldsworthy Lowes "Goldie" Dickinson, ca.1923, the same year she visited Harrison in Paris. This photo was taken at Ottoline Morrell's Garsington estate. From Virginia Woolf's Monk's House Album 4.

spectacles in order to be real. Speaking from her own experiences as a
witness to war, covering the Bosnian war in Sarajevo, Sontag would have
found support, transpersonally, in the work of both Woolf and Harrison,
who each witnessed the devastation of war first hand—Harrison in the
attack on Scarborough in 1914 and Woolf in the bombing of her London
home during "The Blitz" in 1940. Sontag writes:

> To speak of reality becoming a spectacle is a breathtaking provincialism.
> It universalizes the viewing habits of a small, educated population living
> in the rich part of the world, where news has been converted into enter-
> tainment [. . .] (110)

Woolf and Harrison write in concert with her suspicions, her dread of
the abdication of reality. In addition to her skepticism surrounding an
academic climate devoted to intellectual abstraction, Harrison's work
on ritual focused on the *dromenon,* the "thing done" on a daily basis,
and privileged the very real rhythms and practices of daily culture. She
applied these thematics to her pacifism, just as Woolf, with *Three Guineas,* exposed and challenged masculinist fantasies of war.

Building (Transpersonal) Peace

The networking, webbing, the collaborative, collective "talking" of
Woolf's style in *Three Guineas,* which was originally conceived as an
innovative new genre, a novel-essay, connected to what became her novel
The Years, sends the reader back and forth between text and endnotes
and Woolf's scrapbooks and reading notes, in an intertextual, lateral sharing that replicates the ideology of Harrison's position of co-creation and
co-operation. Cross-reading Harrison's essay with Woolf's also speaks to
a future pedagogy and praxis of "positive" peace as formulating analyses
for the conditions to create peace, which have become standard aspects in
the formal discipline of Peace Studies. Like Woolf, Harrison asks:

> And what have we to substitute for competition? Only co-operation. Co-
> operation is a dull, tarnished word, tarred with the brush of utilitarian
> economics. But is it really a cold, dull thing to work together to know, to
> work together to discover, to work together to try and make the world a
> better place for all of us? How savage we are if we can only herd together,
> wolf-like, to fight! (EOW 257)

Both Woolf and Harrison link the idea of war to the dangers of competition, jealousy, and the fostering of intolerance that the university system represents, encourages, and funds. Like Woolf, Harrison also explores the qualities and instincts, psychological, biological, and social, that might help to reveal the sources of violence and war, making a connection between man's "instincts" and the system of education that produces him. Harrison writes:

> And yet our whole education, our public school system, is based on two things: *sich imponiren* of the group—dare at your peril to be different, to have personal distinction—and neck-to-neck competition in work and in games. We teach our children to work, not that they may do their best for sheer love of the thing done, but that they may do better than somebody else. Surely always an ugly thing, for someone else is hurt and diminished. If children are so reared, can we wonder that grown men are at war? (257)

Sich imponiren translates from the German as "to impose oneself." Woolf also critiques the British education system at length and its connection to patriarchy and, by extension, fascism, as she asks "What, then, is this 'university education' of which Mary Kingsley's sisterhood have heard so much and to which they have contributed so painfully?" (TG 31). All men in power, Woolf states, have had a university education. Women, and the state, have paid into that fund. Woolf chronicles "the fact of the immense sum of money that has been spent upon education in the past 500 years" (31) an education that works diligently and relentlessly to "sink the private brother [. . .] and inflate in its stead a monstrous male" (125).

In "Epilogue on the War," Harrison also examines the ways we validate and glorify war. She suggests that the soldier is finally vindicated when his job, the business of war, at last comes about. Invoking the rhythmic, dumb chant of a war song meant to encourage the lemming-like march of soldiers to their deaths, she writes:

> When Tommy goes off to the front, he sings, I am told [. . .] We're here because we're here, because we're here, because we're here." And a very good marching song it no doubt is, for Tommy's business is not psychological analysis. When the officer starts on the same errand, he has the immense personal joy—a joy, perhaps, beyond all others—of feeling that at last his profession, his particular job in life, has not only become

suddenly real, but *the* reality of the moment—*the* thing that counts.
Consciously or unconsciously, that thought must set his heart aflame.
(EOW 227)

Woolf, too, suggests that because the soldier is trained by profession not
to think, because if he does, he will be killed, then we must do the thinking for him. It is an idea Woolf returns to in her essay "Thoughts on Peace
in an Air Raid," when she writes, "so let us think for him. Let us try
to drag up into consciousness the subconscious Hiterlism that holds us
down. It is the desire for aggression; the desire to dominate and enslave"
(245). In this later essay, she continues to ask her audiences to see the
illogical nature of their question and response: "Who is Hitler? What is
he? Aggressiveness, tyranny, the insane love of power made manifest, they
reply. Destroy that, and you will be free" (245). Harrison also speaks of
the fallacious, insane reasoning behind the idea that war can bring about
peace and freedom and be a benefit to civilization:

> War is ennobling, we are told, so long as the rules of civilized war are
> observed—so long as we "play the game." Civilized war! No such thing
> exists. War may be necessary—it is always barbarous. It is no real settle-
> ment of any difficulty—no real adaptation of national need to national
> environment. (EOW 257)

Both Harrison and Woolf add, satirically, disclaimers in the beginnings
of their essays that they may indeed not be qualified to speak on matters
of foreign policy, given the fact that they are women and excluded from
the education and political power so generously gifted to their male counterparts. However, they note, they each feel qualified to speak, as human
beings, on human nature. As Harrison writes, "the only way to allay
this irritation is to track out the cause and try to find the human need
that called for the reaction" (EOW 238), and if we are able to "show
the meaning and function of patriotism, its wrongness and its rightness.
When we are truly patriotic, war will, I believe, end" (225). Woolf also
explores definitions of "patriotism" and poses the question,"But the educated man's sister—what does patriotism mean to her? Has she the same
reasons for being proud of England, for loving England, for defending
England?" (TG 12). She is preoccupied with conventional definitions
of patriotism, and their connection to motivations for going to war. In
"Thoughts on Peace in an Air Raid," Woolf asks what interior process
spurs on the air force pilot up in the sky? "[H]e is driven by voices in himself—ancient instincts, instincts fostered and cherished by education and

tradition" (246). She questions, "Is he to be blamed for those instincts? Could we switch off the maternal instinct at the command of a table full of politicians?" Woolf then fantasizes about a world in which women are asked to turn off their maternal instincts:

> [B]ut if it were necessary for the sake of humanity, for the peace of the world, that child-bearing should be restricted, the maternal instinct subdued, women would attempt it. Men would help them. They would honour them for their refusal to bear children. They would give them other openings for their creative power. That too must make part of our fight for freedom. We must help the young Englishmen to root out from themselves the love of medals and decorations. We must create more honourable activities for those who try to conquer in themselves their fighting instinct, their subconscious Hitlerism. We must compensate the man for the loss of his gun. (247)

In order to compensate man for the loss of his weaponry, Woolf turns to our basic human instinct to create, an idea she encounters as she listens to the planes overhead in the midst of an air raid. "The emotion of fear and of hate is [. . .] sterile, unfertile. Directly that fear passes, the mind reaches out and instinctively revives itself by trying to create. Since the room is dark it can create only from memory" (247). In order to help men turn away from acting on their militaristic desires, "we must give him access to the creative feelings. We must make happiness. We must free him from the machine. We must bring him out of his prison into the open air. But what is the use of freeing the young Englishman if the young German and the young Italian remain slaves?" (247–48). Woolf's revision of the world calling for a radical and international pacifism in *Three Guineas* was both unwelcome and unsettling to a country galvanized by national pride in the First World War and a country, she cautioned, whose patriarchal values embodied the same brand of fascism it claimed to be opposing, en route to a second one. From the vantage point of gender, tyranny made its homeland in England and English culture, making boundaries and conceptions of nation-states meaningless to those they oppressed and hostile to conditions necessary for building peace.

To "Think Peace into Existence": Transpersonal Global Pacifisms

Woolf's pacifism took the form of her pen, and her pacifist essays

became her "fight with the mind" (TOP 244) to "think peace into existence" (TOP 243) while the planes dropped bombs overhead. Trespass-
ing, transcending, extending, and dissolving boundaries were mutual,
shared projects of Harrison and Woolf, who, as feminist outsiders, challenged their oppression with their work and exposed the dangers and
narrowness of patriarchy's nationalistic and militaristic agendas. Like
Woolf, Harrison discusses the importance of extending pacifism across
all borders as she bemoans the loss of the privileging of internationalism, the loss of "the old ideals of the "citizen of the world" (EOW 238).
Herd mentality and the projection of the state's needs upon the individual
feed the fuel and psychology of war. War mentality instructs that "before
all things be local, parochial, patriotic—i.e., dwell on your differences,
and be prepared to fight for them; cultivate the small, combative herd-
emotions, and for your religion [someone outside of yourself] will provide it for you. Your god must be the projection of the state, [. . .] and
as combative." This god, according to Harrison,

> demands, he necessitates, immediate unquestioning faith, faith so unques-
> tioning that it is a mainspring of action, faith wholly dogmatic and non-
> intellectual, whose only function is to pull the trigger. Such faith is in its
> final analysis a local affirmation of self-confidence, "la croyance c'est la
> patrie." (238)

The War Spirit "above all, craves for action, and only for such thinking
as is immediately translatable into action" (241). It is in fact anti-thinking
and can only lead to and foster militarism. Harrison adduces Dostoevsky
as an example of a great writer who uncharacteristically held reactionary views tied to the Russian state that abused him. "Dostoevsky stands
for patriotism, and reactionaries are all ardent patriots. Their enthusi-
asm is national rather than international" (242). "[W]e have been perhaps not wholly surprised to find that the man [Dostoevsky] who created
these amazing figures was himself not only epileptic and dissolute, but
also an arch-egotist to the verge of madness—[. . .]he appears in his
letters, supremely a patriot in the narrowest sense. He really hated the
international ideal," and yet his own country in a mock execution had
"Dostoevsky [stand] up in his shirt against the prison-wall to be shot"
(244). He was then forced to live abroad where, as Harrison writes, "his
utter inability to see any good in foreign lands would be childish if it
were not the source of such poignant misery" (244). Despite his treat-
ment, Dostoevsky, the reactionary, "anti-intellectualist, Collectivist of the

small group, the nation, a patriot through and through," still loved Russia; therefore, Harrison instructs us that we have to learn from all these reactionaries and nationalists. Everyone feels love of country. Germany's love of country is now "alas! the handmaid of war" (245). For Harrison and her intellectual colleagues and "us older liberals," patriotism "was not an inspiring word. It spelled narrowness—limitations. We aspired to be citizens of the world" (242). But through Dostoevsky's example, she has learned that to be patriotic, to love one's country is not harmful; it is the idea of *sich imponiren,* to impose oneself, that "sins worst against patriotism" (245). Dostoevsky, in other words, was an equal opportunity hater of "others," but he did not *sich imponiren* as he "was Russia for the Russian [. . .]. He never tried to impose Russianism as a gospel or a panacea, and, [. . .] he never even tried to infuse the Russian spirit as the salt of the earth" (246). According to Harrison,

> *Sich imponiren* is the very spirit of war; true patriotism, national differentiation, of peace. [. . .] War, which seems to be nurtured by patriotism— which seems the uttermost expression of it, turns at last on patriotism and slays it. The patriot loves his country because it is different from others, because of its local colour, flavour, smell, because of its living personality. But let that country "impose itself," make other countries obey its laws, accept its customs, adopt its very language, and all these distinctions, lovely and beloved, lapse into a grey uniformity. (246)

In "Thoughts on Peace in an Air Raid," Woolf also yearns for a celebration of diversity, as she envisions a scenario that if the Englishman shoots down the German plane, the two pilots will become friends as men, not soldiers, and the Englishwoman will make him tea. That, according to Woolf, "would seem to show that if you can free the man from the machine, the seed does not fall upon altogether stony ground. The seed may be fertile" ("Thoughts on Peace in an Air Raid" 248), for "Unless we can think peace into existence we—not this one body in this one bed but millions of bodies yet to be born—will lie in the same darkness and hear the same death rattle overhead" (243).

Three Guineas yearns for a re-visioning of society along pacifistic communal lines invoked earlier by Harrison in "Epilogue on the War: Peace with Patriotism," when Woolf replies to her correspondents that "we can best help you to prevent war not by repeating your words and following your methods but by finding new words and new methods. We can best help you to prevent war not by joining your society but by

remaining outside your society but in cooperation with its aim. That aim
is the same for us both" (TG 170). She pleads with us in concert with
Harrison to listen "to the voices of the poets, answering each other, assuring us of a unity that rubs out divisions as if they were chalk marks only;
to discuss with you the capacity of the human spirit to overflow boundaries and make unity out of multiplicity" (169). And it is in this spirit of
co-operation and creativity that Harrison writes, "we must live and let
live, tolerating—nay, fostering—in the life of individuals and of nations
an infinite parti-coloured diversity, and so at last win Peace with Patriotism" (EOW 259). Both essays speak to future agendas in Peace Studies
today, which view peace as an interdisciplinary and international effort
to develop a special set of concepts, techniques, and data to better understand and diffuse conflict. The First World War was a turning point in
Western attitudes towards war, and both Harrison and Woolf can be seen
as an important and prescient part of the processes and discourses that
led to the creation of the discipline. In terms of academic contexts today,
Peace Studies has become a complex and nuanced area of inquiry based
on peace research and peace as a pedagogical activity. The stated objectives of the discipline, that "peace is a natural/social condition whereas
war is not; that war is considered a sin, a perception held by a variety
of religious traditions worldwide; that peace is a prime force in human
behavior; and finally that there is not one conception of peace, but many"
(Dietrich et al.) are positions of global pacifism articulated and outlined
by Harrison and Woolf in "Epilogue on the War" and *Three Guineas,* as
transpersonal witnesses to their era yearning for change.

CHAPTER 5

To Russia with Love

Literature, Language, and a Shared Ideology of the Political Left[1]

IN TERMS OF Russian language, Russian literature, and leftist politics, Virginia Woolf and Jane Harrison's worlds intersected transpersonally in two ways—with Harrison's publication in 1915 of "Russia and the Russian Verb: A Contribution to the Psychology of the Russian People," which she expanded into *Aspects, Aorists, and the Classical Tripos* in 1919, a copy of which Virginia Woolf owned, and, in 1924, with the Woolfs' Hogarth Press publication of Harrison's translation of *The Life of the Archpriest Avvakum, by Himself*. Both *Aspects* and *Avvakum*, one of the earliest examples of Russian autobiography, complicate our understanding of Harrison and Woolf's engagement with Russian literature and language, as well as, our understanding of the British vogue, at the time, for "all things Russian."

---

1. A version of this chapter appeared as "The Writer, the Prince and the Scholar: Virginia Woolf, D. S. Mirsky, and Jane Harrison's Translation from the Russian of *The Life of the Archpriest Avvakum, by Himself*—A Revaluation of the Radical Politics of the Hogarth Press." *Leonard and Virginia Woolf, The Hogarth Press and the Networks of Modernism*, ed. Helen Southworth. Edinburgh: Edinburgh University Press, 2010.

In addition to being linked by these two publications, however, they each were involved in helping to support Russian refugees and in cultivating networks of Russian literary émigrés, connecting them politically to left-wing figures, policies, and "all the new thinking" coming out of Paris at the time, where Jane Harrison was living, and where Virginia Woolf visited her in 1923. It had also become a point of personal gall and political embarrassment to left-leaning British pacifists such as Woolf and Harrison that Britain was allied with Russia's oppressive Tsarist regime in the early years of World War I. The 1917 Bolshevik Revolution represented a promise of reform and positive change to Harrison and Woolf, and translating Russian became a way in, not only potentially to a different literature and literary method, but also to what they each perceived initially as an alternative to patriarchy and oppression.

Shared Connections:
Cultivating Russian Literary and Political Networks

For Virginia and Leonard Woolf, whose newly minted Hogarth Press began publishing translations of Russian works in 1917, the Bolshevik Revolution meant freedom and a welcome release from the tyranny of Tsarist Russia. Leonard Woolf wrote in his autobiography of 1911–1918, *Beginning Again,* that "the outbreak of the Russian Revolution of 1917 produced the same feeling of liberation and exhilaration" as he imagined the French Revolution of 1789 produced in young revolutionaries in the early stages of the war. He noted that, "In the long, grim history of despotisms the Tsarist regime of the 19th century must take a high place for savage, corrupt, and incompetent government" (208–9). In the summer of 1917, Leonard organized a convention "*to hail* the Russian Revolution and to Organise the British Democracy *to follow Russia,*" an event he described as "one of the most enthusiastic and emotional that I have ever attended" (211; emphasis in original). With Oliver Strachey, and with Virginia Woolf's support, he helped to found the left-wing 1917 Club and had their first meeting on 19 December. Virginia opened her 1918 diary with an entry on 4 January of "special events" and "three facts of different importance," (D 1: 99), with the establishment of the 1917 Club among them, along with "talk of peace," and the breaking of her eyeglasses. Virginia used the 1917 Club as an outlet and space to write letters and meet with "a knot of very youthful revolutionaries" (D 1: 99), as well as left-wing politicians, intellectuals, and artists, who were

both members of the Club or passing through. Although Rebecca Beasley argues that "it would be difficult to claim a coherent shared project" in the establishment of the 1917 Club, she admits "in the last years
of the war, the left-wing literary groupings of pre-war Britain were pro-
pelled, by their opposition to the government, to the war, and by their
support for the Russian Revolution, into something like an intelligentsia"
(28). In my view, these were transpersonal networks of support fueled,
informed, and promoted by Virginia and Leonard's political values, as
well as Jane Harrison's, and the 1917 Club was an example of this shared
political vision. Virginia Woolf, although often expressing exasperation
with the younger generation of "Bunnies" or "cropheads" she met there,
deemed the Club "a success" initially, and both she and Leonard stayed
connected to it for over a decade.

Harrison was also energized by the 1917 Revolution, and sought
to cultivate and expand her associations with Russian artists and intellectuals living in exile in Paris and London, and their respective circles
often overlapped. In her essay "Bears in Bloomsbury: Jane Ellen Harrison
and Russia," Marilyn Schwinn-Smith notes Harrison's role "in facilitat-
ing a connection" between Bloomsbury and Russian émigrés (119), and
G. S. Smith sees her role as significant amidst "like-minded intellectuals"
(D. S. Mirsky 98) in helping to shape British literary attitudes towards
Russia even before World War I. But, by 1914, bewildered and deeply
wounded by her intellectual colleagues rallying cry to war (see Chapter
5), Harrison began living in Paris with her former student and companion, the poet and novelist Hope Mirrlees, in the Hôtel de L'Élysée at 3
Rue de Beaune, and by October, both had enrolled in a Russian language
class around the corner from their apartment at the École des Langues
Orientales.

Harrison returned briefly to teach Russian at Newnham College
shortly before she retired in 1922. Although Smith asserts without evidence to support it that Harrison could not be said to have "mastered"
Russian (D. S. Mirsky 97), by all accounts at Newnham, her method of
teaching the language was effective. As early as 1915, Harrison's instruc-
tion enabled Professor Elsie Butler to join the Scottish Women's Hospital
Unit in Russia, and in two weeks she was able to read Turgenev with
Harrison's help. Butler recounts, "it was as if she held the key not merely
to the language she was expounding to me but to all languages—to language itself—a pattern in the chaos; the soil became transparent and one
found oneself looking straight down to the roots. Metaphysically and literally Jane made me dig for those roots" (Stewart 173). Harrison applied

similar "direct" methods in teaching Greek (see Chapter 1) to the lessons she gave in Russian. Another student, Jessie Stewart, wrote, "In Russian, by a process of agglutination, heaped-up prefixes and suffixes almost obliterate it, but it is there—a hard core. With innumerable illustrations from other languages, [Harrison] drove home the basic significance of each—her method was grammatically formal and extraordinarily educative, evolved out of her intellectual curiosity to get behind phenomena to the cause" (173). Butler went on to become an expert in German language and literature, holding two prestigious Chairs in German Studies at Cambridge University, but credited Harrison with her knowledge of Russian, and the time she spent in Russia as a personal high point in her life.

In 1922, Harrison officially retired from Cambridge with much bitterness that her Ritualist colleagues were not appointed to positions she felt they deserved and because the university continued to deny women degrees, a refusal, which, in turn, affected the eligibility of women to continue to study at the British School in Athens, despite Harrison's repeated attempts to have the wording revised to include, promote, and encourage the inclusion of women. She was also outraged by the attack at Newnham by male students that followed their negative vote (Briggs *Reading* 89). Her departure in effect marked the end of her research into Greek ritual, as she chose to spend the last years of her life devoted to the study of Russian literature and language and in cultivating her Russian contacts. During the spring and summer of 1924, she translated *Avvakum* for Woolf's press with Mirrlees and with the help of Russian literary critic, D. S. Mirsky, who wrote the Preface, as well as with the aid of Russian poet and folklorist Alexei Remizov. During this time, she also translated a book of 25 folktales, again with Mirrlees as co-translator and with the help of Remizov, called *The Book of the Bear*, published by Nonesuch in 1926.

Similar to the 1917 Club, Harrison and Mirrlees's various residences in Paris between 1914 and 1926 became significant meeting places for the Russian literary scene and for leading left-wing intellectuals, authors, artists, and philosophers. Virginia Woolf was traveling alone in Paris before being joined by Leonard in the spring of 1923, when together they visited Harrison and Mirrlees in their flat, as she wrote to tell her sister Vanessa on 28 April: "I had a very amusing time in Paris, and saw a good deal of Hope and Jane and met various oddities," one of whom, Maria Blanchard, a Spanish painter, had paid a compliment to Vanessa's artwork. She continues, "there were also some friends of Clive's friends—and a lot of chatter" (L 3: 32) she is eager to relay to her sister when she has more time. In addition to the Woolfs and many members of both "old" and "new" Bloomsbury who were also associated with the 1917 Club, Harrison and Mirrlees's circle included Prince Mirsky, Remizov and his wife Serafima Pavlovna Dovgello, the Russian philospher Lev Shestov, and other notable members such as David Garnett, Gilbert Murray, Logan Pearsall Smith, Charles de Bos, Paul Valéry, Jacques Rivière, Jean Schlumberger, and the Russian poet Marina Tsvetaeva (Smith, "Prince D. S. Mirsky" 234). They also knew Gertrude Stein and Alice B. Toklas, having met them during the war, while Stein and Toklas were staying at Mirrlees's mother's house at Hope's invitation. Stein wrote in *The Auto-biography of Alice B. Toklas* of not being enamored of Jane Harrison, in another example of Stein's ego clashing with another intellectual who perhaps enjoyed more public adulation and respect for her work than had Stein at that time. After the war, Mirrlees wrote her highly experimental poem *Paris* (1919) while living with Harrison. It was a poem which Virginia Woolf handset and published at Hogarth in 1920. Hope's reputation as a poet also connected Harrison and Woolf during this period to the avant-garde poetry scenes in both Paris and London.

Harrison and Mirrlees's contacts, however, were largely enriched and extended by Harrison's international reputation as a scholar and public intellectual and by her invitation to the Pontigny Décades in 1923 and 1924. The Décades were dialogues comprised of three sessions of ten days each, a yearly gathering of the intellectual elite of Europe who convened to discuss philosophical questions in informal conversations, or *entretiens*. They were begun by philosopher Paul Désjardins in 1910 and lasted until his death in 1940 and the Gestapo's confiscation and burning of the Pontigny archive. Pontigny was revived, but in a much altered form, in 1943 in the final years of the war at Mount Holyoke College in the United States, when London's *Times Literary Supplement* reported on March 3 that "a modern counterpart of the Aristotelian Lyceum or the Platonic Academy has found sanctuary in more congenial surroundings than contemporary France can offer to seats of free thought."

Harrison's involvement at Pontigny marked the height of its influence, and put her, at the age of seventy-two, in agreement and alignment with the ideals of this intellectual collective, most of whom were linked to reformed socialism. In addition to literary questions, the Pontigny conversations dealt with enduring issues of moral and historical significance. The theme of the first décades Harrison attended from 23 August to 2 September 1923 was related to the issue of translation. The question "*Le trésor poétique réservé ou de l'intraduisible,*" or "in the poetry

of a people, is there a private treasure impenetrable or untranslatable
to others?" Just as Woolf struggled with the faithfulness of a translated
text, whether from the Greek or from the Russian, Harrison grappled
at Pontigny with questions comparing classic translations of texts to
other more recent incarnations and asked as a member of the collective
whether or not "the notion of perfect comprehension itself is a mirage?"
(Robinson *Life and Work* 293). The dialogues also centered on definitions of nationalism and poetry, and whether it was possible that there
was "an invisible global family of those who find their world enlarged
by the poetry of another people?" (293). The contacts Harrison made at
Pontigny encouraged her long held interest in Russian letters and led her
to choose the text of *Avvakum* to translate.

It was at Pontigny that she met Shestov and, most likely through him,
D. S. Mirsky, although she was probably familiar with Mirsky's work
when he made his debut in the English press writing about Russia in
1920. Harrison began an intense correspondence with Mirsky,[2] after the
meeting she arranged at her flat between him and the Remizovs. In a letter dated 7 April 1924, she invited the Remizovs to tea on 9 April, and
wrote in the postscript in French "Ce sera un grand plaisir—de recevoir
Madame aussi. Nous attendons le prince Mirsky qui vous adore!" [It will
be a great pleasure to receive Madame as well. We expect Prince Mirsky, who adores you] (Remizov Papers). Throughout their relationship,
they were mutually supportive of each other's work. Harrison helped
him edit his major books, *Contemporary Russian Literature: 1881–1925*
(1926) and *A History of Russian Literature: From the Earliest Times to
the Death of Dostoevsky (1881)* (1927), both of which he dedicated to
her. She was also financially supportive of his Russian language journal,
Vyorsts (Milestones), and it was most likely through her connections
that Mirsky not only received support and guidance from Leonard and
Virginia Woolf, but also received an invitation to the next session of the
Décades in August 1924.

Changing (Red) Tides: On Translating Russian and Capturing the Voice of *Avvakum*

The opening of the 1917 Club also coincided with the Woolfs meeting
and befriending S. S. Koteliansky, a Ukranian Jew, familiarly known as

2. See Smith, "Forty-Seven Letters to D. S. Mirsky."

"Kot," who arrived in London in 1911 as a political refugee from Ostropol. Koteliansky's contact with the Hogarth Press and his role in helping Virginia and Leonard Woolf translate Russian is well documented.[3] He was responsible for bringing most of the translations from Russian literature to the press, and he collaborated with both Leonard and Virginia in their early translations and made connections for them with Maxim Gorky and other Russian authors inside Russia and in exile in Paris and London. Virginia Woolf's contact with Harrison, however, involved the press's last Russian translation, which was one of the few translations brought to the press not by Kot, but by Jane Harrison.

The publication of *The Life of the Archpriest Avvakum, by Himself* marked a point of transition for Harrison and Woolf, and for Mirsky, for that matter, whom Harrison enlisted while they were at Pontigny together in 1924 to write The Preface, and the text was unlike any of their other Russian translations. Not only did it chronologically stand at the outer edge of their Russian list, but it was also distinctive in terms of genre, content, and the political values attached to it by virtue of Mirsky's involvement in the nationalist Russian Eurasian Movement and Harrison's sympathy for Russia. *Avvakum* was politically very different from the Russian books brought to the Woolfs by Koteliansky, which, in my view, at least, partially explains its erasure from J. H. Willis's history of the press, *Leonard and Virginia Woolf as Publishers: The Hogarth Press, 1917–41*. Unlike Mirsky's politics, which were in a continuous state of revision in relation to the changes taking place in Russia, Koteliansky's politics were clear and much more in keeping with Leonard Woolf's socialism and ethnicity. We learn that Kot "had been overjoyed by the revolution that had brought Kerensky to power, but almost from the first had been appalled by the ascendancy of Lenin, Trotsky, and (worst of all) Stalin" (Carswell 260). Mirsky, on the other hand, was a member of the aristocracy and, as such, had initially fought on the side of the Imperial Army in 1917 against the Bolsheviks. He continued to refer to himself as anti-Communist as late as 1925 (Smith, *D. S. Mirsky* 126) until he became radicalized after Lenin's death in 1924 and during the translation process and publication of *Avvakum,* and began to politically identify with Bolshevism and ultimately, and fatally, Stalin.

In addition to the political contexts surrounding its translation and publication, the fact that *Avvakum* was an autobiography would have appealed to Virginia Woolf because of her long-standing interest in writ-

---

3. See L. Marcus, Introduction.

ing lives. She would also go on to publish Harrison's memoirs *Reminiscences of a Student's Life* in 1925, foreshadowing her plea in her tribute to Harrison in *A Room of One's Own* urging us to "think back" through the biographies and autobiographies of our mothers (in Harrison's case, of our intellectual mothers), but also demonstrating that their relationship was ultimately transpersonal, one of intellectual friendship and shared ideas.

Harrison's *Avvakum* was also unusual and in contrast to Hogarth's other Russian titles, because it was a life story told in unadorned, common language—there is little time spent on description of any kind as the extremist, Avvakum, gives a first-hand, personal account of the suffering he endured for the Russian Orthodox, "Old Believer," religion he practiced and promoted. As Russia itself was undergoing major political and historical change in the aftermath of the 1917 Revolution, *Avvakum* represented a return to an "authentic" Russian voice and an alternative to both the excessively "soulful" voice of the Dostoevskyites (which Woolf, Mirsky, and Harrison were becoming disenchanted with and averse to) and, at the other end of the spectrum, the "soul-less" voice on the literary horizon of the Communist "New Man," which Mirsky, at the time of *Avvakum's* publication, in any case, feared.

For Mirsky, who consistently "denigrated his aristocratic origins" (Smith, *D. S. Mirsky* 210), *Avvakum* represented his desire to promote a "true" Russian voice. During the translating of *Avvakum,* Mirsky still maintained ties and interests in Russian nationalism with his involvement in the Eurasian Movement leading up to the book's publication in October 1924, as he continued to struggle with forming a response to his post-Revolutionary homeland. The Eurasian Movement "accepted the Bolshevik Revolution, but rejected Communist power and ideology and argued for a future Russia based on Orthodoxy and on what they saw as the nation's true cultural identity as neither European nor Asian" (Smith, "Prince D. S. Mirsky"). *Avvakum* met these nationalistic criteria. The text, however, also marked a turning point for Mirsky, as his ties to the movement began to dissolve. After Jane Harrison died in 1928, Mirsky began research on a biography of Lenin, which transformed his politics yet again, and he chose to return to Stalinist Moscow in 1932 under the patronage of Maxim Gorky. When Gorky died in 1936, Mirksy, without the protection of his patron, was denounced, arrested, and sent to a labor camp where he died in June 1939. Smith wrote that "his arrest, death, and deletion from the public record provides one of the most telling examples of the way Stalinism destroyed its most able and enthusiastic devotees"

("Prince D. S. Mirsky" 232). It was a fate Virginia Woolf foretold, when she wrote of seeing Mirsky for the last time:

> Mirsky was trap-mouthed; opened & bit his remark to pieces: has yellow misplaced teeth; wrinkles his forehead; despair, suffering, very marked on his face. Has been in England, in boarding houses for 12 years; now returns to Russia 'for ever.' I thought as I watched his eye brighten & fade—soon there'll be a bullet through your head. That's one of the results of war: this trapped cabin'd man. (D 4: 113)

The passage also illustrates Woolf's own disillusionment with the 1917 Revolution, which, with Stalin's succession, poisoned any hope she may have seen for a new form of society. Leonard Woolf also mourned Mirsky's departure from the cultural and intellectual environment of Harrison's salon and "that he should have been drawn into the spider web of Soviet Russia to be destroyed there fills one with despair" (*Downhill* 26–27).

For Harrison, *Avvakum* was her first full-length published work related to her study of Russia. Both Leonard and Virginia Woolf deeply respected Harrison's scholarship, politics, and reputation, but *Avvakum* also represented a love of language, and a unique vernacular voice, which Harrison's translation captured, and that both Woolf and Harrison valued. *Avvakum* was also an attempt by Harrison and Mirsky to complicate a stereotypical view of Russian literature as exotic held by both British and French reading audiences who had been encountering the novels of Dostoevsky for the first time in translation.

During his tenure in the Eurasian Movement, for example, Mirsky relentlessly argued for the destruction of the stereotype of the Russian character as "soulful" and against one-dimensional thinking in reviews of Russian literature. In terms of language and style, for both Mirsky and Remizov, as Marilynn Schwinn-Smith notes, "live, colloquial speech was the *sine qua non*" (127). These were qualities that Harrison and Woolf sought out in their own work and had resonance for them, for Harrison in her translation work and for Woolf in her own literary method. In a paper that would later become Woolf's famous essay "Mr. Bennett and Mrs. Brown," "Character in Fiction," delivered on 24 May 1924 to the Heretics Society in Cambridge, a group whose inaugural address was given by Harrison, Woolf elevated Mrs. Brown, "an old lady in the corner opposite" [. . .] to the stuff of fiction, "to express character" rather than tell the hero's story and "celebrate the glories of the British Empire" (102).

Avvakum, in this sense, met these standards of authenticity with its perspective and vernacular voice, as Woolf sought to articulate her own views and literary method in her essays.

After *Avvakum's* publication, Harrison continued to be attentive to Mirsky's position on language, when she wrote, "What you say about 'ornamental prose' is a real help to me" (Smith, "Forty-Seven Letters to D. S. Mirsky" 82). During her work on the translation, Mirsky often tried to convince Harrison to see a more complete picture of Russia than the more exotic portrait put forth by contemporary British and French audiences. She was at first resistant, writing on 14 May 1924, "o yes I know full well there is another side to the Russian character but then that is a side that we English & the Germans & French possess too so it does not interest me. It gives me nothing fresh to live by" (JH Papers). But their mutual respect and the high esteem in which he holds her is clear from their letters and from his 1930 tribute to Harrison at the second Jane Harrison Memorial Lecture. Until his conversion to hardline Soviet Marxism, Harrison remains an exception for him. Honoring her, in a tribute he wrote to her upon her death entitled "Jane Harrison and Russia," he wrote, "And indeed can one imagine the unerring taste of Jane Harrison being drawn by that cheapest and vulgarest of French inventions—"the Slav soul!" (JH Papers). In her memoirs, Harrison also worked to clarify her position in relation to Russian as "other:"

> And let there be no misunderstanding. It is not "the Slav soul" that drew me. Not even, indeed, Russian literature. Of course, years before I had read and admired Turgenev and Tolstoy and Dostoevsky, but at least by the last two I was more frightened than allured [. . .]. No, it was not these portentous things that laid a spell upon me. It was just the Russian language. If I could have my life over again, I would devote it not to art or literature, but to language. Life itself may hit one hard, but always, always one can take sanctuary in language. Language is as much an art and as sure a refuge as painting or music or literature. It reflects and interprets and makes bearable life; only it is a wider, because more subconscious life. (R 79)

The language, the voice, convinced Harrison, who described her upbringing in the "narrow school of Evangelicalism—reared with sin always present, with death and judgment before you" (80), to translate the life of an Orthodox religious zealot like Avvakum. As Mirsky explained in his

Preface, "In the Eastern Church the Writ and the Liturgies were translated into the vernacular of every newly converted nation" (8). It is important to realize, according to Mirsky, that Avvakum's "fanaticism, though historically conditioned by patriotic and nationalistic arguments, was primarily and fundamentally religious and not patriotic. Russia was holy to him because it was the vessel of orthodoxy, not orthodoxy because it was Russian" (Preface 17). Mirsky brings up Avvakum in nearly every preface he writes, as he emphasizes his relevance to contemporary writers. He appeals to Russian writers to look to Avvakum as an example for their own art, which he feels is overburdened by political and sociological doctrine. Writing of Avvakum, Mirsky states, "His groundwork is the spoken language of his time, that is, a language essentially the same as the spoken language of to-day" (26). In *Russia: A Social History,* Mirsky writes that Avvakum "introduced into his written works the spirit of popular preaching and the language of the street. He was the first to use colloquial Russian for literary purposes" (172). This is an idea that appealed to Harrison, who spent much of her professional life in conflict with the strict grammarians of the Classical departments of Oxbridge.

Harrison was proud of her translation, which was "linguistically [. . .] a phenomenal achievement" (Robinson *Life and Work* 296). She wrote to Gilbert Murray, "As a prize for goodness of heart I send you the Archpriest Avvakum. If you don't think he is a loveable old bear our acquaintance ceases automatically" (Stewart 193). One of her former students also wrote that "the erudition and skill of [*Avvakum*] caused Jane's friends in Paris to rank her Russian work on a level with her early books" (174). *Avvakum* ultimately fell into obscurity, tainted by Mirsky's Soviet conversion, but it continues to be an example of Virginia Woolf's transpersonal connection to Harrison's work and example and to her own understanding of Russian literature, language, and politics.

Russian "Aspects" and Russian "Soul"

Like Harrison, Virginia Woolf held Russian literature in high regard. She often used the writings of Tolstoy, Dostoevsky, and Chekov, for example, as well as many other more obscure authors like Saltikov and Militsina, as standards by which to measure English literature in her own reviews, essays, letters, and diary entries. In her 1919 essay "The Russian Point of View," published in *The Common Reader* in 1925, Woolf, as was not

unusual in British criticism of Russian writers, identifies an abiding spirituality and understanding of "the soul" she finds lacking or culturally
unacceptable, if not unattainable, in English literature.

Both Harrison and Woolf's understanding of Russian literature as
"soulful" and as exotic "other" was part of the British (and French) trend
during the early decades of the twentieth century, but their study of and
understanding of Russian letters changed over time, as they each grew
to reject this stereotypical, reductive view. Initially, as Schwinn-Smith
writes, "Harrison took up the study of Russian to get at the literature,
to read Tolstoy, Dostoevsky and Chekhov in the original" (123), which
reminds us that Woolf first took up the Greeks, to read and translate the
Classics denied her as a woman. Laura Marcus writes, "While there were
scattered English translations of Dostoevsky's work in the late-nineteenth
century, these came much later than the translations in France and Germany, and were frequently out of print" (Introduction vii), and much
of the characterization of the Slav soul was based on reviews of French
translations of mostly nineteenth-century Russian novels. European reaction to Russian literature became known as The Dostoevsky Cult, which
was at its peak between 1912 and the early 1920s (L. Marcus, Introduction ix). Harrison and Woolf's involvement can be seen as both a part of
this trend, but also as working against and complicating these views.

Both Harrison and Woolf took up their study of the Russian language
at nearly the same time and for the same reasons, in order to bypass the
obstacles of mediating story from one language into another. As a linguist,
Harrison was well aware of the challenges of authority in a translated
text. In 1919, Woolf articulated her position as well, when she wrote:

> When you have changed every word in a sentence from Russian to
> English, have thereby altered the sense a little, the sound, weight, and
> accent of the words in relation to each other completely, nothing remains
> except a crude and coarsened version of the sense. ("The Russian Point
> of View" 174)

The challenges of reading works in translation, of the inability to "trust
ourselves not to impute, to distort, to read into them an emphasis which
is false" were also central themes in Harrison's *Aspects, Aorists, and the
Classical Tripos,* which was published in the same year as "The Russian
Point of View." Woolf was also familiar with *Aspects*'s earlier incarnation, "Russia and the Russian Verb." If we read Woolf's reading of the
Russians through Harrison as transpersonal, adding Hogarth's acquisition

of *Avvakum,* we have a more complex picture of her response to Russian literature and letters. We see her perspective of Russia as soulful, changing over time and becoming more informed and nuanced, as she reads the Russians through Harrison's *Aspects.*

Unfairly, in my view, Harrison's essay has been narrowly characterized as promoting a portrait of Russian literature as "soulful" with Harrison's remark that "the Russian stands for the complexity and concreteness of life—felt whole, unanalyzed, unjudged, lived into . . . " (*Aspects* 35). G. S. Smith, for example, links her published essay to the romanticized view of Russia Harrison often spoke about in her personal correspondence (98). The essay itself, however, is a treatise on language and the relationship between language and psychology. *Aspects* turns, as does much of Harrison's best scholarship and prose, "on the imaginative art" of research, putting forth "a reality seen through a temperament" and has "a fleet-footed subtlety and elegance of logic that is characteristic of her scholarly demonstrations," as Mirsky noted in his tribute (JH Papers).

Rather than promoting the Slav soul, the essay ostensibly argues for the inclusion of Russian in the curriculum at Cambridge. Harrison proposes that Russian should be equally weighted alongside ancient Greek in the Classical Tripos and that "an accurate knowledge of the Russian and Greek languages together with an intimate understanding of the two civilizations should furnish a humanistic education at once broad and thorough" (*Aspects* 36). The essay demonstrates Harrison's linguistic abilities and her appreciation for the simplicity of the structure of the Russian language at its core. She begins *Aspects* by pointing out that she was indeed interested in "getting at the literature," but this hid her true desire, which was the language itself, for "to fall in love with a language is not to fall in love with a literature. It is well to note—a fact too often forgotten—that a rich language does not necessarily mean a rich literature" (5). She explores the language from a philosophical viewpoint, and "the dominance of 'aspect' over tense and of 'imperfective' over 'perfective,' as having more to say about life and time and culture than simply the "ideas of completion or non-completion" which lie at the grammatical root of Russian aspects (9–11). She magnifies her discussion to also include group psychology. For Harrison, "Language is the *un*conscious or at least subconscious product of the group, the herd, the race, the nation. Literature is the product more or less conscious of the individual genius, using of course the tools made by the blind herd, but, after the manner of live organisms, shaping these tools even as he uses them" (5). What lies behind Russian aspects and this idea of process, of the accomplished and unaccomplished act, is a psychology of a people and a philosophy and science of human existence. *Aspects* is an essay with a profoundly interdisciplinary focus, which ultimately argues for a policy change within an academic department, but it is a critique of Russian literature and language, which resonated with Virginia Woolf, who was also seeking to articulate her response to Russian literature.

In concert with Harrison, Woolf writes of the challenges of reading works in translation. In "The Russian Point of View," she points out that not only do we have the physical distance separating Europe and Russia, "but a much more serious barrier—the difference of language" (173). As she will go on to write in "On Not Knowing Greek" of the obstacles to truly understanding the language, "since we do not know how the words sounded" (23), she says that our ability to understand and comment on Russian literature "has been formed by critics who have never read a word of Russian, or seen Russia, or even heard the language spoken by natives" ("The Russian Point of View" 174). Woolf speaks of Russian soulfulness in the essay, but with all of the admitted pitfalls of reading works in translation. Of Chekhov, she writes, "The mind interests him enormously; he is a most subtle and delicate analyst of human relations. But again, no; the end is not there. Is it that he is primarily interested not in the soul's relation with other souls, but with the soul's relation to health—with the soul's relation to goodness? [. . .] The soul is ill; the soul is cured; the soul is not cured [. . .]. In consequence as we read these little stories about nothing at all, the horizon widens; the soul gains an astonishing sense of freedom. In reading Chekhov we find ourselves repeating the word 'soul' again and again" (173). About Dostoevsky's novels Woolf writes that they "are seething whirlpools, gyrating sandstorms, waterspouts which hiss and boil and suck us in. They are composed purely and wholly of the stuff of the soul. Against our wills we are drawn in, whirled round, blinded, suffocated, and at the same time filled with giddy rapture" (178). Her characterizations of soulfulness in Russian literature are consistently put forth as being on "a tangent far from the truth" (182), and are more a comment and critique of that depiction as being mediated through the flawed art of translation.

After the publication of *Avvakum* in 1924, Harrison's death in 1928, and the drastic and catastrophic changes brought about by the Stalinism of the 1930s, Russian literature brought conflicting associations for Virginia Woolf. Laura Marcus writes that for Woolf "Dostoevsky [. . .] became unreadable [. . .] for her in the 1930s" ("European Dimensions"

354). She tries Turgenev, but her ambivalence towards Dostoevsky and her early attraction to his work and other Russian writers fades, as she writes in 1929 in "Phases of Fiction" about Dostoevsky: the violence "lays bare regions deep down in the mind where contradiction prevails"; "the crude outer sign of the vice and the virtue we meet, at full tilt, in the same breast" (126–27). She acknowledges Dostoevsky's abilities, but also points out that, "We cannot read to the end without feeling as if a thumb were pressing on a button in us, when we have no emotion left to answer the call" (128). Woolf expresses a readerly fatigue she has come to associate not only with Dostoevsky, but with the Russian psychological novelists in general: "This emptiness and noise lead us to wonder whether the novel of psychology, which projects its drama in the mind, should not [. . .] vary and diversify its emotions, lest we shall become numb with exhaustion" (128).

Woolf and Harrison each became involved in Russian translation as a bridge and connection to the literature and language, but also the politics, of another culture. The publications of both *Aspects* and *Avvakum* illustrate the intricate networks of Russian intellectuals both were engaged in and supported and promoted. Their interests in Russian literature and language and the points of contact through their scholarly and cultural productions demonstrate their shared literary and political involvement in the alternative perspectives and social systems Russia offered, but never, ultimately, fulfilled.

AFTERWORD

Modernism's Transpersonal *and*

Re-connecting Women's Lives/Women's Work and the Politics of Recovering a Reputation

IN HER PREFATORY NOTE to *Ancient Art and Ritual* (1913), Jane
Harrison writes, "The point of my title and the real gist of my argument
lie perhaps in the word '*and*'—that is, in the intimate connection which
I have tried to show exists between ritual and art. This connection has, I
believe, an important bearing on questions vital to to-day" (v). She agrees
that "the title of this book may strike the reader as strange and even dis-
sonant" and asks, "What have art and ritual to do together?" (9–10).
It is her objective, in this explanatory text meant to articulate *Themis*'s
major themes, published a year earlier in 1912, "to show that these two
divergent developments have a common root, and that neither can be
understood without the other." "It is at the outset," she writes, "one and
the same impulse that sends a man to church and to the theatre" (9–10).
    Similarly, in the spirit of the word *and*, the aim of this study has been
to show the intimate connection between two major feminist intellectuals, Virginia Woolf and Jane Ellen Harrison, as beginning on the vertical
axis of mentorship, but ultimately illustrating a transpersonal relationship
that in turn revised both their classicism and their understanding of their
own times. It was a project I came to from the murky, chaotic waters of

my own emotions, a woman's intuition, a grope, a hunch, encouraged by
the work, in many cases transpersonally, of decades of feminist scholarship and critical thinking, to argue that whenever Virginia Woolf thinks
about the Greeks in relation to her work, she does so through Jane Harrison's pioneering research on the matrifocal origins of Greek religion. The
impulse, furthermore, that sends Woolf to the theater, to the performance
and art, let's say, of her entire modern literary project, which is rife with
instances of Greek mythology, also sends her to the "church" of Harrison's politics, her feminism, pacifism, and her radical views on religion
and family life. When I say *church*, however, I mean in the sense of the
word's earliest beginnings, from the Greek, *kyros*, which I translate as
"power," rather than "Lord" or "master," and as akin to the Latin *cavus*,
or "hollow," more at "cave." For Harrison's "church" or "cave"[1] is not
based on the sermonizing, sin, or conversion that shaped her childhood,
but resonates with Woolf as the *locus*, or power base, of her yearned-
for "human intercourse," a notion Virginia Woolf considered as a serious form of social action, a shared laboratory of ideas, with Chloe and
Olivia lighting "a torch in that vast chamber where nobody has yet been"
(AROO 83).

In deploying Nancy K. Miller's definition of "transpersonal" as "a connection sideways" characterized by friendship and work to the Harrison–
Woolf encounter, we understand then that thinking/reading/writing
transpersonally means asking how lateral connections, our intellectual
"chosen relations," inform individual, cultural, political, and social
identity. By cross-reading Harrison and Woolf as transpersonal, we recognize Harrison as sharing in Woolf's modernist story. Reading their relationship transpersonally, as a "feminist friendship," we have seen that
Woolf's use of Jane Harrison's revisions of the pantheon of the heroic
Olympians fueled not only her literary aesthetic, but also a politics she
encountered, developed, and shared by way of Harrison's example as a
public intellectual and international scholar.

And yet, today, Harrison's work and reputation continue to provoke
either hostility or silence, thus creating an intellectual climate that per-
sists in diminishing and dismissing her example. In between panel presentations at a recent International Virginia Woolf Conference, Bonnie Kime
Scott and I, whose paths crossed by coincidence during a coffee break,
each made note of the fact that we had sat in on three different paper

---

1. Indeed, Harrison called her room at Newnham "her cave," because she claimed
that the guardians of Plato's cave in his *Republic* were Orphic initiates, a topic she favored
over the more highly regarded Olympians (Robinson, *Life and Work* 187).

presentations on two different panels on Virginia Woolf and the Classics and not one made mention of Jane Harrison. Her erasure is baffling, especially to critics such as Scott, Jane Marcus, Martha Carpentier, and others, mostly feminist and cultural theorists, whose work this study is indebted to, and who have made important contributions over the years to keep Jane Harrison's contributions and reputation alive.

Furthermore, with the exception of the archivists at Newnham College, who with very little funds meticulously prepared and now house and maintain her papers, Harrison is little known at either Newnham or Girton, the two women's colleges where one would expect to find support among students and faculty for her work. In her essay "Virginia Woolf, Cambridge and *A Room of One's Own*: 'The Proper Upkeep of Names'" (1996), Jane Marcus recounts her experience attending the sixty-fifth anniversary of *A Room of One's Own* in 1993 and admiring the portrait of Jane Harrison by Augustus John which was then hanging in the Senior Common Room at Newnham. When she pointed out "That's Jane Harrison!" no one in the room knew who she was. Marcus writes "not one of her pioneering books was on the reading list of the seminar in feminist Anthropology and none of the graduate students in that class had ever heard of her" (11). I had a similar experience while doing research at Newnham in 2006, when I saw the Harrison portrait behind locked doors in the Faculty Common Room. Biographer and critic Frances Spaulding, whom I ran into by chance on my way to the dining hall (this is often how research happens!), offered to sneak me in, and her eyes lit up at the opportunity to be a bit subversive on behalf of my cause, when she realized I was there to do work on Harrison. I had yet to read Marcus's essay at that point, but found her account of Harrison's obscurity to be alive and well outside of certain small circles in academia. A few faculty members were having tea beneath Harrison's portrait, but none of them knew who she was, nor were they aware that she was the woman in whose name the biennial Jane Harrison Memorial Lecture was given.

The present Cambridge classicist Mary Beard, in her "biography" *The Invention of Jane Harrison* (2000), somewhat disturbingly works the most strenuously to diminish Harrison's scholarship and reputation. Beard casts Harrison's life and work as "mythology" itself, and disparages what she calls a kind of conspiratorial effort on the part of her friends and admirers to have "clubbed together" (1) to "invent" and perpetuate Harrison's "heroization" (8). As a well-known and respected scholar, Beard enjoys the power and status Harrison never had. Her dismissal of Harrison is a denial of her own intellectual origins and of Harrison's pioneering work in her field. Beard's project as she claims is to test the very nature and boundaries of biography as a genre, but she uses Harrison's body of work as a scapegoat instead. Ultimately, the book becomes a rehearsal of a predictable script of hostility aimed at women writers. By not writing a biography of Jane Harrison, Mary Beard denies Harrison her place in history. Jane Harrison becomes an object of ridicule. Her genius is denied.

Beard's hostility towards Jane Harrison has a long and well-documented history. Shelley Arlen's article "'For Love of an Idea': Jane Ellen Harrison, Heretic and Humanist" is one of the rare efforts among critics to examine the misogyny, motivation, and exceedingly emotional attacks on Harrison's life and work from her contemporaries. Despite "emerging as the leader of an intellectual school," being a "precursor of Structuralism" and a founder of Myth-Ritual criticism, Arlen writes, "she is rarely credited with the work she created, inspired, and promoted" (165). Arlen attributes this oversight to the interdisciplinary nature of Harrison's scholarship and the controversial theories and discoveries she developed which posited the existence of women-centered Greek cultures behind the myths. The excessive rumors and hostility she endured, however, were the result not only of her work on ancient Greece, but also "her personal life and her views on feminism, religion, and political pacifism" (166). Although Harrison was a popular lecturer and many of her contemporaries and male and female colleagues championed her work, Arlen demonstrates that "the outraged ones succeeded to a considerable extent in discrediting her," perpetuating a legacy of their own we find repeated today in many of her most recent biographers and "anti-biographers," as in the case of Beard, and, more recently, in the work of MacArthur grant-recipient Joan Breton Connelly, who failed to credit or even acknowledge Harrison or her published work in her *Portrait of a Priestess: Women and Ritual in Ancient Greece* (2007), a study which "re-interprets" the Parthenon frieze and many of the same vase fragments Harrison published on and devoted her life to analyzing. Connelly is working in the discipline of archaeology, a field which Harrison helped to create. Neither Beard nor Connelly, in very real terms, would have been able to complete their work without Harrison's scholarship, research, or her example as a professional woman scholar. To disagree with someone's work is one thing, to ignore it is to participate in a drama of denial that silences women's voices and contributions to culture, history, literature, art, politics, philosophy, and to the narratives and discourses of what we commonly call civilization.

During her own time, Harrison's most virulent opponents were William Ridgeway and Montague Rhodes James. They were highly motivated to discredit her and, as Arlen points out "were not the disinterested seekers after truth they claimed to be, but rather had ulterior motives and private agendas in their rejection of her ideas" ("'For Love of an Idea'" 167). One of Harrison's most strident critics, William Ridgeway Disney Professor of Archaeology and Brereton Reader in Classics at Caius College, Cambridge, was described in both *Cambridge Retrospect* and *Cambridge Review* in the following way:

> capable of warm friendship and of unhesitating animosity. Nobody would call him unprejudiced, and he could provoke the mildest and most tranquil people.
>
> He was always deep in politics, national, ecclesiastical, logic, and academic, restlessly fitting every new problem into his large framework of loves and hates. (Glover 76; Robertson)

Although Ridgeway's theories on the origins of tragedy were far less valid than those of the Ritualists, his attacks upon their work, especially upon Jane Harrison's arguments, were well known and played out in the pages of the *Cambridge Review*, where during spring 1911 it was noted that "[h]e brought some of his heavy guns to bear upon Miss Harrison" (News and Notes, *Cambridge Review* 16 Feb. 1911; 23 Feb. 1911; 9 March 1911). He had a reputation for being dramatic, dare we say emotional, as he ridiculed his adversaries and promoted his own ideas. As Arlen notes, "Ridgeway's animosity toward Harrison had political grounds as well: he had little tolerance for women in the academy, and he despised pacifists" ("'For Love of an Idea'" 178). He was active in the National League for Opposing Women's Suffrage and a vocal opponent of women's education and their admission into university. On 22 November 1920, Ridgeway wrote to *The Times*:

> We do strongly object to any injury being done to the higher education of men by giving women a voice in the control of the men's curricula and examinations. [. . .] If women had full membership, there would be a tendency on their part to modify the curricula and examinations for the benefit of their own sex.

Ridgeway firmly believed that women's education would adversely affect society as a whole, be a distraction to men at college, and be a harmful waste upon their nerves and psychological makeup. Alongside this irrational fear was the idea of education as serving to masculinize women, or conversely the equally disparaging contention and double bind that a woman's scholarly output would be overly feminized and inherently flawed by her emotional makeup.

Jane Harrison is often cited as one of the best examples of a scholar who was able to successfully integrate the intellect with the emotional aspects of being a woman, a notion supported by critics such as Martha Vicinus and Harry C. Payne, who considered her scholarship "a successful synthesis of sex in intellect" (qtd. in Vicinus 162). Harrison's struggle for this balance and "synthesis," however, was hard won, and her ability to wed passion with intellect on the page in her highly attractive, readable prose and in the lecture hall, with her inspirational delivery and demeanor, were frequently attacked in the press. Both her personal life and her work suffered a public hostility that relentlessly tried to marginalize her work and damage her reputation.

Although Robert Ackerman suggests that because she was a woman, Harrison was allowed far greater emotive range as a scholar, it was a gift for which she was frequently and publicly disparaged. Ackerman writes that "because she was a woman I am sure (without being able to prove it) that to some extent at least her world found her behavior charming where the same behavior in a man would have been thought childish or bizarre" (*Myth and Ritual School* 71). He goes on to note her ability to "think in pictures—eidetic imagery" as "childish" and "primitive" and to categorize her natural gift at personifying inanimate objects like her books, for example, giving nicknames to her friends, or her playful fondness for bears as being somewhat "embarrassing." These references, her fondness for bears, for example, are only found in her personal correspondence, not in her published work. He does allow that these characteristics "tempered a profoundly intellectual nature" and that "she was able to hold her own at the top of a male profession that at the time employed perhaps the most rigorous scholarly criteria of all the various divisions in the world of humane letters" (71–72). I take issue, however, with Ackerman's characterization of these abilities in Harrison as "childish" and part of a female emotional makeup that was tolerated by male scholars. On the contrary, the overwhelming evidence of Harrison being taken to task for too much emotion in her work suggests not that she was "allowed" to be more emotional in her work than her male counterparts, but that she was targeted and marginalized *because* she was a woman. Hugh Lloyd-Jones in his contribution to *Cambridge Women:*

Twelve Portraits (1996) also implies that her attitude towards her work was "tolerated" because of her gender, that she had "a rare kind of imaginative flair that has been denied to many persons with a firmer grasp of Greek grammar and of systematic thinking" (32). Both of these perspectives lack an understanding of women's experience and women's lives, and perhaps without meaning to serve to dismiss or ignore the complexities and breadth of the theories and contributions of a scholar who performed her research according to a principle (read feminist) that stated, "knowledge is never, or very rarely divorced from emotion and action" (SSF 48).

In addition to his misogyny, Ridgeway was a belligerent adversary of peace activism, especially the U.D.C. (Union for Democratic Control). He viewed Newnham College as a hotbed of "Pro-German agitation." In a letter to the *Cambridge Review,* 14 February 1917, he wrote:

> Another member of the Newnham staff also notoriously connected with the U.D.C. [. . .] who had recently made a speech at a public gathering at Newnham [. . .] glorifying the Hon. Bertrand Russell, who had recently been convicted and punished for seeking to stop [military] recruiting. (224)

In this example, Ridgeway was referring to Jane Harrison, who had spoken out on behalf of Lord Russell's reinstatement in a bid for academic freedom, but, as Arlen points out, Ridgeway was "incorrect on two counts. Harrison was never a U.D.C. member, and she did not press her pacifistic views in wartime" upon her students ("For Love of an Idea" 179), unlike Ridgeway, who denied any student who was a U.D.C. member access to his classes. Ridgeway, exhaustively and emotionally, attacked Harrison's political views as immoral and her feminist theories on Greek ritual as "debauching young minds wholesale" (qtd. in Pfaff 256).

Her other most vocal opponent, Montague Rhodes James, Provost of King's College, Cambridge and its former Vice-Chancellor, was a religious conservative, outspoken against women receiving degrees at Cambridge, and a known misogynist. In *Montague Rhodes James,* his biographer Richard William Pfaff quotes a poem about M. R. James written by a colleague who portrayed him as "James the Greater / Who's orthodox and woman hater" (220). Although he claimed little interest in politics, James felt so offended by Harrison's article in the prestigious *Classical Review* in 1917 titled "The Head of John the Baptist," which applied Harrison's theory of the Year-Spirit to Salome's dance in a performance she had seen of Oscar Wilde's *Salome,* that he "instantly took a pen and dipped it in gall and flayed her" (qtd. in Pfaff 255), calling the essay as an outright attack on Christianity. His attack, which also parodied her rhetorical style and "emotional" scholarship, was supported by William Ridgeway and played out in the pages of both the *Classical Review* and the *Cambridge Review.* As Arlen notes, however, "Harrison remained unmoved. She thanked James for his correction of minor inaccuracies, which, she reminded readers, 'nowise invalidate, or even affect, my argument'" ("For Love of an Idea" 181) and, gesturing towards future generations of scholars, wrote on 31 March 1917 in *The Classical Review:*

> To me the keenest joys of science [. . .] are always perilous, and I hope
> to die commending these perilous joys to a generation better equipped,
> and I trust more valorous, than my own

Arlen's essay illustrates the power of the male academic establishment to "make or break a reputation," as she also places Harrison's critical reception within an "androcentric positivism" that claimed scholarly investigations should be conducted with dispassion and disinterest, which were not considered qualities of the female mind. Harrison eventually felt forced to abandon Greek scholarship, left Cambridge and London for Paris, and turned her sights to the study of Russian literature and language.

Despite the damage done to her reputation, Jane Harrison read as a success in Virginia Woolf's eyes, becoming a role model of a professional woman and public intellectual unafraid to wed the emotional to the intellect in order to find her own voice. Furthermore, although Woolf continues to be placed among the "dramatis personae" of Bloomsbury, she more accurately belongs within a transpersonal community of independent women scholars with Harrison at its matrifocal center, a circle vibrating with a Harrison-inflected understanding of the classics, marked by intellectual vigor, defiance, and an affection between women based on their work.

As significant as I suggest Harrison's contributions are to the very fabric of Woolf's intellectual and political life and to her cultural and literary output, I also see Harrison as an important figure and public intellectual with an international reputation informing much of the political and literary climate of the early twentieth century. And yet her work continues to be unacknowledged, attacked, or unknown. Our critical understanding of modernist texts shifts and is given added dimension by bringing her Greek research, Russian study, and explorations in the fields of psychology, sociology, archaeology, and linguistics into dialogue not only with Woolf, but with other modernist authors who borrowed from her and whose literary production and political views were furthered by her example. In addition to the need for an updated and more accurate full-length biography of Harrison, with few exceptions, more critical work has yet to be done, linking her in a meaningful way to H. D., Ezra Pound, T. S. Eliot, James Joyce, D. H. Lawrence, Katherine Mansfield, Amy Lowell, Mina Loy, May Sinclair, and Gertrude Stein, among many others in literature; to Sigmund Freud and Carl Jung, in psychology; and Henri Bergson and Saussure in linguistics. Bonnie Kime Scott and others are beginning to see Jane Harrison as a source of eco-feminism in modernist writers.[2]

Despite the personal and professional hostility she endured during her own lifetime, Jane Harrison was heartened by a new generation of readers who reminded her that after encountering her work they had become "free-thinkers" (T 538) ever since. Just as Woolf was creating her modernism out of a narrative that had yet to be experienced and enjoyed by women in a patriarchal and militaristic state, Harrison's research insisted she "set sail in seas as yet for me uncharted" (T 540). Joining Harrison and Woolf with a modernist, transpersonal 'and' demonstrates an intimacy that each enjoyed both within and between the boundaries of their work. After Harrison's death in 1928, her connection to Virginia Woolf was duly noted. In her portrait of Harrison, published in 1959, Harrison's former student Jessie Stewart invoked Virginia Woolf's name when she remembered Harrison as being "Lady Themis [. . .] Potnia Theron, the Lady of the Sprites," but she asked of her audience, "of that tradition, let Virginia Woolf speak" (187). This study encourages an end to the critical history that has set aside, ignored, or dismissed Harrison's work, as it participates in an act of feminist reclamation Virginia Woolf theorized in her own essays and fiction. By recognizing Harrison as both mentor and transpersonal friend, we change the way we read and understand Virginia Woolf, as their encounter gives us insight into our critical understanding of the boundaries and sources of Woolf's literary modernism and political ideals.

---

2. See Scott, *In the Hollow of the Wave.*

BIBLIOGRAPHY

Archival Sources

Case, Janet, Papers. Girton College Archives, Girton College, Cambridge.

Harrison, Jane Ellen, Papers. Newnham College Archives, Newnham College, Cambridge.

Mirrlees, Hope, Papers. Hornbake Library, University of Maryland.

Mirrlees, Hope, Papers. Newnham College Archives, Newnham College, Cambridge.

Monks House Papers. Manuscript Collections. University of Sussex Library.

Remizov, Alexei, Papers. Amherst Center for Russian Culture, Amherst College.

Woolf, Virginia, and Leonard Woolf, Papers. Henry W. and Albert A. Berg Collection. New York Public Library.

Secondary Sources

Ackerman, Robert. "The Cambridge Group and the Origins of Myth Criticism." Diss. Columbia U, 1969.

———. "Jane Ellen Harrison: By Myth Begotten." *Religion* 31 (2001): 67-74.

———. Personal interview. 22 June 2006.

———. *The Myth and Ritual School: J. G. Frazer and the Cambridge Ritualists.* New York: Routledge, 2002.

Aeschylus. *The Oresteia.* Trans. Robert Fagles. New York: Penguin Books, 1979.

———. *The Oresteia.* Trans. Richmond Lattimore. Chicago: U of Chicago P, 1955.

———. *The Oresteia.* Trans. Alan Shapiro and Peter Buritan. Oxford: OUP, 2003.

———. *The Oresteia.* Trans. Arthur Verrall. London: Macmillan, 1893.

Alley, Henry. "A Re-discovered Eulogy: Virginia Woolf's Miss Janet Case: Classical Scholar and Teacher." *20th Century Literature* 28.3 (Autumn 1982): 290–301.

Annan, Noel. *The Dons: Mentors, Eccentrics, and Geniuses.* U of Chicago P, 1999.

Arlen, Shelley. *The Cambridge Ritualists: An Annotated Bibliography of the Works by and about Jane Ellen Harrison, Gilbert Murray, Francis M. Cornford, and Arthur Bernard Cook.* Metuchen, NJ: Scarecrow Press, 1990.

————. "'For Love of an Idea': Jane Ellen Harrison, Heretic and Humanist." *Women's History Review* 5.2 (1996): 165–90.

Beard, Mary. *The Invention of Jane Harrison.* Cambridge, MA: Harvard UP, 2000.

Beasley, Rebecca. "Russia and the Invention of the Modernist Intelligentsia." *Geographies of Modernism.* Ed. Peter Brooker and Andrew Thacker. New York: Routledge, 2005. 12–28.

Beer, Gillian. *Virginia Woolf: The Common Ground.* Edinburgh: Edinburgh UP, 1996.

Bell, Quentin. *Virginia Woolf: A Biography.* New York: Harcourt, 1972.

Berman, Jessica. *Modernist Commitments: Ethics, Politics, and Transnational Modernism.* New York: Columbia UP, 2012.

Black, Naomi. "Introduction." *Three Guineas* by Virginia Woolf. Oxford: Blackwells, 2001. xlvi–lvi.

Blotner, Joseph L. "Mythic Patterns in *To the Lighthouse*." *PMLA* 71.4.1 (September 1956): 547–62.

Breton Connelly, Joan. *Portrait of a Priestess: Women and Ritual in Ancient Greece.* Princeton, NJ: Princeton UP, 2007.

Briggs, Julia. "The Novels of the 1930s and the Impact of History." *Cambridge Companion to Virginia Woolf.* Cambridge: Cambridge UP, 2000. 72–90.

————. *Reading Virginia Woolf.* Edinburgh: Edinburgh UP, 2006.

————. *Virginia Woolf: An Inner Life.* New York: Harcourt, 2005.

Burton, John, and E. A. Azar. *International Conflict Resolution: Theory and Practice.* Boulder, CO: Lynne Rienner Publishers, 1986.

Butler, Judith. *Frames of War: When Is Life Grievable?* New York: Verso, 2009.

Calder, William M., III, ed. *The Cambridge Ritualists Reconsidered: Proceedings of the First Oldfather Conference.* Illinois Classical Studies Supplement 2, Illinois Studies in the History of Classical Scholarship 1. Atlanta: Scholars Press, 1991.

Caramagno, Thomas C. *The Flight of the Mind: Virginia Woolf's Art and Manic Depressive Illness.* Berkeley: U of California P, 1995.

Carpentier, Martha C. *Ritual, Myth, and the Modernist Text.* Vol. 12. Library of Anthropology Series. Amsterdam, NL: Gordon and Breach, 1998.

Carswell, John. *Lives and Letters: A. R. Orage, Beatrice Hasting, Katharine Mansfield, John Middleton Murry, and S. S. Koteliansky, 1906–1957.* New York: New Directions, 1978

Chapman, Wayne K., and Janet M. Manson, eds. *Women in the Milieu of Leonard and Virginia Woolf: Peace, Politics, and Education.* New York: Pace UP, 1998.

Cook, A. B. *The Rise and Progress of Classical Archaeology.* Cambridge: Cambridge UP, 1931.

————. *Zeus.* Cambridge: Cambridge UP, 1914–40.

Cook, Blanche Wiesen. "Female Support Networks." *Women's America: Refocusing the Past.* Ed. Linda Kerber and Jane DeHart-Matthews. 2nd ed. New York: Oxford UP, 1987. 43–60.

————. "'Women Alone Stir My Imagination.'" *Signs: Journal of Women in Culture and Society* 4.4 (1979): 718–37.

Cooper, Sandi E. "Jane Addams' Newer Ideals of Peace: A View from the European Peace Movement." American Historical Association, Philadelphia. January 2006.

———. "Peace as a Human Right: The Invasion of Women into the World of High International Politics." *Journal of Women's History* (July 2002): 9–25.

Cornford, F. M. *The Origin of Attic Comedy.* London: E. Arnold, 1914.

———. *From Religion to Philosophy: A Study in the Origins of Western Speculation.* 1912. Princeton, NJ: Princeton UP, 1991.

———. *Thucydides Mythistoricus.* London: E. Arnold, 1907.

———, trans. and ed. *The Republic of Plato.* Oxford: OUP, 1945.

Cramer, Patricia. "Jane Harrison and Lesbian Plots: The Absent Lover in Virginia Woolf's *The Waves.*" *Studies in the Novel* 37.4 (Winter 2005): 443–63.

Cuddy-Keane, Melba. "The Politics of Comic Modes in Virginia Woolf's *Between the Acts.*" 105 *PMLA* (1990): 273–85.

DeSalvo, Louise. *Virginia Woolf: The Impact of Childhood Sexual Abuse on Her Life and Work.* New York: Ballantine, 1989.

Dietrich, Wolfgang, et al., eds. *The Palgrave International Handbook of Peace Studies: A Cultural Perspective.* London: Palgrave Macmillan, 2011.

Eliot, T. S. "The Interpretation of Primitive Ritual." Manuscript. John Hayward Bequest, Modern Archive of Kings College, Cambridge University.

———. *Selected Essays.* London: Faber and Faber, 1951.

———. "Ulysses, Order, and Myth." *Selected Prose of T. S. Eliot.* Ed. Frank Kermode. New York: Farrar, Straus, Giroux, 1975. 175–78.

———. *The Waste Land. Collected Poems: 1909–1962.* New York: Harcourt, 1963.

———. *The Waste Land: A Facsimile and Transcript of the Original Drafts Including Annotations of Ezra Pound.* Ed. and introd. Valerie Eliot. New York: Harvest/Harcourt, 1971.

Euripides. *The Bacchae, Electra, Iphigenia at Aulis. Ten Plays.* Trans. Moses Hadas and John McClean. New York: Bantam Classics, 1972.

Fernald, Anne. "O Sister Swallow: Sapphic Fragments as English Literature." *Virginia Woolf: Feminism and the Reader.* New York: Palgrave Macmillan, 2010. 17–50.

Forster, E. M. *Virginia Woolf.* Rede Lecture, Cambridge University 29 May 1941. New York: Harcourt, 1942.

Gadd, David. *The Loving Friends: A Portrait of Bloomsbury.* New York: Harcourt Brace, 1974.

Galtung, Johan, and Carl G. Jacobsen. *Searching for Peace: The Road to TRANSCEND.* London: Pluto Press, 2000.

Gilbert, Sandra M., and Susan Gubar. *No Man's Land: The Place of the Woman Writer in the Twentieth Century.* Vol. 1, *The War of the Words.* New Haven: Yale UP, 1988.

Glover, T. R. *Cambridge Retrospect.* Cambridge: Cambridge UP, 1943. 76.

Goldman, Jane. *The Feminist Aesthetics of Virginia Woolf: Modernism, Post-Impressionism, and the Politics of the Visual.* Cambridge: Cambridge UP, 1998.

Gordon, Lyndall. *Virginia Woolf: A Writer's Life.* New York: Norton, 1984.

Grattan-Guinness, Ivor. *Psychical Research: A Guide to Its History, Principles, and Practices.* Northampton, U.K.: Aquarian Press, 1982.

Gregory, Eileen. *H. D. and Hellenism: Classic Lines.* Cambridge: Cambridge UP, 1997.

Gruber, Ruth. *Virginia Woolf: The Will to Create as a Woman.* 1935. New York: Carroll & Graf, 2005.

Gualtieri, Elena. "*Three Guineas* and the Photograph: The Art of Propaganda." *Women Writers of the 1930s: Gender, Politics, and History.* Edinburgh: Edinburgh UP, 1999. 165–78.

Gubar, Susan. Introduction. *A Room of One's Own*. By Virginia Woolf. New York: Harcourt, 2005.

Harris, Ian, Fisk, Larry J. and Carol Rank. "A Portrait of University Peace Studies in North America and Western Europe at the End of the Millennium." *International Journal of Peace Studies*. 3.1 (1998). Online.

Harrison, Jane Ellen. *Alpha and Omega*. London: Sidgwick, 1915. New York: AMS, 1973.

———. *Ancient Art and Ritual*. London: Williams, 1913. New York: Greenwood, 1969.

———. *Aspects, Aorists, and the Classical Tripos*. Cambridge: Cambridge UP, 1919.

———. *Epilegomena to the Study of Greek Religion*. Cambridge: Cambridge UP, 1921.

———. "The Head of John the Baptist." *Classical Review* 30 (1917): 216–19. Noted in *Cambridge Review*, 21 February 1917, 233.

———. *Introductory Studies in Greek Art*. London: Unwin, 1885. New York: Macmillan, 1892.

———. "The Judgment of Paris: Two Unpublished Vases in the Graeco-Etruscan Museum at Florence." *Journal of Hellenic Studies* 7 (1886): 196–219.

———, trans. *Manual of Ancient Sculpture*. By Pierre Paris. London: Lippincott, 1890.

———. "Mystica Vannus Iacchi." *Journal of Hellenic Studies* 23 (1903): 292–324.

———. *Mythology*. London: Harrap, 1924. New York: Harcourt, 1963. Revised and republished in 1927 as *Myths of Greece and Rome*; previously published in 1905 as *The Religion of Ancient Greece*.

———. *Myths of the* Odyssey *in Art and Literature*. London: Rivingtons, 1882. New Rochelle, NY: Caratzas, 1980.

———. "Pandora's Box." *Journal of Hellenic Studies* 20 (1900): 99–114.

———. "The Pictures of Sappho." *Woman's World* 1 (1888): 274–78.

———. "The Pillar and the Maiden." *Proceedings of the Classical Association* 5 (1907): 1–13.

———. *Prolegomena to the Study of Greek Religion*. Cambridge: Cambridge UP, 1903.

———. *Reminiscences of a Student's Life*. London: Hogarth Press, 1925.

———. Report of the Curricula Committee, "General Meeting." *Proceedings of the Classical Association* 3 (1906): 65–66.

———. "Some Fragments of a Vase Presumably by Euphronios." *Journal of Hellenic Studies* 9 (1888): 143–46.

———. *Themis: A Study of the Social Origins of Greek Religion*. Cambridge: Cambridge UP, 1912. London: Merlin, 1963. New ed., pub. with *Epilegomena to the Study of Greek Religion*.

———. "Unanism and Conversion." *Alpha and Omega*. London: Sidgwick, 1915. 42–79.

Harrison, Jane Ellen, and Hope Mirrlees, trans. *The Life of the Archpriest Avvakum, by Himself*. London: Hogarth Press, 1924.

———, trans. *The Book of the Bear, Being Twenty-One Tales Newly Translated from the Russian*. London: Nonesuch Press, 1926.

Harrison, Jane Ellen, with D. S. MacColl. *Greek Vase Paintings*. London: Unwin, 1894.

Harrison, Jane Ellen, with Margaret de G. Verrall. *Mythology and Monuments of Ancient Athens: Being a Translation of a Portion of the* Attica *of Pausanias*. London: Macmillan, 1890.

Heilbrun, Carolyn. *The Last Gift of Time*. New York: Ballantine, 1997.

Henig, Sandra. "Queen of Lud: Hope Mirrlees." *Virginia Woolf Quarterly* 1 (1972): 8–23.

Hite, Molly. "Introduction and Notes." *The Waves* by Virginia Woolf. New York: Harcourt, 2006.

Humm, Maggie. *Modernist Women and Visual Cultures: Virginia Woolf, Vanessa Bell, Photography, and Cinema.* New Brunswick, NJ: Rutgers UP, 2003.

Hurst, Isobel. *Victorian Women Writers and the Classics: The Feminine of Homer.* Oxford: OUP, 2006.

Hutton, Lizzie. "The Example of Antonia White: Revaluations." *New England Review* 26.1 (2005): 121–29.

Hyman, Stanley Edgar. *The Armed Vision: A Study in the Methods of Modern Literary Criticism.* New York: Knopf, 1948.

Koestenbaum, Wayne. *Double Talk: The Erotics of Male Literary Collaboration.* New York: Routledge, 1989.

Kolocotroni, Vassiliki. "This Curious Silent Unrepresented Life: Greek Lessons in Virginia Woolf's Early Fiction." *Modern Language Review* 100.2 (April 2005): 313–22.

Koulouris, Theodore. *Hellenism and Loss in the Work of Virginia Woolf.* Burlington, VT: Ashgate, 2010.

Latimer, Tirza True. *Women Together/Women Apart: Portraits of Lesbian Paris.* New Brunswick, NJ: Rutgers UP, 2005.

Lauter, Estella. "Anne Sexton's 'Radical Discontent with the Awful Order of Things.'" *Women as Mythmakers: Poetry and Visual Art by Twentieth-Century Women.* Bloomington: Indiana UP, 1984. 23–46.

Lee, Hermione. *Virginia Woolf.* New York: Vintage, 1999.

Lehman, John. *Thrown to the Woolfs: Leonard and Virginia Woolf and the Hogarth Press.* New York: Holt, 1979.

———. *Virginia Woolf and Her World.* New York: Harcourt, 1974.

Lloyd-Jones, Hugh. "Jane Ellen Harrison 1850–1928." *Cambridge Women: Twelve Portraits.* Eds. Edward Shils and Carmen Blacker. Cambridge: Cambridge UP, 1996. 29–72.

Macciocchi, Maria-Antonietta. "Female Sexuality in Fascist Ideology." *Feminist Review* 1 (1979): 67–82.

Macmillan, Margaret. *Paris 1919: Six Months That Changed the World.* New York: Random House, 2002.

Maika, Patricia. *Between the Acts and Jane Harrison's Con/spiracy.* Ann Arbor, MI: UMI Research Press, 1987.

Marcus, Jane. *Art and Anger: Reading Like a Woman.* Columbus: Ohio State UP, 1988.

———. *Hearts of Darkness: White Women Write Race.* New Brunswick, NJ: Rutgers UP, 2004.

———. Introduction and annotations. *Three Guineas.* By Virginia Woolf. New York: Harvest/Harcourt, 2006.

———. *Virginia Woolf and the Languages of Patriarchy.* Bloomington: Indiana UP, 1987.

———, ed. *New Feminist Essays on Virginia Woolf.* Lincoln: U of Nebraska P, 1981.

———. "Pargeting 'The Pargeters': Notes of an Apprentice Plasterer." *Bulletin of the New York Public Library* 80 (1977): 416–35.

———. "Quentin's Bogey." *Critical Inquiry* 11 (March 1985): 486–97.

———. "Storming the Toolshed." *Signs: Journal of Women, Culture and Society* 7.3 (1982): 622–40.

———. "Virginia Woolf, Cambridge, and *A Room of One's Own:* 'The Proper Upkeep of Names.'" London: Cecil Woolf-Bloomsbury Heritage Series, 1996.

———. "*The Years* as Greek Drama, Domestic Novel, and Götterdammerung." *Bulletin of the New York Public Library* 80 (1977): 276–301.

Marcus, Laura. "The European Dimensions of the Hogarth Press." *The Reception of Virginia Woolf in Europe.* Ed. Mary Ann Caws. London: Continuum, 2002. 328–56.

———. Introduction. *Translations from the Russian: Virginia Woolf and S. S. Kotelian-sky.* Ed. Stuart N. Clarke.Southport, U.K.: The Virginia Woolf Society of Great Britain, 2006. vii–xxvii.

Marcus, Sharon. *Between Women: Friendship, Desire, and Marriage in Victorian England.* Princeton, NJ: Princeton UP, 2007.

Meisel, Perry, and Walter Kendrick, eds. *Bloomsbury/Freud: The Letters of James and Alix Strachey, 1924–1925.* New York: Basic Books, 1985.

Miller, Nancy K. "A Feminist Friendship Archive." *Professions 2011.* New York: Modern Language Association of America, 2011. 68–76.

———. "Getting Transpersonal: The Cost of an Academic Life." *Prose Studies* 31.3 (December 2009): 166–80.

Mirrlees, Hope. *The Counterplot.* New York: Knopf, 1924.

———. *Lud-in-the-Mist.* 1926. Cold Spring, NY: Cold Spring Press, 2005.

———. *Madeleine: One of Love's Jansenists.* 1919. Iowa City: U of Iowa Libraries, 2004.

———. *Moods and Tensions: Poems.* 1976.

———. *Paris: A Poem.* London: Hogarth Press, 1919.

Mirsky, D. S. *A History of Russia.* London: Benn's Sixpenny Library, 1927.

———. *Jane Ellen Harrison and Russia.* Cambridge: W. Heffer & Sons, 1930.

———. *Lenin.* Boston: Little, Brown, 1931.

———. Preface. *The Life of the Archpriest Avvakum by Himself.* Trans. Jane Harrison and Hope Mirrlees. London: Hogarth Press, 1924.

———. *Russia: A Social History.* London: Cresset Press, 1931.

Murray, Gilbert. *Aeschylus, The Creator of Tragedy.* Oxford: Clarendon Press, 1940.

———. *Aristophanes: A Study.* New York: OUP, 1933.

———. *The Classical Tradition in Poetry: The Charles Eliot Norton Lectures.* Cambridge, MA: Harvard UP, 1927.

———. *Euripides and His Age.* Home University Library of Modern Knowledge 73. London: Williams, 1913.

———. "Excursus on the Ritual Forms Preserved in Greek Tragedy." *Themis: A Study of the Social Origins of Greek Religion.* By Jane Ellen Harrison. Cambridge: Cambridge UP, 1912. 341–69.

———. *Five Stages of Greek Religion: Studies Based on a Course of Lectures Delivered in April 1912, at Columbia University.* New York: Columbia UP, 1925.

———. *Four Stages of Greek Religion.* New York: Columbia UP, 1912.

———. *Greek Studies.* Oxford: Clarendon Press, 1946.

———. *The Rise of the Greek Epic.* Oxford: Clarendon Press, 1097.

Nelson, Deborah. *Pursuing Privacy in Cold War America.* New York: Columbia UP, 2002.

Nicolson, Nigel. *Portrait of a Marriage.* New York: Atheneum, 1973.

Ostriker, Alicia Suskin. "Anne Sexton and the Seduction of Audience." *Seduction and Theory.* Ed. Diane Hunter. Urbana: U of Illinois P, 1989. 154–69.

Pawlowsky, Merry. "Exposing Masculine Spectacle: Virginia Woolf's Newspaper Clippings for *Three Guineas* as Contemporary Cultural History." *Literature and Digital Technologies: W. B. Yeats, Virginia Woolf, Mary Shelley, and William Gass.* Ed. Karen Schiff. Clemson, SC: Clemson U Digital Press, 2003. 33–49.

Peacock, Sandra J. *Jane Ellen Harrison: The Mask and the Self.* New Haven, CT: Yale UP, 1988.

Peters, Julie Stone. "Jane Harrison and the Savage Dionysus: Archaeological Voyages, Ritual Origins, Anthropology, and the Modern Theatre." *Modern Drama* 51.1 (Spring 2008): 1-41.

Pfaff, Richard William. *Montague Rhodes James.* London: Scolar Press, 1980.

Prins, Yopie. "Greek Maenads, Victorian Spinsters." *Victorian Sexual Dissidence.* Ed. R. Dellamora. Chicago: U of Chicago P, 1999. 43–81.

———. "Otototoi: Virginia Woolf and the 'Naked Cry' of Cassandra." *Agamemnon in Performance.* Ed. Edith Hall and Fiona Macintosh. Oxford: Oxford UP, 2005. 163–85.

———. "The Sexual Politics of Translating *Prometheus Bound.*" *Classical Reception and the Political.* Spec. issue of *Cultural Critique* 74 (Winter 2010): 1–17.

———. *Victorian Sappho.* Princeton, NJ: Princeton UP, 1999.

Robertson, D. S. "Sir William Ridgeway." *Cambridge Review,* 15 October 1926, 12.

Robinson, Anabel. *The Life and Work of Jane Ellen Harrison.* Oxford: OUP, 2002.

———. "Something Odd at Work: The Influence of Jane Harrison on *A Room of One's Own.*" *Wascana Review* 22 (1987): 82–88.

Schlesier, R. "Prolegomena to Jane Harrison's Interpretation of Ancient Greek Religion." *The Cambridge Ritualists Reconsidered.* Atlanta, GA: Scholars Press, 1991. 185–226.

Schwinn-Smith, Marilyn. "Bears in Bloomsbury: Jane Ellen Harrison and Russia." *Virginia Woolf: Three Centenary Celebrations.* Ed. Maria Candida Zamith and Luisa Flora. Porto: Faculdade de Letras da Universidade de Porto, 2007. 119–44.

Scott, Bonnie Kime, ed. *Gender in Modernism: New Geographies, Complex Intersections.* Urbana: U of Illinois P, 2007.

———. *The Gender of Modernism: A Critical Anthology.* Bloomington: Indiana UP, 1990.

———. *In the Hollow of the Wave: Virginia Woolf and Modernist Uses of Nature.* Charlottesville: UP of Virginia, 2012.

Silver, Brenda. *Virginia Woolf's Reading Notebooks.* Princeton, NJ: Princeton UP, 1983.

Smith, G. S. "Jane Ellen Harrison: Forty-Seven Letters to D. S. Mirsky, 1924–1926." *Oxford Slavonic Papers* ns 28 (1995): 62–97.

———. *D. S. Mirsky: A Russian-English Life, 1890–1939.* Oxford: Oxford UP, 2000.

———. "Prince D. S. Mirsky." *The Dictionary of Literary Biography.* Vol. 317: Russian Émigré Writers. Ed. Maria Rubins. New York: Thomson Gale, 2005. 230–36.

Smith, G. S., and Richard Davies. "D. S. Mirsky: Twenty-Two Letters (1926–34) to Salmoneya Halpern; Seven Letters (193) to Vera Suvchinskaya (Traill)."*Oxford Slavonic Papers* ns 30 (1997): 89–120.

Snaith, Anna. "Wide Circles: Three Guineas Letters." *Woolf Studies Annual* 6 (2000): 1–68.

Sontag, Susan. *Regarding the Pain of Others.* New York: Picador, 2003.

Sophocles. *Antigone, Oedipus the King, Electra. Three Tragedies.* Trans. H. D. F. Kitto. Oxford: OUP, 1982.

Spalding, Frances. *Insights: The Bloomsbury Group.* London: National Portrait Gallery, 2005.

Spater, George, and Ian Parsons. *A Marriage of True Minds: An Intimate Portrait of Leonard and Virginia Woolf.* New York: Harcourt, 1977.

Staveley, Alice. "Marketing Virginia Woolf: Women, War, and Public Relations in *Three Guineas.*" *BookHistory* (2009): 295–339.

Stewart, Jessie. *Jane Ellen Harrison: A Portrait from Letters*. London: Merlin Press, 1959.

Trotter, David. "The Modernist Novel." *The Cambridge Companion to Modernism*. Ed. Michael Levinson Cambridge: Cambridge UP, 1999.

Vicinus, Martha. *Independent Women: Work and Community for Single Women, 1850–1920*. Chicago: U of Chicago P, 1985.

Vickery, John B. *The Literary Impact of* The Golden Bough. Princeton, NJ: Princeton UP, 1973.

Willis, J. H., Jr. *Leonard and Virginia Woolf as Publishers: The Hogarth Press, 1917–41*. Charlottesville: UP of Virginia, 1992.

Wilson, F. M. "Friendships." *A Newnham Anthology*. Ed. Ann Phillips. Cambridge: Cambridge UP, 1979: 67.

Wilson, John C. "Preface." *Epilegomena to the Study of Greek Religion* and *Themis: A Study of the Social Origins of Greek Religion*. Hyde Park, NY: University Books, 1963. vii–xii.

Wisor, Rebecca. "Versioning Virginia Woolf: Notes towards a Post-eclectic Edition of *Three Guineas*." *Modernism/Modernity* 3.16 (September 2009): 497–535.

Woolf, Leonard. *Beginning Again: An Autobiography of the Years 1911 to 1918*. New York: Harcourt, 1963.

———. *Downhill All the Way: An Autobiography of the Years 1919 to 1939*. New York: Harcourt, 1967.

———. *The Intelligent Man's Guide to the Prevention of War*. London: V. Gollancz, 1933.

———. *The Journey Not the Arrival Matters: An Autobiography of the Years 1939 to 1969*. New York: Harcourt, 1969.

———. *Quack! Quack!* London: Hogarth Press, 1935.

Woolf, Virginia. "The Art of Biography." *The Death of the Moth*. New York: Harcourt, 1942. 187–97.

———. "The Art of Fiction." *The Moment and Other Essays*. New York: Harcourt, 1947. 106–112.

———. *Between the Acts*. London: Hogarth, 1941.

———. *The Diaries of Virginia Woolf*. Ed. Anne Olivier Bell and Andrew McNeillie. 5 vols. New York: Harcourt, 1977–84.

———. *Flush, a Biography*. London: Hogarth, 1933.

———. *Jacob's Room*. 1922. New York: Harcourt/Harvest, 1978.

———. "The Leaning Tower." *The Moment and Other Essays*. New York: Harcourt, 1947. 128–54.

———. *The Letters of Virginia Woolf*. Ed. Nigel Nicolson and Joanne Trautmann. 6 vols. New York: Harcourt, 1975–80.

———. "A Letter to a Young Poet." *The Death of the Moth*. New York: Harcourt, 1942. 208–226.

———. *Melymbrosia*. Ed. and introd. Louise DeSalvo. San Francisco: Cleis Press, 2002.

———. "Memories of a Working Women's Guild." *The Captain's Deathbed and Other Essays*. New York: Harcourt, 1950. 228–48.

———. "The Modern Essay." *The Common Reader*. 1925. New York: Harvest/Harcourt, 1953. 211–222.

———. "Modern Fiction." *The Common Reader*. 1925. New York: Harvest/Harcourt, 1953. 146–54.

———. *Moments of Being: Unpublished Autobiographical Writings*. Ed. Jeanne Shulkind. New York: Harcourt, 1976.

———. "Mr. Bennett and Mrs. Brown." 1924. *The Captain's Deathbed and Other Essays*. New York: Harcourt, 1950. 94–119.

———. *Mrs. Dalloway*. 1925. Annotated with an introduction by Bonnie Kime Scott. New York: Harcourt, 2005.

———. "The Narrow Bridge of Art." 1927. *Granite and Rainbow*. New York: Harcourt, 1958. 11–23.

———. *Night and Day*. 1919. New York: Harcourt, 1948.

———. "On Not Knowing Greek." *The Common Reader*. 1925. New York: Harvest/Harcourt, 1953. 23–38.

———. *Orlando, a Biography*. London: Hogarth, 1928.

———. *A Passionate Apprentice: The Early Journals, 1897–1909*. Ed. Mitchell A. Leaska. New York: Harcourt, 1990.

———. "The Perfect Language." *Essays of Virginia Woolf*. Vol. 2. Ed., Andrew McNeille. London: Hogarth, 1987: 114–19.

———. "Phases of Fiction." *Granite and Rainbow*. New York: Harcourt, 1958: 93–145.

———. "Professions for Women." *The Death of the Moth and Other Essays*. New York: Harcourt, 1942. 235–42.

———. *A Room of One's Own*. 1929. Ed., with introduction and annotations, Susan Gubar. New York: Harvest/Harcourt, 2005.

———. "The Russian Point of View." *The Common Reader*. Ed. Andrew McNeillie. New York: Harcourt, 1925. 173–82.

———. *The Second Common Reader*. 1932. New York: Harcourt, 1986.

———. "Slater's Pins Have No Points." *The Complete Shorter Fiction of Virginia Woolf*. New York: Harvest/Harcourt, 1985. 215–220.

———. "A Society." *The Complete Shorter Fiction of Virginia Woolf*. New York: Harvest/Harcourt, 1985. 124–36.

———. "Thoughts on Peace in an Air Raid." *The Death of the Moth and Other Essays*. New York: Harcourt, 1942. 243–48.

———. *Three Guineas*. 1938. With an introduction and annotation by Jane Marcus. New York: Harvest/Harcourt, 2006.

———. *To the Lighthouse*. London: Hogarth, 1927.

———. *The Voyage Out*. London: Duckworth & Co., 1915.

———. *The Waves*. 1931. Introd. Molly Hite. New York: Harcourt, 2006.

———. "Women and Fiction." 1929. *Granite and Rainbow*. New York: Harcourt, 1958. 76–84.

———. "Why?" *The Death of the Moth and Other Essays*. New York: Harcourt, 1942. 227–34.

———. *The Years*. London: Hogarth, 1937.

Wussow, Helen. "Virginia Woolf and the Problematic Nature of the Photographic Image." *20th Century Literature* 40.1 (Spring 1994): 1–14.

INDEX

Ackerman, Robert, 14, 20–21, 23–24,
28, 31–32, 69,173; *Cambridge
Group and the Origins of Myth Criticism,* 28; *Myth and Ritual School:
J. G. Frazer and the Cambridge Ritualists,* 28; on Nietzsche, 69, 69n2
Acropolis, 22, 38, 72–74, 91
Aeschylus, 14, 45, 50, 51, 69, 73, 87–91,
101–5, 108, 110, 137; *Agamemnon,*
87; *Choephori,* 87, 101–5, 108, 110,
137; *Prometheus Bound,* 75; Walter
Headlam's translation of, 90; wom-
en's translation of, 69, 73, 87–90.
See also Agamemnon Notebook,
89–90; Libation Bearers Notebook,
90, 101–5
Aeschylus in Athens (1941) (Thomson),
31
aestheticism, 20–21, 49
Agamemnon Notebook, 89–90
anthropology, 7, 18, 24, 30–32, 72, 171;
movement, 30–32
Antigone (Sophocles), 50, 51, 53, 76, 78,
137
Apollo, 56, 64, 69, 69n2, 70, 88, 104
archaeology, 6, 7, 8, 18, 18n5, 21, 23–24,
30, 32, 28, 47, 129, 171–72, 176

Arlen, Shelley, 7n3, 18, 25, 120, 171–72,
174–75; on Harrison's structural-
functionalism, 25
asceticism, 26
atheism, 12, 32, 120, 131; Harrison's, 32,
120, 131; Woolf's, 12, 131
Athena, 48, 50, 51, 67, 70, 74, 84, 88,
111; Janet Case as, 48; Woolf as,
111
Athens, British School of: women's eligibility at, 156
Atossa, 51
audience, 11, 16–17, 118, 120–22; as
feminine collective, 120–22; Harrison's, 16–17
autobiography, 10, 115, 124, 153, 154,
159; academic, 115; *Downhill All the
Way* (Leonard Woolf), 9, 154; Russian, 153, 159–63

Bacchus, 7. *See also* Dionysus
Beard, Mary, 29, 41, 170–71; and Harri-
son's reputation, 170–71
Bell, Clive, 41, 156
Bell, Julian, 41, 54; pictured, 41
Bell, Vanessa, 43, 57, 82, 117, 156

feminism, 6, 32–33, 115–17, 169; and
audience, 87, 120–24; of Clytemnes-
tra, 50; of Aristophanes, 50
Fernald, Anne, 53, 63, 78–79
Forster, E. M., 2n1, 62, 65, 81
Frazer, Sir James G., 28, 31–32, 64; *The
Golden Bough*, 31
Freud, Sigmund, 25, 34, 49n8, 176
The Furies (Aeschylus), 87–88, 101,
110–11

Gaia, 75
Gardner, Ernest, 19
Garnett, David, 157
gender, 3, 6, 8, 67, 75; bias 14–18; per-
ception 125; politics 51; roles 78, 80,
116, 120; and war 136–41
German Archaeological Institute, 21
Girton College, 49, 53, 59, 116–17, 170
The Golden Bough (Frazer), 31–32
Gorky, Maxim, 159–60
Greece: Greek art, 7–8; Greek education
(Woolf's), 38–61; Greek language,
6–7, 71; Harrison's travels, 15–21,
32; Harrison's passion for, 11; in
Jacob's Room, 97–101; Woolf's
emphasis on, 78–79; in *The Waves*,
110–13; Woolf's travels, 57–58, 113
Gruber, Ruth, 111
Gubar, Susan, 64n1, 119–20

H.D. (Hilda Doolittle), 176
Hamilton, Edith, 51
Harrison, Jane Ellen, "abstraction,"
144; actor, 49; Alcestis, figure 4, 52;
Alpha and Omega (1915), 8, 267,
32, 70, 112, 116, 134; *Ancient Art
and Ritual* (1913), 7, 54, 106, 111,
168; archaeology, 6–8, 18, 18n5, 21,
23–24, 30; *Aspects, Aorists, and the
Classical Tripos* (1919), 7; atheism,
32, 120, 131; biography, 12, 29, 30;
Book of the Bear (1926), 11, 156;
childhood, 11–14, 20; death, 7–9,
12, 29–30, 72, 166–67, 176; "direct
method," 45–49; *dromenon*, 67, 73,
111, 146; "Epilogue on War: Peace

with Patriotism," 26, 37, 134–36,
152; *Epilegomena to the Study of
Greek Religion* (1921), 7, 21, 25–27;
on gender, 14–18, 51, 78, 80, 116,
120, 126; Gertrude Stein, 157; *Greek
Vase Painting* (1894), 21, 23; "holophrase," 34, 62, 68; *Introductory
Studies in Greek Art* (1885), 17, 21;
Jane Harrison Memorial Lecture,
162, 170; Leonard Woolf remem-
brance, 9; *Life of the Archpriest
Avvakum, by Himself* (1924), 5,
11, 153–67; *liknons,*16; *Mythology
and Monuments* (1890), 21–22, 32,
49n8, 58, 91; *Myths of the Odyssey in Art and Literature* (1882), 21;
pacifism, 153–67; "Pandora's Box,"
56–57, 98, 119; pedagogy, 14–18,
36, 38–61, 146; "Pictures of Sappho," 59; "Pillar and the Maiden"
(1903), 25–26, 70; Pontigny
Decades, 37, 157–59; *Prolegomena to the Study of Greek Religion*
(1903), 7, 11, 19, 21, 24–26, 51, 58,
63, 67–71, 87, 106; *Reminiscences of
a Student's Life* (1925), 5, 39; Russia,
5–7, 15, 20, 25–26, 32, 37, 150–51,
153–165, 175–76; Salome, 175; "Scientiae Sacra Fames," 11, 37, 115–33;
Shestov, Lev, 157–58; "Some Fragments of a Vase Presumably by Euphronios," 56; as a student, fig. 1, 13;
Themis: A Study of Greek Religion
(1912), 7, 21, 24–27, 31, 34, 39, 50,
65, 67–78, 84–87, 89; Themis, *see*
Chapter 2; Themis pictured, fig.6, 76;
Women's Penny Paper, 15; "Unanism
and Conversion," 25; Unbounded
Whole, 35, 105, 110–14; "world
soul," 114
Heilbrun, Carolyn, 10
*Hellenism and Loss in the Work of Vir-
ginia Woolf* (2011) (Koulouris), 53
Heretics Society, 161. *See also* Cambridge
University
Hermes, 16, 76
Homer, 68, 75, 91
hero's journey, 31
Hurst, Isobel, 59

Olympians, 37, 39, 68–69, 71–73, 75, 84, 87, 169. *See also* Greece
Orestes, 11, 87–89, 101–5, 110
Orpheus, 56
Oxford, 120

pacifism, 153–67
Pall Mall Gazette, 17, 19, 121
Pandora's Box, 56, 57, 98, 119. *See also* Harrison, Jane Ellen
Paris salons, 116, 155
Parthenon, 8, 15
A Passionate Apprentice (Woolf), 40, 57
Pater, Clara, 20, 23, 40, 41n3, 42
Pater, Walter, 20, 23
Pausanias, 75
Peace Studies, 134–52, 154, 174: activism, 174; Addams, Jane, 135; Burton, John, 136; Fawcett, Millicent, 135; Galtung, Johan, 136; International Peace Research Institute, Oslo, 136; Jacobs, Auletta, 135; National Union of Women Suffrage Societies (NUWSS), 135; negative and positive peace, 135; Pizan, Christine de, 135; Wald, Lillian, 135; Women's League for International Peace and Freedom, 135; Women's Peace Party (WPP), 135; Women's Suffrage and Political Union (WSPU), 135
Peacock, Sandra J., 29
Penelope, 41n2, 53
Petrie, W. M Flinders, 19
philology, 7
photography, 142
polis, 7, 77
Pontigny Decades, 37, 157–59
Pound, Ezra, 2, 62, 176
Pre-Raphaelites, 20
Primitive Culture (1871) (Lang and Tylor), 25
Prins, Yopie, 20, 47, 51, 53, 73–75, 90
Prolegomena to the Study of Greek Religion (1903) (Harrison)
Prometheus, 53
Prometheus Bound (Case), 51
Protestantism, 9
Proust, Marcel, 127, 130

psychology, 3n2, 6, 26–27, 30, 32, 65, 129, 165–67; Russian verb and, 153; of war, 150

Quakerism, 60, 110–11

Radcliffe-Brown, A. R., 25
Raverat, Gwen (née Darwin), 8–9, 12
Raverat, Jacques, 8–9, 12
Reminiscences of a Student's Life (Harrison), 5, 39
Remizov, Alexei, 33n6, 156–58, 161
Ridgeway, William, 172, 174–75
Riviere, Jacques, 157
Robinson, Annabel, 11, 29–31, 45–46, 115
A Room of One's Own (Woolf). See Woolf, Virginia
Russia: 1917 Club, 154–58; aristocracy, 159–60; Bolsheviks, 154; Communism, 158; Dostoevsky Cult, 164; Eurasian Movement, 159–61; Lenin, Vladimir, 159–60; nationalism, 160; Orthodoxy, 160, 163; Shestov, Lev, 157–58; Stalin, Joseph, 159–60; stereotype, 161–62; translation, 153–55; 157–58; Russian Revolution (1917), 37, 154–161; Tsarist regime, 154

Sackville-West, Vita, 55, 116
Sapphism, 55
Sappho, 59, 128
Saussure, Ferdinand de, 176
Schlumberger, Jean, 157
Schwinn-Smith, Marilyn, 155, 161, 164
Scott, Bonnie Kime, 3, 31, 35n8, 169, 170, 176n2
Sexton, Anne, 3n2
Shakespeare, Judith, 125–26
Shakespeare, William, 28, 81, 94, 110, 127, 130
Shaw, George Bernard, 131
Sinclair, May, 176
Smith, G. S., 155, 157, 158n2, 159–62, 165
Smith, Logan Pearsall, 157

CLASSICAL MEMORIES/MODERN IDENTITIES
Paul Allen Miller and Richard H. Armstrong, Series Editors

This series consistently explores how the classical world has been variously interpreted, transformed, and appropriated to forge a usable past and a livable present. Books published in this series will detail both the positive and negative aspects of classical reception and will take an expansive view of the topic. Therefore, it will include works that examine the function of translations, adaptations, invocations, and classical scholarship in the formation of personal, cultural, national, sexual, and racial identities. This series's expansive view and theoretial focus thus separate cultural reception from the category of mere *Nachleben*.

Virginia Woolf, Jane Ellen Harrison, and the Spirit of Modernist Classicism
JEAN MILLS

Humanism and Classical Crisis: Anxiety, Intertexts, and the Miltonic Memory
JACOB BLEVINS

Tragic Effects: Ethics and Tragedy in the Age of Translation
THERESE AUGST

Reflections of Romanity: Discourses of Subjectivity in Imperial Rome
RICHARD ALSTON AND EFROSSINI SPENTZOU

Philology and Its Histories
EDITED BY SEAN GURD

Postmodern Spiritual Practices: The Construction of the Subject and the Reception of Plato in Lacan, Derrida, and Foucault
PAUL ALLEN MILLER

CPSIA information can be obtained
at www.ICGtesting.com
Printed in the USA
FSOW02n0812180217
30962FS